Lightbulb Moments in Human History

From Cave to Colosseum

Lightbulb Moments in Human History

From Cave to Colosseum

Scott Edwin Williams

Winchester, UK
Washington, USA

JOHN HUNT PUBLISHING

First published by Chronos Books, 2023
Chronos Books is an imprint of John Hunt Publishing Ltd., No. 3 East St., Alresford,
Hampshire SO24 9EE, UK
office@jhpbooks.com
www.johnhuntpublishing.com
www.chronosbooks.com

For distributor details and how to order please visit the 'Ordering' section on our website.

ISBN: 978 1 80341 200 9
978 1 80341 201 6 (ebook)
Library of Congress Control Number: 2022933233

A CIP catalogue record for this book is available from the British Library.

Design: Matthew Greenfield

Other than illustrations in the public domain, all other images have been licenced from Adobe Stock, iStock, or Dreamstime. Cover images licenced from: Andrey_Arkusha, rodjulian, StockImageFactory, philipus, olly, and GeorgiosArt - Adobe Stock. Fotomolos - Dreamstime. mmac72 - iStock

UK: Printed and bound by CPI Group (UK) Ltd, Croydon, CR0 4YY
Printed in North America by CPI GPS partners

Contents

Introduction: Walking on the Moon 1

Chapter One: (I'm an) Apeman – Remote Prehistory and the Palaeolithic Era 24
A Brief Interlude I: Calling Occupants of Interplanetary Craft 54
Chapter Two: We Built this City – The Neolithic Revolution 58
Chapter Three: By the Rivers of Babylon – Ancient Mesopotamia 79
A Brief Interlude II: Little Egypt 100
Chapter Four: Walk Like an Egyptian – Ancient Egypt 102
Chapter Five: Another Brick in the Wall – Ancient China 122
Chapter Six: While my Sitar Gently Weeps – Ancient India 142
A Brief Interlude III: (It's no) Sacrifice 160
Chapter Seven: I Left my Heart in Chichén Itzá – Ancient Mesoamerica 163
A Brief Interlude IV: Personal Jesus 182
Chapter Eight: My Sweet Lord? – The Biblical World 184
Chapter Nine: Greece is the Word – Ancient Greece 205
Chapter Ten: Rome (If You Want to) – Ancient Rome 242

Conclusion: Getting Better – The End of the Beginning 276
Acknowledgments 281
References 283

In Loving Memory of my parents
Frederick Edwin Williams
and
Bettina Amy Williams
Thank you both for everything

Introduction

Walking on the Moon

When I was a six-year-old, ginger-haired boy obsessed with dinosaurs and cavemen, the biggest idea in human history became reality.

Before dawn on Monday, 21 July 1969, I jumped out of bed and careened barefoot into the kitchen with one question on my mind.

Mum was already at the stove, her beloved AM radio playing in the background.

"Have they landed yet?" I asked.

"I haven't really been listening." Mum was paying more attention to the frying eggs.

Dad walked in, buttoning his shirt. "Have they landed yet?"

I shrugged.

We turned our attention to the radio. There was a lot of static, beeps, and men saying things I didn't understand, and then:

Houston, Tranquility Base Here. The Eagle has Landed.

That I understood. Armstrong and Aldrin had landed on the Moon. What a relief. I'd been worried the astronauts would suffer the same fate as the lizard I'd tried to launch a month before during the Queen's Birthday fireworks. Enclosed in a gumball capsule insulated with modeling clay and strapped to a skyrocket, I'd sent the reptilian Neil Armstrong soaring skywards, only for the inevitable explosion to ensure 'Neil' didn't make it back to Earth alive.

In a few hours, the commentator informed us, Neil and Buzz would step outside the *Eagle*, the lunar module, and step onto the Moon's surface.

"Come on, get your uniform on, Scotto!"

"But Mum, I want to watch the moonwalk on TV!" I could see Dad was sympathetic, but he knew better than to contradict Mum.

"If you don't go to school, you'll never get to the Moon yourself."

Snap. If I was going to grow up to be an astronaut, I needed to do well at school. I trudged off to get dressed.

It was difficult to concentrate in class. The moonwalk was all some kids could talk about. Others not so much:

"Who cares?" said Stevie, who always looked grubby no matter how early in the day.

All I could think about were the astronauts in the *Eagle*, readying themselves for the EVA, which I knew stood for Extra-Vehicular Activity. Luckily, my teacher, Mrs Landy, decided that this historical event was must-see TV. I was jammed into a classroom, eyes glued to a flickering black and white television mounted on a tall, wheeled, metal stand. It must have been a huge deal, because teachers only rolled out the TV set for special occasions.

"Quiet down, boys and girls! You're about to watch something very special," Mrs Landy said, struggling to adjust the rabbit ears to fine-tune the snowy picture. I sat with the other Grade One students in Cronulla Public School, waiting for Neil Armstrong to step off the foot of the Lunar Module.

"Boring!" Stevie was wriggling next to me and taking core samples from deep inside his nose.

"Shut up." I dug him in the ribs. "Just watch."

The TV commentator breathlessly informed us that Neil Armstrong was exiting the lunar module. I watched in awe as the blurry footage showed Armstrong climbing down the ladder before stopping and hesitating at the bottom rung. Then, at 12:56 p.m. Sydney time, he stepped into history.

Fig. 1: One can quibble about what he said next, but 'Mankind' was acceptable in the 1960s (Merlin74 and S.E.W.)

And that was it. A human was on the Moon. Humanity had succeeded in its greatest technological achievement. At that moment, a small but significant part of my brain was frozen in time.

When it comes to space, I will forever be six years old. That's why I'm not angry when billionaires like Elon Musk, Jeff Bezos, and Sir Richard Branson spend their billions on seemingly quixotic trips into the void. Because, if I had billions of dollars, that's exactly what I'd do.

As I grew older, I began to wonder how we went from caveman to spaceman in such a geologically short span of time. In particular, how did the sequence begun millions of years ago with primitive stone tools develop into a technology capable of landing humans on another celestial body? These two disparate achievements share one similarity at the core of their DNA.

Each was the brainchild of humanity.

Fig. 2: Everything that has gone before has led to this
(Kovalenko 1 and S.E.W.)

Humans had accomplished this amazing achievement by building on the discoveries of their predecessors. The heritage of space travel was traceable: Before being headhunted by NASA, Wernher von Braun had developed rocket technology for the Nazis, but he owed a debt to the pioneering rocketry of Robert Goddard. Both Von Braun and Goddard built on the work of the medieval Chinese rocket makers, and also owed much to the work of Sir Isaac Newton.

Of course, Sir Isaac had his own debts.

Lightbulb Moments: On the Shoulders of Giants

If I have seen further, it is by standing on the shoulders of giants.

Sir Isaac Newton wrote these words in 1675, 294 years before the Moon landing. He was acknowledging the debt his lightbulb moments, the laws of motion and universal gravitation, owed to giants such as Galileo and Copernicus.

Newton understood that only a handful of new ideas truly stand alone. Occasionally, very occasionally, someone gets a flash of inspiration that leads to a genuinely new breakthrough, but otherwise, we build on the work of others. When conceiving big ideas, we humans walk the fine line between inspiration and plagiarism towards immortality. This is one of humanity's superpowers.

So, what do I regard as 'lightbulb moments?' They are big ideas that initiate world-changing paradigm shifts. Therefore, throughout this book, I'll use the terms 'lightbulb moments' and 'big ideas' interchangeably. Sometimes they are creative flashes of epiphany. Sometimes they arise in response to existential problems. Sometimes, they've been hiding in plain sight just waiting for someone to notice. They are neither good nor evil, but can make civilizations rise or fall. They can be crude, three-million-year-old stone tools, spiritual concepts, mind-bending thought experiments, or the International Space Station.

Most lightbulb moments are elaborations on existing ideas. One such example is writing, which started life in Mesopotamia around 3400 BC as a practical method of doing business, and evolved into a powerful method of storytelling. Others are created through the synthesis of two or more existing ideas. Collective learning is an excellent example of this process. Three big ideas: spoken language, the invention of writing, and the development of teaching combine to give us the even bigger idea from whence, arguably, all other big ideas are born. Through collective learning, human ingenuity spans the sciences, religion, philosophy, engineering, law, the humanities, and the social sciences.

Collective learning allows humans to preserve and share information. It allows them to pass it down to their descendants, providing a link from the past and a connection to the future. Collective learning means each generation doesn't have to literally reinvent the wheel.

Or the toaster.

Collective learning also means that ideas can be continually refined, which is a critical process in progress. For example, the concept that 'All men are created equal' has changed the way we look at the world. But it took a long time for people to consider that 'all *humans* are created equal,' and honestly, we haven't done a very good job following through on that.

For 99.9999% of human history, women, poor people, and anyone who wasn't white weren't considered equal. While we might be closer than ever before to getting there, we're not close enough. Once conceived, the concept of human equality grew and spawned other big ideas, such as communism, modern democracy, the human rights, women's rights and anti-slavery movements.

However, not all big ideas are intrinsically positive. The invention of writing, for example. How can the idea that gave us *The Hobbit, Harry Potter* and *Hamlet* be anything but good? Well, *Mein Kampf*, anyone? Writing is only as virtuous as the person who puts pen to paper. The same goes for rockets. The only differences between a Moonshot and a ballistic missile launch are intent, trajectory, and payload.

The Four Domains of Lightbulb Moments

Throughout this book, I will categorize lightbulb moments into four domains: STEM (Science, Technology, Engineering, and Mathematics), Religion, Educational, and Cultural. Like the examples below, all of history's big ideas can be sorted into at least one of these domains (see Table 1). Many can be categorized under more than one domain, such as religious education (Religious and Educational), or building megaprojects like Stonehenge (Religious, Cultural, and STEM).

STEM	Religious	Educational	Cultural
Tool use	Life after death	Speech	War
Mathematics	Hinduism	Writing	Political theories
Agriculture	Buddhism	Teaching	Sports
Weaving	Judaism	Reading	Art
Pottery	Christianity	Collective learning	Narratives

Table 1: The Four Domains of Lightbulb Moments (S.E.W.)

I'm not suggesting this is groundbreaking stuff. It's just a convenient way for me to explain my thinking. I offer no judgments as to whether one domain's ideas are of greater value than others, as that would be unconsciously biased towards concepts I find important.

From time to time, I'll refer to these domains, but I'll do so as little as possible. Years of wading through educational theories have given me a deep loathing of all domains, taxonomies, stages, cycles, and hierarchies, yadda, yadda, yadda. They are usually the realm of self-important, self-promoting egotists, and I don't take myself that seriously. For that reason, I absolutely, positively refuse to personalize them as *Williams'* Four Domains of Lightbulb Moments. In fact, if I start referring to them as such, I give permission for you, dear reader, to approach me at a book signing and punch me in the head.

When it comes to assessing the impact of these lightbulb moments, it is most easily done through the lens afforded by Big History.

Big History

When it comes to history, big is the new small.

Since history was first recorded, historians maintained a laser focus on minutiae, which has reliably bored the shit out of generations of schoolchildren. In the race for tenure and relevance, historians zoomed in closer and closer. Close enough to see the clogged pores in Henry VIII's nose. Historical periods had the crap analyzed out of them, spawning extreme specialties and obscure papers, such as *Devourers of Men's Flesh: The Uncanny Representations of Irish Cannibalism in the Elizabethan Era* by Marzena Keating.

Against this backdrop, enter Big History, a term coined in the 1990s by historian David Christian. Big History is a way of looking at long periods of time from a satellite's view to assemble a big picture view of the past.

Big History examines history from the Big Bang to the present day. Rather than sweating the small stuff, big historians use a multidisciplinary approach combining scientific, sociological, historical, and geographical concepts to investigate long-term trends and patterns. Big History is structured around eight fundamental thresholds, which are:

1: The Big Bang
2: The First Stars
3: New Chemical Elements
4: The Earth and Solar System
5: Life on Earth
6: Humans
7: Agriculture
8: The Modern Revolution.

The limited scope of *Lightbulb Moments in Human History* means we can safely ditch the first thirteen-or-so billion years and enter at Threshold 6: Humans. Depending on which version of the theory you see, sometimes Threshold 6 is called 'Collective Learning.' Those who've been paying attention will notice I've already used that term a number of times. That's because, from a Big History perspective, collective learning is what separates humans from most life on Earth. However, as we will see in Chapter One, not *all* life...

My Lightbulb Moment

Lightbulb Moments in Human History is a big and often chequered history of some of humanity's biggest ideas. It is not and cannot be a complete history of every consequential idea of all time. In keeping with the theme of accessibility, I've only chosen big ideas I found impactful and interesting. There have been enough dry histories full of dates, wars, and kings. Having said that, sometimes there will *be* dates, wars, and kings, but only when they are accompanied by compelling and/or amusing stories. When an historical story is contested, I make no apologies for choosing the more entertaining option.

At this point, I should offer full disclosure: I'm a Gen X white straight cisgender male who was born in the 1960s into a middle-class family in an affluent area of an affluent country. As such, this book comes with a huge dollop of implicit biases, which I've tried to minimize.

In this endeavor, I stand precariously on the shoulders of giants. Unlike Sir Isaac, my 'giants' aren't all scientists: I drew influence from the works of writers such as Yuval Noah Harari, Jared Diamond, Marlene Zuk, David Christian, Susan Wise Bauer, Emma Southon, and Rutger Bregman. Equally, I'm influenced by those of a less serious bent, such as Monty Python's Flying Circus, and writers like Greg Jenner, John O'Farrell, and Mark Forsyth. I did extensive research, but I wanted this to be an accessible history, so I haven't burdened it with loads of footnotes. However, for those interested, I include an extensive bibliography.

Fig. 3: For better or worse, this book is the result of my lightbulb moment (rodjulian and S.E.W.)

I believe that lightbulb moments usually make the world a better place. While it may be naïve to think that human ingenuity will solve the ills of the world, to be fair, it wouldn't be the first time human ideas came to the rescue. In 1798, English economist Thomas Malthus predicted that agricultural production would not be able to keep up with population growth, and this would inevitably lead to worldwide famine and death. Given the farming methods of Mathus' day (and his overestimation of population growth), he had a point. Fast forward to today, however, and big ideas have enabled humans to implement agricultural and technological improvements that have increased the productivity of farms, thus avoiding the Malthusian Trap.

Progressivist views of the world were popular in the eighteenth and nineteenth centuries, but fell into disrepute in the twentieth. It is fashionable to simply deny that the human condition is improving. Many reputable academics hold complex philosophical views. I could go down the rabbit hole here, but I'd be talking in ever-decreasing circles about stuff the general reader might find tedious (and would give me a headache).

In the world of professional historians, the idea of viewing history as a perpetual series of improvements has long since fallen out of favor. The concept is often dismissed in universities as oversimplified, 'weak' history. *Ouch*. In my defense, I believe history is more like the stock market: ups and downs, but with a steady long-term uptick.

However, I understand where the historians are coming from: For 95% of our history, humans were hunter-gatherers. If human history is indeed an unbroken sequence of growth, how do we account for millennia of seemingly zero development? Collective learning started off at a crawl. From our perspective, for thousands of years, humanity's intellectual property seemed limited to knowledge of survival tactics and how to flake the perfect stone tool. However, as we'll see, even though early humans weren't splitting the atom, they did the heavy lifting of inventing language, teamwork, and many other things we take for granted. These were big ideas without precedent.

In time, humankind's collective knowledge grew until it hit critical mass. This is when I believe human ingenuity stepped up a gear, and it had overwhelmingly positive consequences.

It seems my sunny outlook isn't for everyone. In his book *Bad Ideas? An Arresting History of Our Inventions,* Robert Winston explained his gloomier perspective: "Ever since the hand-axe human progress has, in one sense, been downhill. The hand-axe led to the battle-axe, and the atlatl led to the catapult." While Winston claims not to view the future of humanity pessimistically, his point is well-taken. There are consequences for any technological advances humans make.

Not all of them are good. Even seemingly benign inventions can have a dark side: knives spread butter, but they can also kill.

It's really no surprise some people feel this way. Viewed in isolation, humanity seems to be attracted to the lowest common denominator. We've recently witnessed the rise in Reality TV Presidents, anti-vaxxers, flat-Earthers, climate change deniers, and people who believe that shape-shifting reptilian humanoids are taking over the world. So it's tempting to believe we are living in a real-life version of Mike Judge's 2006 film, *Idiocracy*, where so-called stupid people have taken the ascendancy due to the devolution of humankind. In fact, the White House of *Idiocracy* was frighteningly prescient of the shitshow of Trump's West Wing.

Fig. 4: I, for one, welcome our Trumpian/Reptilian overlords to our Flat Earth (By Taras, auntspray, Kalifer and S.E.W.)

My belief is that human ingenuity propels civilization's upward trajectory. When humanity stumbles into a pothole, it eventually climbs out and moves slowly but inexorably towards better ideas. Socially, scientifically, and even politically. Yes, these blips can be glaring. Sometimes, it seems like human achievement is in a permanent death spiral. However, when viewed through the lens of Big History, these are minor corrections.

I'm not for one moment saying that times aren't tough right now. Our confidence has been shaken on a number of fronts. Climate change looms, causing us to rethink our way of life. The information revolution and globalization have displaced many jobs. Social media has given a platform to people who *really* shouldn't have one. The twenty-four-hour news cycle means that we are bombarded with almost constant negativity. People are worried and looking for easy answers, enabling populist politicians to position themselves to take advantage.

If it's any comfort, humanity has risen above such stumbles before. The European Middle Ages following the Fall of Rome saw a noticeable decline in civilized values, but people clawed back knowledge over time and the Renaissance was a high-water mark. At the beginning of the Industrial Revolution, living standards for workers initially dipped; unemployment was rife until the developed world reorganized itself to suit the new paradigm. The early-to-mid twentieth century suffered through two world wars, a depression, and the Holocaust; yet it wasn't long after that average living standards for most of the world hit the highest level ever.

We must remember that every time there's been a reversal, humans have always recovered and rebuilt. New technology and ideas in public policy emerge to meet the challenges.

Yes, things seem bleak right now, but in time, a new and better equilibrium will be reached. While I'm confident that education and creativity will allow us to solve our multitude of problems, the solutions won't just magically appear, and there will be pain along the way. We face real problems that will require some heavy-duty big ideas to find a solution. Recovery isn't guaranteed but, given what we've seen over the arc of history, it's likely.

Of course, life isn't significantly better for everyone. Everyday life in the developing world remains a struggle, but even there, infant mortality has dropped and life expectancy has risen (in Somalia life expectancy has risen from 33 years of age in 1950, to almost 58 years today). While things are better than they were, I don't claim 58 years to be acceptable.

Even the developed world has problems. Significantly, at the time of writing, we are two years into a global pandemic that has ravaged the world. Millions have died worldwide. Not only has the pandemic caused a severe health crisis, it's also given every conspiracy theorist a soap box. We've heard that COVID-19 is a hoax; that the life-saving vaccines (an absolute triumph of fast-moving human ingenuity) were really the delivery system for Bill Gates' mind-control chips; and we've seen people take horse-worming medicine at the behest of unqualified right-wing TV hosts, moronic podcast stars, Russian troll farms, and misguided Facebook friends. Deliberate, damaging misinformation is perpetuated by powerful people who should (and sometimes *do*) know better.

I don't have the answer to combatting the use of lies to manipulate the population, but I have confidence that things will change. There will be rocky years ahead, but eventually, things will get better. Our better angels, which have been put to flight by our demons, will return. Rutger Bregman in his book *Humankind* makes the case that when given a choice, most humans will be decent, cooperative, and kind. He may well be right.

If all that wasn't enough, we must also address global warming. It's an existential crisis; but with hard work, luck, and a combination of creativity, sustainable living practices, and yet-to-be-discovered green technologies, we'll beat that problem too. However, if the worst comes to worst, humans will be forced to develop new ways of living on our planet. The only people who have a hope of solving these problems are people with big ideas.

Even if we drag ourselves back from the brink of global warming, the human population will eventually exceed the

Earth's optimal carrying capacity, if it hasn't already. Perhaps colonizing the Moon and Mars will, in time, reduce pressure on the Earth's population. Again, it will be our best and brightest who will make this a reality. So, no matter what happens, our long-term survival as a species depends on human ingenuity.

If all this sounds overly optimistic, remember the strides humanity has made in the last hundred years. The world of today with cars, cell phones, space travel, and miraculous medical treatments, would be unrecognizable to our recent ancestors.

Canceling History?

Within living memory, humans led very different lives to ours, with different priorities and philosophies. Judging certain historical figures or events by today's standards often leads to false conclusions. That's why, although I'm a liberal, I challenge the recent rise of the extreme cancel-culture view of history.

A very personal example of how different our lives and values can be is my grandmother. She was born in 1895 and grew up during the height of the White Australia Policy. She lived through World War I, the Spanish Flu Epidemic, the Great Depression, and World War II. She was born before the invention of the automobile and lived to see humans on the Moon. Nanna was in her late sixties when I first remember her as a kindly, if opinionated, older lady. She could also be a terrible racist, often making me wince with her opinions. While I'm not trying to excuse her, I know that if she'd been born a generation later, she would have held different, less intolerant views. I still cherish her memory and keep a photo of her in my home. I'm not going to 'cancel' my nanna. She was a product of her place and time.

Today, however, some proponents of 'cancel culture' want to purge certain historical figures. Now, there's nothing wrong with looking at history through an updated lens. It's helpful in bringing new understanding and perspective. We don't need public statues of Confederate generals, in the same way, we don't need statues of Pol Pot, Joe Stalin, or Justin Bieber.

However, many historical figures, like say, Winston Churchill, have been mythologized. Yet they were often far from saints. No doubt, Churchill was the bulwark against Nazism who saved Britain in its 'finest hour.' But he was also the man who said: "I hate Indians. They are a beastly people with a beastly religion." If that wasn't bad enough, he routinely described various people of color as 'uncivilised,' 'barbarians,' and 'savages.' However, looking at Churchill, or any other luminary from the past, with a critical eye differs greatly from attempting to delete them from history.

Fig. 5: Winston was a deeply problematic hero with plenty of statues (V.J. Matthew and S.E.W.)

If *Lightbulb Moments in Human History* has a bias towards Great Men over Great Women, it is *not* because only men can be great. It is because for most of recorded history women have not been afforded the opportunity of being great. They have been marginalized second-class citizens whose words and deeds were rarely recorded. Lack of gender equality reduced the number of people who were educated. Big ideas without education are possible, but unlikely, because innovation correlates strongly with education.

Imagine a world where women had always received the same education as men. For every Caesar, Shakespeare, and Darwin there would be at least one female equivalent. It is a similar story with socio-economic and racial factors. Include hypothetically educated men and women from all races and classes and imagine where our society would be today.

Humanity missed out on those great minds for thousands of years, but they're no longer lost to the future. In Ancient Egypt, the literacy rate was around 3%, a figure mostly composed of upper-class men. Ancient Rome's literacy rate was between 5% and 30%, depending on where you lived in the empire. Compare that to 2015, when UNESCO estimated the global literacy rate for all people aged 15 and over was 86.3%. This improvement is a major reason for my optimism about the trajectory of the educated mind and the prospect of even bigger ideas.

Getting Better all the Time?

Life, in the words of Lennon and McCartney, is 'getting better all the time.' Over the millennia, the human condition has improved dramatically in almost every conceivable metric: literacy, life expectancy, infant mortality, famine, poverty, war, work health and safety, housing, technology, and education.

Looking at the last two hundred and twenty-one years, the statistics speak for themselves. Life expectancy at birth in 1800 was around 40 years of age; today the worldwide average is 73 years of age. The global infant mortality rate in 1800 was 43%, while today it has dropped to 3.8%. The worldwide literacy rate in 1800 was 12.05%; today, it's 86.25%. In 1800, 81% of people worldwide lived in extreme poverty; today the figure is 9.2%. These rates are by no means a mic drop, but they illustrate my point.

In *The Better Angels of Our Nature*, Steven Pinker showed how violence—including war, deaths by terrorism, and rates of homicide—has steadily declined over the years, despite the public perception to the contrary. In most Western countries, same-sex couples can marry. Even discrimination due to sexism and racism has decreased, although we must continually strive for further improvement.

On average, people's daily lives are at an historical high. When the current era is studied by future historians, on statistics alone, they'll view it as an improvement on what came before. However, there are also anecdotal factors.

Let's face it, in the developed world, our *minimum* expectations are so much greater than our ancestors' wildest desires. We expect to live in a McMansion when they just hoped for a roof over their heads. We *need* a vacation around the world; they'd have been happy for a weekend off work. We expect Instagrammable food presentation, while they just hoped not to starve. There's a reason many of today's petty complaints are written-off as 'First World problems.'

Humanity's lightbulb moments have played no small part in these impressive advances.

Lightbulb Moments in Human History is organized into familiar historical eras. It covers many significant ancient civilizations, in chronological order wherever possible. This is the first in a series of books and deals with the big ideas of prehistory and the ancient world, up to the fall of Rome. The next installment will carry the story from medieval times up to the late Victorian era. Another will deal with the twentieth century up to the present, and then speculate on the lightbulb moments we can expect in humanity's future.

The story of civilization is a story of advancement. The human need for self-improvement is deeply embedded in our collective psyche. Parents work to ensure their children's lives are better than theirs. All major religions seek to move their adherents towards enlightenment. Corporations strive to maximize their stock values. Inventors are still trying to build a better mousetrap. There's a reason self-help books are such a popular genre, because individuals always want to 'level-up.' So do civilizations.

Of course, there are exceptions: If you were born after the fall of Rome, you'd probably wish you'd been born earlier; but from a Big History perspective, life has improved from generation to generation. A Roman from the first century AD who lived with running water and bathhouses would've been overjoyed not to be an Egyptian in 2500 BC, dodging crocodiles while bathing in the Nile. Citizens of Renaissance Florence would've thanked their lucky stars that they lived in their beautiful city and hadn't been born during the squalor of Medieval York. The intelligentsia of Victorian England, of course, felt superior to them all.

Fig. 6: Haughtius Maximus was not impressed (jonnyjim and S.E.W.)

But who alive today would seriously want to live in Victorian England? Before you jump up screaming, "Me! Pick me!" remember it was a time before antibiotics and effective anesthesia. It was the time of unbearable pollution and London's 'Great Stink'. Cholera, smallpox, typhoid, and scarlet fever went largely unchecked, and even a simple scratch could cause fatal sepsis. Seventy-hour, six-day working weeks were commonplace. Child labor was rife, and industrial health and safety laws non-existent. The infant mortality rate was 15%. It's no surprise that the average life expectancy in Victorian England was barely 42 years.

Fig. 7: Josiah the hipster volunteering for an early grave (lorado and S.E.W.)

In 2023, there are many, particularly politicians, who would love to take us all back to the 1950s. But would *that* be a good idea? In the 1950s, over 30% of Western homes didn't have indoor plumbing and 25% didn't even have a flush toilet. In 1959, 20% of homes had no telephone, and only 60% had a television. It wasn't unusual for kids to die of measles or whooping cough. Heart conditions that can be routinely treated today were often fatal. The road deaths were through the roof, because cars had no seat belts or airbags. Computers took up a whole room and cost millions of dollars. Women were expected to give up their jobs when they married. Gay men remained closeted, so they didn't have to endure the same fate as Alan Turing in 1952: chemical castration. Segregation still existed in many American states, and in Australia, the indigenous people were not even counted as citizens of their own country.

The Elephant in the Room

Even though we're *not* living in a post-racial world, things are improving. Although not fast enough, to be sure. However, in part, because the Black Lives Matter movement highlighted critical problems that still need solving, there's a greater level of awareness than ever before. This augurs well for the future, but right now, the world is clearly going through something significant.

A big idea is suffering its birth pangs.

As a result, when writing a book such as *Lightbulb Moments in Human History*, which takes a lighthearted view of cross-cultural historical events, I find myself negotiating a minefield. Sure, it's safe for me to poke fun at Christianity and white, Western society, whatever the era, because I'm nominally Christian, white, and Western. It's also safe to make jokes about Mesopotamia, Ancient Egypt, and Ancient Rome because there's no one alive from those eras to be offended. However, similar comments about events in Ancient China or Ancient India are more problematic. If I make light of something Confucius said, is that racist? Is a wry examination of the unusual genesis of the Hindu god Ganesha culturally insensitive? Inevitably, some people will answer a resounding 'YES!'

But please bear with me.

I'm aware that 'humor' has been used throughout history to subjugate minorities. Everything from the blackface in minstrel shows to the yellowface in *Breakfast at Tiffany's,* and beyond. I do not intend to offend, so I want to avoid anything discriminatory. In a 2020 Guardian article, *No joke: ironic racism in comedy is just not funny,* Jason Osamede Okundaye rebukes writers and performers who use racist characters ironically to mock racism, as "(t)his allows comedians and actors to 'safely' perform absurd racist tropes through the malicious deception of an actually racist audience, therefore creating distance between artist and artwork." Point taken.

However, the task I've undertaken is writing a lighthearted history of big human ideas. Not all big ideas are from white, Western people, so I am left with a conundrum. I can write fun, snarky chapters about white people and 'straight' chapters about other cultures. Or treat all subjects equally and damn the consequences. I believe one thing that unites all human beings is a sense of humor, and I also think it is paternalistic not to treat all cultures the same. So I am applying the same gently mocking tone to ALL cultures alike.

Nevertheless, it's inevitable that despite my intentions, I'll upset someone. Let me be clear, if you are a holier-than-thou white person being offended on behalf of somebody else, I simply don't care. However, if in my ignorance I genuinely offend your culture, I sincerely apologize.

Fig. 8: Karen gets her knickers in a twist
(MangoStar_Studio and S.E.W.)

One small step...

Lightbulb Moments in Human History melds many of my lifelong obsessions: prehistory, ancient history, art history, printing, science, cartooning, education, space, and (with a bit of luck) comedy, together in one package. It's taken two years to write but has been a lifetime in the making. All my explanations, caveats, and justifications have been made. Giant's shoulders have been stood upon.

Now it's time to take one small step.

Chapter One

(I'm an) Apeman
Remote Prehistory and the Palaeolithic Era

I assure you I'm not unhinged.

This is a serious question: Did animals come pre-programmed with behaviors that would eventually allow humans to evolve into ideas-machines? In the time-honored words of click-bait advertising, *the answer might surprise you*.

Don't worry, I don't think animals have the cognitive firepower to have 'ideas' let alone epoch-making ones. However, I don't apologize for beginning a book entitled *Lightbulb Moments in Human History* by discussing particular traits in non-human animals.

Why? Well, for one thing, humans are animals too, and many 'ideas' we attribute to our higher-order thinking skills have their roots much further back in our evolution. Some of these ideas, such as basic communication and certain types of learning, are actually adaptations due to natural selection and evolved over millions of years. However, natural selection is not the end of the story.

Cognitive psychologist Douglas Wylie from the University of Alberta believes that the brains of animals such as chimpanzees, as well as some types of birds, share a similar structure to humans. In particular, Wylie is referring to the cerebellum, which, in some mammals and birds, is more enlarged and folded. More folds means more surface area. More surface area means more neurons. More neurons mean more connections and better cognition. The cerebellum is the part of the brain that controls motor learning and motor control, which are the cognitive skills required for tool use. Wylie theorizes that this similarity in formation of the cerebellum may account for how some animals, like humans, use tools.

But isn't tool use the brainchild of humanity? Well, yes... and no.

For the bulk of human history, we believed that our use of tools set us apart from the beasts. Yet, as we looked more closely at the natural world, it became clear that tool use by animals was not uncommon. Turns out we weren't so bloody special after all. Of course, the tools these animals use aren't power drills or chain-saws. Dictionaries more or less define a tool as: "an implement, usually one held in the hand, used to carry out a useful function." Given the hand-held specification, these definitions imply tool use is the domain of primates.

Indeed, monkeys and apes have often been seen using tools in the wild. Not only has it been observed, but the idea of tool use has been intentionally transmitted by some primates through a kind of cultural learning. However, it's not only primates that use tools. Animals such as octopuses, dolphins, and crows have utilized tools for the acquisition of food and water, for construction and hunting, and even for self-defense.

In order to accommodate the variety of tool users, Benjamin Beck, a comparative psychologist who specializes in animal cognition, revised the definition. Using Beck's interpretation, a tool must: "(i) not be part of the animal itself; (ii) not be attached to the environment; and (iii) be manipulated to achieve some beneficial outcome." This definition opens up a whole world of animal tool use.

And there are some interesting cases...

Under the Sea: Poisonous Whips, Coconut Shells and Fake Noses

My personal favorite non-human tool user is the Blanket Octopus, which avails itself of an extremely unusual defensive weapon. When threatened, these eight-armed ninjas rip off the venomous tentacles of the nearest Portuguese man-of-war (to which the octopus has a natural immunity) and wield them like a venomous cat-o'-nine-tails. The soon-to-be-sorry predators beat a hasty retreat. The Blanket Octopus can also use these poisoned whips-from-hell for hunting prey.

While we're on the subject of octopuses: Dr Julian Finn and fellow researchers from Museums Victoria have documented a species called the Indonesian Veined Octopus, which carries around coconut shells it can quickly assemble into a personal air-raid shelter. These octopuses display amazing foresight in carrying the makeshift sanctuaries for potential future use. Finn wrote: "(T)he discovery of this octopus tiptoeing across the sea floor with its prized coconut shells suggests that even marine invertebrates engage in behaviours that we once thought the preserve of humans."

It's more than a little creepy as well.

However, octopuses aren't the only undersea tool users. When Spotted Dolphins in Shark Bay, Western Australia want dinner, they have to hunt. Unfortunately, their prey take refuge around rugged rocks and sharp coral on the seafloor. No matter. These ingenious dolphins tear off hunks of marine sponge and wear them like a fake nose to protect their beaks while they feed. Once upon a time, it seems, a clever dolphin invented this technique and it caught on. Now all Shark Bay dolphins hunt in that way. This is the first documented use of tools by the creature often touted as the second most intelligent creature on Earth.

Fig. 1: A slightly inaccurate artist's rendering of a sponge-wearing dolphin (federicoriz and S.E.W.)

A New Reason for Ornithophobia?

Birds from the corvid family, such as crows and ravens, have long been renowned for their intelligence. They not only use tools, but they also *create* tools. In 2002, Oxford researchers observed Betty the New Caledonian Crow making a hooked tool from some wire in her cage and using it to get some otherwise unattainable meat. This was seen as unusual until it was discovered that New Caledonian crows have *always* been hardcore tool-users. If Alfred Hitchcock had known about their ability to make potential weapons, it would've added a new and disturbing angle to *The Birds*.

Birds also build nests, but whether these are considered tools is hotly debated by scientists. By Beck's definition, nests are definitely tools, but researchers such as St. Amant and Horton do not agree. While one might assume that nest-making is innate, there is circumstantial evidence that male bowerbirds learn bower construction through observation. These bowers are exceedingly clever constructions. The golden bowerbird builds a tower of sticks around a pole, then pimps out its bachelor pad with colorful feathers, leaves, flowers, berries, and other objects to attract the ladies.

Fig. 2: The golden bowerbird is a player (Archivist and S.E.W.)

Don't take Parenting Advice from a Meerkat

Ok, so we've established that animals can use tools, but can they pass this learning on to others? We've already noted that apes learn by observation and Spotted Dolphins appear to have transmitted knowledge of sponge use for fishing. Can animals *teach?*

The answer is a qualified 'yes.' But it's not teaching like *we* know it.

Let's look at the cute, but neurotic meerkat. We've become used to these guys as adorable, eccentric characters in insurance commercials on TV, but as parents, meerkats are proper bastards. Older meerkats have to teach their young how to catch and kill one of their main food sources, the scorpion. But how do parents do that without putting their kids in danger? Initially, adult 'teacher' meerkats kill the scorpion before providing it to their pups. Later, they give them a live, but immobilized scorpion. Gradually, the teachers introduce their pupils to less and less impaired scorpions, until finally, they present them with a fully functional, sting-you-in-the-face one. Natural selection deals with the students who can't manage this task.

No wonder meerkats always look nervous.

Fig. 3: Meerkats are paranoid for good reason
(Egor Kamelev and S.E.W.)

Monkey See/Monkey Do

Strangely, our closest relatives, the great apes, don't show compelling evidence of teaching behavior. Young apes are adept at gathering information by observing the behavior of more experienced apes, but the latter are not actively teaching. Rather, they are just going about their daily lives and being mimicked by the younger apes. The young apes show definitive evidence of learning, but the older apes aren't explicitly teaching.

When it comes to apes teaching, the most significant example comes from animals in captivity. Washoe the chimp was captured by humans who intended to shoot her into space. For unknown reasons, she was reprieved and instead taught American sign language (famous quotes: "You, Me out go," "Time Eat," and the ever-popular "You Me Peekaboo"). Then Washoe tried to teach an infant chimp in her care to use this sign language. She was observed shaping the infant's fingers into the sign 'food.' Why Washoe didn't just teach the baby a less polite signal is unsure.

Fig. 4: A message to the researchers (by Baris-Ozer and S.E.W.)

If Vervet Monkeys Could Talk, They'd Slur Their Words

Another big idea that we erroneously believe sets humans apart from animals is language. Let's be clear: No animal comes close to sophisticated human speech. However, several creatures including whales, dolphins, and even bees, can communicate information. The one most closely related to humans is the vervet monkey.

Research has shown that vervet monkeys have distinct calls that warn others and distinguish whether they have seen a wild cat, a snake, or an eagle. When the troop members hear these calls, they react in ways that show they are taking appropriate evasive action based on the differing threats these predators pose. Young vervets cannot naturally make the sounds and appear to learn the proper calls. It is unclear how the learning takes place, although it is hypothesized that reinforcement from adults plays a part. However, it's more than appearing to have an embryonic language that makes these little monkeys seem humanlike. They also display other human traits such as anxiety and social drinking.

Fig. 5: A vervet enjoying a glass of well-structured merlot (By Leonard Zhukovsky and S.E.W.)

Vervet monkeys love drinking so much, they're often used by

scientists in studies of alcoholism in humans. In the wild, they sourced alcohol from rotting fruits fermenting on the forest floor. Nowadays, they find it easier just to steal it from humans. When one considers the vervet's entire 'language' is based on screaming warnings about impending doom, you really can't blame them for drowning their sorrows.

Not So Unhinged After All?

Clearly, some traits we often view as fundamentally human—tool use, teaching, and communication—have their genesis in animals. This is our baseline. With tool use, communication, and teaching hard-wired into our ancestors' DNA, millions of years of evolution have fine-tuned them to the point where its most recent iteration, *Homo sapiens*, has become the most intelligent species on the planet.

This is despite damning evidence found at MAGA rallies and in internet comment threads.

Hominids

So Easy, Even a Caveman Could Do it?

Ever since Darwin told us we had apes as distant ancestors, modern humans have been uneasy and a little defensive. We mocked the simian nature of *Australopithecus*. We jeered at the brow-ridges and stocky frame of the Neanderthals. And the less said about *Homo erectus* around an adolescent boy, the better. As far as relatives go, these apemen are the embarrassing cousins we'd rather not acknowledge.

However, it is very wrong to write off these relatives as dull brutes who lived short and squalid lives, even though that's how we characterized them for many years. More recently, this idea has been rejected by some modern scholars who now tend to view hunter-gatherer lifestyles as idyllic, with loads of free time and an excellent diet. To my mind, both of these extremes miss the mark: Our ancestors were neither brutes nor noble savages.

They were a little of both. Most of all, they were trailblazers who began the process of collective learning.

Unfortunately, popular culture has done its bit to undermine our respect for our hominid forebears. In a meme made famous by 1950s cartoons, cavemen with names like Grog and Ugg sporting unkempt mullets and wearing fetching off-the-shoulder animal skins fight off a *T. Rex* with stone-tipped spears. This image is amusing and about as anachronistic as it gets. At least 65 million years separate any form of prehistoric human from encountering any form of dinosaur.

Fig. 6: Despite what you've seen on TV, this didn't happen (by Kovalenko I and S.E.W.)

Another well-known trope is the caveman 'seducing' his intended mate with a club, then dragging her senseless body back to his cave by the hair. This is a deeply troubling image in this day and age (as it should have been in *any* day and age). However, I don't want to kink-shame people. If consenting adults get off on rough play, well good luck to them. And as long as all parties are on board, turnabout is fair play.

Fig. 7: Ugg and Mrs Ugg get kinky
(by franckreporter and S.E.W.)

These depictions fueled the perception that early humans were clumsy and slow-witted. Admittedly, there's some validity to that view. For a start, *Australopithecines* weren't skilled conversationalists. Experts believe they were about as vocal as a modern chimpanzee. But that doesn't mean *Australopithecines* couldn't be inventive. Stone implements still exist from at least 3.3 million years ago. There's also evidence that they were teaching each other how to make these tools. Researchers suggest that behavioral changes in *Australopithecus afarensis* associated with the development of stone-age tech, may have, over eons, driven the emergence of the *Homo* genus. However, if one invited an *Australopithecus* to a dinner party, it would be more likely to throw its feces at the guests than engage in witty repartee.

Fig. 8: Grog knew exactly how to liven up Karen and Kevin's barbecue... (jacoblund, Ershova_Veronika and S.E.W.)

Of course, it's unlikely that this theoretical dinner party would've been any more successful with *Homo habilis, Homo erectus,* or even Neanderthal guests of honor. If our previous experience with inebriated monkeys is any sign, these guys would have hit the bottle. One can only imagine how a drunk, powerful Neanderthal could trash a joint.

But would that be a fair assessment?

For many years, Paleoanthropologists believed Neanderthals were too stupid and ungainly to use and make efficient tools or cooperate to hunt megafauna. However, recent discoveries bring into question the idea that Neanderthals were stone-age Homer Simpsons. It is now theorized they created art, cared for their elderly, and possibly even invented language.

Language is a game-changer: There's no more direct way to impart information than through verbal communication, and information is crucial. It permits individuals to make better choices. Language allows one to convey details about the availability of food, the location of predators, or other environmental conditions that are vital to a creature's survival. The development of true language was a significant evolutionary advantage. The reasons are many, but principally, speech allows the dissemination of information without the constant need for reinvention.

For animals living in social groups, there are distinct advantages to learning information from older and more experienced animals, as knowledge gathered over many years is transmitted without the risks inherent with trial-and-error experimentation. In fact, language's ability to impart knowledge provides a species with an evolutionary advantage. Let's face it, it would have been a lot more effective for Grog to scream: "Ugg! Cave bear! Run!" rather than to convey this life-or-death information through the subtle art of mime.

Fig. 9: Marcel versus the cave bear
(shymar27, zinkevych and S.E.W.)

Even without speech, there are other ways that teaching could have occurred in both non-human primates and early humans. One of the most significant drivers of human evolution was the efficient transfer of information among a group. Humans can transfer information in many ways, most of which show a capacity for symbolic communication. Symbolic communication is most often achieved through the use of vocalization in primates, and it is theorized that hominids had this ability, too. By vocalization here, I mean screeching and whooping, not engaging in learned discourse.

Other methods of teaching include demonstration, where a teacher shows how to perform everyday tasks; positive feedback, where a teacher uses positive sounds or body language to show approval of a student's performance; or negative feedback, in which the instructor beats the shit out of an underperforming student.

So, what does this say about the potential for proto-humans to pass on their technological breakthroughs? We can only make educated assumptions about the behavior of our forebears based on limited evidence. However, it is plausible to speculate that most hominids could engage in any of these types of education. Just as we see now, older, more experienced members of the group could transfer knowledge to less experienced members of the group. Theory has it that the inherent value of these elders as a type of brains trust is the reason that some Neanderthal and *Homo erectus* skeletons show clear evidence of having been cared for well after their youthful, productive days were over.

Homo Sapiens: Out of Africa

Homo sapiens emerged in Africa around 150,000 years ago, but their improbable journey to become the dominant species on the planet was not smooth. These guys were physically indistinguishable from modern humans, yet it took 70,000 years for their technical progress to match their genetic progress. Until then, *Homo sapiens* was an unimpressive animal that was pathetically weak compared to most predatory species. They were almost driven to extinction with, at one stage, as few as 10,000 individuals left. While it took *Homo sapiens* some time to hit their stride, when the Great Leap Forward took place, their progress was exponential.

Those who've watched Stanley Kubrick's *2001: A Space*

Odyssey will remember the blockish alien monolith that sparked intelligence in early humans. It was a great movie, but this was not what I meant by Great Leap Forward. For a start, the cavemen in *2001* appear to be *Australopithecines,* and the Great Leap Forward happened millions of years after that. Instead, several big ideas and chance occurrences helped propel human development over millennia.

Fig. 10: If only human intelligence was so easily sparked (Jakaria3704, rolffimages and S.E.W.)

Meet the Flintstones

When I think about the technology of early humans, my mind almost inevitably goes to the words 'stone age.' This is probably the result of my childhood exposure to *Flintstones* cartoons. These

1960s icons of pop culture were deliberately anachronistic, but one technology that was frequently shown was the stone wheels of Fred Flintstone's car. And while six-year-old me understood there had been no Palaeolithic cars, I never doubted the existence of the Palaeolithic wheel. How could there not have been? It seems like such an obvious invention. But it wasn't.

Humans were keen observers of the environment and plagiarised many early engineering ideas from Mother Nature. However, there's no analog to the wheel in the living world. Animals have wings, fins, flippers, and legs, but there are none with wheels. So, the wheel is far from the brainchild of primitive man. Of course, primitive humans may have rolled heavy objects on wooden logs, but if they did, they left no trace. The first evidence we have for the wheel is around 5,500 years ago, but more on that later.

A Bunch of Prized Tools

There is, however, plenty of evidence of other technological innovations of early humans. All hominids used stone tools, and as humans evolved, so did the sophistication of their tools. The tools we use today are the direct descendants of the first crude stone tools.

The first human tools uncovered by archaeologists were simple, often just crudely shaped hunks of rock or sharp stone flakes. These so-called Oldowan tools (the name taken from Olduvai Gorge in Tanzania where they were first discovered) were used for a million-year period over humanity's evolution, starting around 2.6 million years ago.

It's easy to imagine the progression. The first tool was the most important: A rock in the fist gave a hominid the power to do things it couldn't do with its hand alone. A plain old rock has limited practical applications, but once that first tool was invented, humans would have seen the potential for other labor-saving devices. This would have driven innovation. Each subsequent generation of tools inspired the next.

That doesn't mean human tools evolved quickly, though. For hundreds of thousands of years, technology remained virtually unchanged. Then one day, a flash of inspiration, blind stroke of luck, or a new pressing need, led to an improvement. Early Palaeolithic humans started off with unrefined tools, usually hand axes and hand-held spears, but over long periods refinements were made. Later, in the middle and upper Palaeolithic, came innovations such as harpoons, nets, spear throwers, and eventually, the bow and arrow.

Over time, *Homo sapiens'* capacity to accumulate and transfer knowledge, manufacture tools, and coordinate via communication, improved their ability to hunt and make war. This advanced technology likely had dire consequences for the Neanderthals, as we shall see.

Language and Collective Learning

In short, the Great Leap Forward around fifty thousand years ago, gave modern humans the push to increase their knowledge of the physical world and build intellectual capital. As we have seen, modern humans are evolutionary outliers, and their use of language is unmatched in the animal world. We've seen varied forms of communication among non-human animals. However, human language is unique in its power to communicate complex information about objects and events happening outside the immediate time or place. So, it is reasonable to surmise that this advanced mode of communication led to the capacity to teach and build a body of knowledge.

In his fascinating book, *Origin Story*, the 'big history' historian David Christian notes that "these linguistic enhancements allowed humans to share information with such precision and clarity that knowledge accumulated from generation to generation." He terms this ongoing accumulation of knowledge *collective learning*, and believes it has driven change "as powerfully as natural selection."

Because of language, humans could accumulate knowledge within communities, between neighboring communities, and even across generations. This was only possible because language gave us the power to teach abstract concepts. Humans could recount cautionary tales that happened a long time ago or in faraway places, share the location of valuable resources, pass on traditions, coordinate strategies, or instruct others on how to perform a useful skill.

Over tens of thousands, or even hundreds of thousands of years, hominids developed and then refined many life-altering practices and inventions: Horse-riding and rudimentary medicine were both major advances that gave our species an edge. The capacity to communicate and teach these ideas was essential to the continuation and eventual supremacy of humanity.

The controlled use of fire, the domestication of dogs, the invention of art, the development of tools, as well as the rise of humor and religion, all had far-reaching evolutionary consequences.

Quest for Fire

The use of fire by hominids was a paradigm-shifting innovation. Controlled fire provided warmth and light, protection from the weather and from nocturnal predators, and, eventually, a way of cooking food. Caves used by hominids usually show traces of wood ash and burned animal bones. In time, the judicious use of fire allowed our ancestors to migrate out of warmer climates and into cooler regions.

Obviously, hominids didn't 'invent' fire, but they demonstrated the ability to exercise some control over it early in human evolution. Recent uncontested evidence suggests that the controlled use of fire dates back nearly 1.5 million years. However, the progression from control of fire to being able to *create* fire is significant. It required hundreds of thousands of years to develop. There is no archaeological proof that humans could produce fire from scratch until Neolithic times. Fire-starting kits containing fire drills, flint, and pyrites have been unearthed in Neolithic sites in Europe from around 12,000 years ago.

Fire creation was a life-or-death skill for humans trying to endure the ice age.

There is evidence that *Homo erectus* began cooking food around two million years ago. As a result, anthropologist Richard Wrangham argues that cooking has played an essential role in human evolution. While this is a contentious view, it may help to explain the growth in the brain size of hominids. The human brain requires more energy than any other organ. Until the widespread use of cooking, humans couldn't afford the luxury of wasting energy on excess grey matter. Cooking enabled humans to digest food faster. This, in turn, allowed for the evolution of a smaller digestive tract, which then allowed more energy to be diverted to our brains. The theory is that these bigger brains gave us greater cognitive capability, which contributed to the development of language and collective problem-solving.

Cooking may also explain the evolution of smaller teeth and jaws, as massive choppers were not necessary to chew cooked food. Some of these adaptations are extremely ancient, going back to before *Homo sapiens* and Neanderthals split from a common ancestor, approximately half a million years ago.

Modern humans and Neanderthals managed to co-exist for hundreds of thousands of years, until around 40,000 years ago, when Neanderthals went extinct. What happened? Many paleontologists believe that *Homo sapiens* essentially ethnically cleansed their competitors out of existence. This theory relies on the idea of conflict between the two branches of hominid due to competition for limited resources. Climate change or natural disasters might easily have upset the balance between *Homo sapiens* and *Homo neanderthalensis*, thus bringing them into conflict.

Given what we know about humans, bloody murder doesn't seem out of the question. However, it's possible that deliberate genocide was not the reason for the downfall of the Neanderthals. Modern humans may have simply out-competed them for scarce resources, leading to their demise.

There are several explanations that might account for *Homo sapiens'* triumph in such a war of attrition. Their more sophisticated technology probably played a part, as did their domestication of dogs (more about that, shortly). Both would enhance the hunting ability of modern humans in a time of scarcity. There is a belief that Neanderthal's more powerful bodies required more energy than their competitors' did, which gave *Homo sapiens* a competitive advantage. Some scientists theorize that modern humans reproduced more quickly, which could have played a part in the demise of their heavy-browed cousins.

There are intangibles: Did humanity's ability to be creative, as well as to learn and transfer information, play a part? Were Neanderthals less able to adapt because of a lack of creativity? Were modern humans more intellectually agile in their approach to the problems they encountered? Unless we clone a Neanderthal, we can never be certain of the answer, although I'm not for a moment saying we *should* clone one of these guys.

Scientists sequenced the Neanderthal genome in 2010. In a technical sense, the cloning of a Neanderthal is within the realm of possibility. Of course, that would be deeply unethical, because the process requires a human egg and a human surrogate to carry this hybrid Neanderthal/human embryo. Who's to say that someone as unscrupulous as Vladimir Putin wouldn't try to clone some Neanderthal super-soldiers?

Anyway, why cook up Neanderthal/human hybrids when they already exist in the world? I hate to break it to you, but you might actually *be* one. Yes, somewhere between 1 and 4 percent of the modern human genome (excluding that of Africans) is attributable to Neanderthals. This is proof positive that modern humans and Neanderthals bumped uglies on a semi-regular basis. There's even a rather far-fetched theory that the disappearance of Neanderthals from the fossil record is because they merged into the *Homo sapiens* population through interbreeding.

This theory has little-to-no support, but I find it interesting, as it goes a long way to explaining a few of my acquaintances.

Three Shamans Walk into a Bar...

If you think humor just *had* to be the invention of the big hominid brain, you'd be mistaken. We know that close primate relatives including chimps and gorillas emit laughter-like sounds in response to 'fun' stimuli, such as tickling and play. Therefore, it's likely that *Australopithecines* would have screech-laughed in similar circumstances. I like to imagine a Neanderthal chuckling at a well-timed fart around the campfire. So, while the sophisticated appreciation of clever wordplay or a well-put-together joke results from a complex cognitive function, it doesn't take a super-brain to laugh. But as language evolved, a new dimension was added to the humour.

*Fig. 11: I didn't say it was **sophisticated** humor*

(zemler and S.E.W.)

Laughter is the usual response to a humorous situation, and it is ubiquitous in all humans (except hyper-religious nut-jobs like the Taliban or members of the Westboro Baptist Church). In fact, humor's presence in human behavior has led some scientists to theorize it was adaptive. Yes, having a sense of humor may have given humans an evolutionary advantage. If so, was Charlie Chaplin more evolved than Adolf Hitler? I can't say for sure, but Charlie got all the girls, passed on his genetic material *eleven* times, and lived to the ripe old age of 88. Hitler had one testicle, was rumored to be asexual, fathered no children, and ended up shooting himself in the head at 56.

Fig. 12: Chaplin vs Hitler: It's really no contest (Public domain)

Let's face it, a 'good sense of humor' is near the top of the list of attractive traits in a mate. Being humorous is often correlated with intelligence, creativity, and empathy. That's because funny people need a unique combination of IQ and EQ to do their thing. Laughter puts others at ease. In social animals such as humans, these are important traits for which evolution would select. Is it any wonder there are no little Hitlers running around?

A Human's Best Friend

> *Remove domestication from the human species, and there's probably a couple of million of us on the planet, max[...] Domestication has influenced the entire earth. And dogs were the first.*
> Greger Larson

The bond between humans and dogs runs deep. Genetic evidence indicates that dogs diverged from the wolf family around 40,000 years ago. Perhaps a human adopted an abandoned wolf pup, or it's possible that wolves foraging through human garbage heaps became acclimated to cavemen. However it occurred, dogs were the only animal that hunter-gatherer humans domesticated.

In 'Stone Age Man Kept a Dog,' an article in *Nature*, Kendall Powell notes that Palaeolithic humans probably selectively bred aggression out of wolves around 15,000 years ago in East Asia. The article examines a study by a team of evolutionary biologists at Sweden's Royal Institute of Technology comparing dog and wolf DNA from all over the world. Their analysis of the results suggested that humans domesticated dogs more than once.

The domestication of dogs turned into an evolutionary advantage for humans. They were likely used as guard dogs, for their herding abilities, and, as we can see from cave art, for hunting. Through a combination of evolution and breeding, dogs and humans have developed a close, almost symbiotic relationship. Eventually, dogs became companions as well as working animals. One thing is clear: The domestication of the dog was the beginning of two big ideas, domesticated animals and pet ownership.

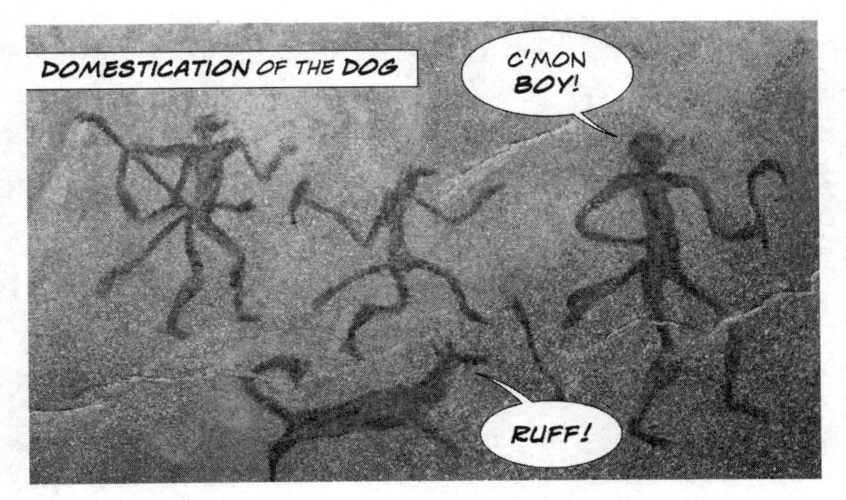

Fig. 13: "Who's a good doggy?" (Gerasimov174 and S.E.W.)

Prehistoric Picassos

The visual arts are a fundamental expression of humanity. They exist in every culture and are a graphic method of communicating feelings and ideas. Before the invention of writing, the visual arts were the only concrete way humans could record events. The most common motifs in cave painting were scenes of humans hunting animals and images of the ubiquitous Palaeolithic graffiti tag, the handprint.

Fig. 14: Fire and cave art: two big ideas (Gorodenkoff and S.E.W.)

There is no definitive explanation of the meaning of these hand stencils. They could be something as simple as the signature on an artwork. Or they could be an 'I stencil therefore I am' statement of self-awareness. Some might also be the tribe's shaman making his/her mark on the cave wall as a part of a ritual. Handprints appear in cave art from all around the world, so it's unlikely their meanings were the same in places as distant as Europe and Australia. Researchers in Cantabria note that handprints can be found in unusual positions, where easier options were available. They hypothesized from this that these stencils might have offered advice about where others could position their hands to safely negotiate a passage through the cave. Kind of like a stone-age game of Twister.

Beautiful, complex cave paintings such as those in the Lascaux Caves in France are often thought to be religious in nature, perhaps linked to shamanic ceremonies. In one version of this theory, suggested by David Lewis-Williams, a shaman enters the caves in a trance state, then paints his visions, perhaps hoping to extract power from the cave walls. If correct, then that was the beginning of the tradition of artists painting while on mind-expanding drugs.

Painting isn't the only visual art that got its start in the Palaeolithic period. There were also sculptures, which frequently took the shape of Venus figurines. These fetishized images of femininity usually display wide hips, large breasts, and a head without facial features. Although these figurines can vary, they often depict feminine forms that, in addition to the hips and breasts, also include exaggerated abdomens, thighs, or vulvas.

Perhaps the most famous sculpture of this type is the *Venus of Willendorf*. It is estimated that this 11-centimeter-tall, oolitic limestone sculpture is approximately 25,000 years old. Were these highly stylized depictions of naked women representations of a mother goddess? Were they toys? Or did cavemen really, really like fuller-figured women? No one is really sure.

Fig. 15: Maybe it was just caveman porn?
(zemler, Neil Harrison and S.E.W.)

Ingesting the In-Laws?

Speaking of mother goddesses, it was during the lower and middle Palaeolithic periods that humans began thinking about religion. Spiritual lightbulbs were popping here, there, and everywhere. Ritual burial first appears during this time; the use of pigments on the body and presence of grave goods may indicate the beginning of a belief in life after death. Apart from providing the dead with useful stuff, there was another way of easing their path into the afterlife: eating them. It's believed that ritual cannibalism involved eating the flesh and chewing on the bones of the deceased, ostensibly to honor them and inherit their qualities. Although extreme hunger may have come into it as well.

Fig. 16: Grandparent: the other white meat (Gorodenkoff and S.E.W.)

Even though we can't be absolutely sure of their beliefs and practices, there's evidence of shamanic practices in the upper Palaeolithic. However, our experience of modern-day shamans can give us clues: One of the shaman's jobs was to communicate with the spirit world. When bad spirits were suspected of causing illness, the shaman attempted to drive them out. The shaman might also have gone on vision quests, perhaps to reveal the future or the will of the gods. Or maybe it was just an excuse to get high.

Obviously, early humans didn't initially have rigidly organized religion as we know it. We're talking about a time before written records, so there are only a couple of ways we can gain an insight into what prehistoric humans may have believed. One is by examining archaeological evidence, which, although helpful, requires a certain amount of supposition. The other is by studying modern hunter-gatherer societies and looking for commonalities. These ways aren't perfect, I'll grant you, but it's the best we can do, and gives as accurate a picture as possible.

Over 99% of human history took place before written records, which is a period of time that makes the building of the Great Pyramid seem like a recent event. It ranges from the lower Palaeolithic period to the Neolithic and incorporates a vast array of beliefs—everything from primitive shamans, the worship of a mother goddess, and sophisticated astronomical placement of stones, to complex oral traditions that were passed down through generations.

However, it is important to note that the ubiquitous nature of religious belief took hold very early in human history. It speaks to two very human desires: to explain the inexplicable and to find meaning in existence. What seems clear is that early humans felt the need to make spiritual sense of the world, and it's a big idea that's continued to the present.

I'd say we've come a long way, because the metaphorical 'Body of Christ' has to be preferable to the literal 'Body of Ugg.'

Hunting and Gathering: It's a lifestyle choice!

The overriding characteristic of the Palaeolithic period was the hunter-gatherer lifestyle. In fact, for the vast majority of human existence, all humans obtained food in the wild by hunting animals and foraging for edible plants. There was an emphasis on gathering because hunting expended large amounts of energy. These hunter-gatherer societies usually comprised fewer than one hundred members, and in good times, enjoyed diverse and plentiful diets. Jared Diamond, evolutionary biologist and doyen of the chin-strap beard, asserts that "[h]unter-gatherers practiced the most successful and longest-lasting lifestyle in human history."

Of course, being a nomadic foraging community had downsides. First, you'd have to love camping and hunting. Also, it wasn't great for the very young or the old and infirm: Infanticide and senilicide (the murder of the elderly if they couldn't keep up with the tribe) were rife. It also mattered very much *where* you were a hunter-gatherer. If you lived in a warm coastal environment, you might live a comfortable, almost affluent existence (by caveman standards). If you lived in a baking desert or in the Arctic, you very much lived a subsistence lifestyle. That's if you survived at all.

So while hunter-gathering was the heavyweight champion when it came to longevity of the lifestyle, the jury's out on whether it was the most successful way of life. It depends on lowering one's definition of 'success' to mere survival. However, in contrast to the Hobbesian belief that the lifestyle would be 'poor, nasty, brutish, and short,' it's clear that on average, hunter-gatherer groups had healthier, longer lives than inhabitants of early farming societies. In fact, by some estimates, after the rise of farming, life expectancy wouldn't return to the same heights until the later Roman Empire.

Despite this 'success,' beginning around 9500 BC, humans all around the world moved slowly but inexorably towards a more sedentary, agricultural lifestyle. In her book *Paleofantasy*, Marlene Zuk skewers the idealized notion of the Palaeolithic as the halcyon days of humankind, in which carefree humans skipped barefoot through the heather and lived off the bounty of the earth. From Enlightenment scholars looking back to the noble savage to the recent trend of hippie-dippy Paleo diets, Zuk demonstrates that this nostalgic yearning for a time when humans were perfectly evolved to live in harmony with nature is pure fantasy.

I agree. If hunter-gathering was so bloody wonderful and idyllic, I doubt that the shift to agriculture would have happened once, let alone many times. Humans and our hominid forebears had been nomadic foragers for millions of years, and that lifestyle had severely limited the population. While this was arguably great for the planet, it wasn't ideal for our development as a species.

The coming shift to an agrarian lifestyle would eventually allow much greater population density and more opportunity for collective learning. The Neolithic Revolution would be the result.

But it came with a downside.

Fig. 17: A great idea that brought about generations of near starvation (Erica Guilane-Nachez and S.E.W.)

A Brief Interlude I

Calling Occupants of Interplanetary Craft

Four years after watching the Moon walk, my interest in ancient civilizations was piqued for all the wrong reasons.

This came in the form of *Chariots of the Gods?* a 1970 documentary based on a book by convicted fraud and pseudo-archaeologist Erich von Däniken. The movie cashed in on the astronaut fever of the Moon landings, so it's really no surprise that I clamored to get taken to see it. Von Däniken's 'big idea,' was that humanity had been visited in the past by ancient astronauts.

My dad took me to see the movie at the Cronulla Odeon, which in 1973 was a shabby art deco cinema whose heyday had been forty years previous. What I saw both transfixed and disturbed me. The creepy premise, unsettling music, and the faux-factual style. I sat riveted through an hour and a half of rock art of supposed 'astronauts,' leading interpretations of religious texts, and extremely dubious archaeological analysis. As one might expect from a movie which had a question mark in its title, almost all of these bogus claims were couched as questions: "The height of the Great Pyramid is nearly one billionth the distance from the Earth to the Sun. Coincidence?" and, in reference to a Mayan carving, "Isn't this a typical position for an astronaut?"

I lapped it up. *Chariots of the Gods?* validated virtually every hope and terror a kid could possess. It was presented as fact, and if aliens had interacted with humans two thousand years ago, why not now? I remember staring out the window into the black of night wondering if one of von Däniken's aliens was staring back at me. Would I be abducted? Vaporized? I was fascinated, but more than a little afraid.

"You know it's not real, don't you?" Dad batted away my fears with a wave of his hand.

"But they made a movie, it must be true."

"You can't believe everything you see."

The problem was that I found it so *convincing*. Von Däniken used flawed logic and misrepresented and even fabricated 'evidence' to make a compelling case for his proposition: Celestial visitors had bestowed advanced technology on early humans. For reasons known only to themselves, these aliens had built Stonehenge, the Great Pyramid, and Machu Picchu, and in fact, every significant ancient site. Y'know, stuff we poor, stupid humans couldn't *possibly* have accomplished for ourselves.

My obsession was so great that, despite my ancient astronaut anxiety, I begged Mum and Dad for a copy of the companion book, which I pored over endlessly. *Chariots of the Gods?* turned out to be a gateway drug to the wide world of wild conspiracy theories. And I fell for it hook, line, and sinker.

It poisoned my mind to the extent that, for a time, my views about the ancient world were severely warped.

Herr von Däniken gifted me something else: an enduring fear. In the movie, von Däniken examined the rock art of Tassili n'Ajjer in Algeria. Understandably, his interpretation was that Neolithic artists were depicting ancient aliens. For nearly fifty years, one of these images has haunted my dreams. So much so, I still can't look at it without a shiver running up my spine. In an attempt to exorcise this demon, I present it here.

Ladies and gentlemen, I give you 'the Great God Mars.'

Fig. 1: I guess you're wondering what the big deal is, yeah?
(Archivist and S.E.W.)

This is how von Däniken describes him:

> *Without overstretching my imagination, I get the impression that the great god Mars is depicted in a space- or diving-suit. On his heavy powerful shoulders rests a helmet which is connected to his torso by a kind of joint.*

Clearly, my cyclopean nightmare *must* be an alien wearing a spacesuit. According to von Däniken, there was simply no other rational explanation. Sure, seasoned archaeologists had vastly differing opinions, but what would *they* know? Didn't they have *eyes?*

Eventually, I learned to think more critically. While I don't rule out the *possibility* that aliens visited us in the past, what is more likely: that Marvin the Martian built monoliths like Stonehenge, or that they were created by the application of collective human knowledge? Rather than picking up our technological and communications skills from beyond the stars, isn't it far more probable that we developed them ourselves by gradually accumulating ideas and skills for hundreds of thousands of years?

After all, that's how a rag-tag collection of ground-dwelling, foraging primates learned to farm.

Chapter Two

We Built this City
The Neolithic Revolution

Aliens had nothing to do with it. Honestly.

The Neolithic or New Stone Age is synonymous with a wide range of significant changes, not least of which was the refinement of stone tools for which the period was named. Larger human settlements, beer, and pottery also arose during this time. As did the human penchant for creating stone monoliths. But perhaps the single biggest innovation of the Neolithic was the advent of agriculture. As we shall see, when that lightbulb moment struck in disparate areas all over the globe, things would never be the same.

Farming: The Biggest Idea Ever?

The emergence of agriculture is often seen as the defining event of the 'Neolithic Revolution,' and like all revolutions, its effect was... well... revolutionary. In fact, archaeologist Steven Mithen claims that the advent of farming was "the defining event of human history."

Nominating the humble science of farming as the most significant human idea ever might seem like a stretch, but Mithen's idea is persuasive. There are many lightbulb moments that we'll investigate in this (and subsequent) books: human speech, religion, writing, education, mathematics, the Industrial Revolution, and the internet, just to mention a few. But it's arguable that none of these would've seen the light of day without the invention of agriculture. There's a strong argument that without it, humans would still be living in small tribal groups and most of our accomplishments would never have occurred.

Of course, it's highly unlikely that a Neolithic 'Archimedes' ran out of his cave screaming: "Eureka! I've invented an entirely new lifestyle that will change the world!" Far more likely, foraging groups gradually began to domesticate animals and plant seeds as a supplement to their hunter-gathering way of life. Given that this shift from foraging to farming took place over generations, the change happened so organically it probably wasn't noticed. Humans transitioned to farming at the same time in many unrelated locations, including the Levant, India, China, and Mesopotamia. In that respect, this lightbulb moment was closer to a searchlight moment.

Eventually, farming changed everything. Small, nomadic hunter-gatherer tribes put down roots and set up villages. Villages became towns. The towns eventually grew into cities. In the long term, agriculture freed some people from the task of providing food so they could undertake other roles: artists, priests, philosophers, and even primitive scientists. In this way, the agrarian lifestyle paved the way for advances in all domains of lightbulb moments.

So, even if our hypothetical caveman Archimedes had burst triumphantly out of his cave proclaiming a change in lifestyle, would this lightbulb moment have been welcomed?

Unlikely.

You see, for such a transformative idea, this lightbulb burned exceedingly dim for hundreds of years, and often mustn't have seemed like a great idea at all. There were some teething problems (if one can count malnutrition and starvation as 'teething problems') as humans learned the vagaries of farming. The much-vaunted 'paleo' diet of the forager was gone, replaced by a reliance on a limited range of crops that didn't provide an appropriate range of nutrition. In these circumstances, a crop failure was disastrous, as there was no fallback position. Also, as humans began to live in closer proximity to each other, infectious diseases took their toll, jumping from person to person, or even jumping species from the newly domesticated animals.

So far, so bad. And it gets worse.

Infant mortality went up. Life expectancy went down. Jared Diamond cites evidence that dramatically shows the effect of this transition: skeletal remains from this time show that after the adoption of farming, average height slumped from 175 cm to 160 cm for men, and 165 cm to 152 cm for women.

Fig. 1: The change from hunter-gathering didn't suit everyone, Part I (Morphart and S.E.W.)

As time went by, humans became more proficient at agriculture, the human population began to increase, and our relationship to the natural environment became more distant. The advent of agricultural practices such as slash and burn methods of land clearing and the overgrazing of cattle had negative environmental impacts. In fact, the genesis of many of our current problems with our relationship with the planet begins at this point.

Adopting agriculture also brought on class divisions and gender inequality. It's conjectured that women became less like the valued partners anthropologists theorize they were in the Paleolithic, and more like the chattel of Neolithic men. Slavery, too, appears to be an invention of agrarian societies.

Clearly, humanity's quality of life had changed, but not (in the short term) for the better. Things looked bleak. If ever there was evidence that human history was *not* a perpetual series of improvements, this was it.

Thank God I'm a Country Boy: The Agrarian Lifestyle

Given the significant downsides, why was farming so transformative for human society? To understand that, we need to look at the growing pressures on hunter-gatherer groups.

Anatomically modern humans had been around for hundreds of thousands of years. They had made little technological progress other than improving their stone tools, but they had little need of technology because the foraging lifestyle had been so good to them. In 1966, American anthropologist Marshall Sahlins coined the term 'affluent hunter-gatherers' to describe these people. According to Sahlins' research, these affluent hunter-gatherers had loads of leisure time and limited wants and needs. It's possible that inhabitants of such foraging communities only needed to work somewhere between fifteen to twenty hours a week to keep themselves fed. Nice work if you can get it.

However, one can imagine that such a chilled-out lifestyle might not be optimal for driving technological advancement. In such an environment, 'If it ain't broke, don't fix it' would probably be an adaptive way of thinking. Yet, eventually, change came in the Neolithic age.

In the Levant, the Neolithic Natufian culture, which dates from 15,000 to 11,500 years ago, seems to bridge this nomadic to agricultural divide. The Natufian settlement of Abu Hureyra provides the earliest evidence of systematic agriculture on Earth. There's clear evidence that it began as a hunter-gatherer settlement, but slowly the inhabitants changed a sedentary, agricultural lifestyle. Archaeologists have uncovered evidence that around 13,000 years ago, they began to cultivate rye. Until other evidence is discovered, this makes the people of Abu Hureyra the world's first known farmers. But this change probably wasn't a conscious choice.

It has been heavily speculated that the metamorphosis from forager to farmer was a result of climate change. This would make sense, as the hunter-gatherer lifestyle had been successful for millions of years and, as we've speculated, it's unlikely 'affluent hunter-gatherers' would have actively sought change. There had to be a good reason. Rather than coming as a fully formed epiphany, farming was likely a series of innovations over a long period to help combat the effects of global cooling.

With energy at a premium, humans needed to find new ways of extracting as much of it from the land as possible. The development of agriculture let them do just that. Farming and animal husbandry allowed humanity to more fully exploit the potential energy that plants had accumulated due to photosynthesis. Cultivating edible plants was a far more effective way of exploiting their energy than gathering them in the wild. And, although humans couldn't digest grass, cows and sheep could, and we could gain the energy they'd obtained from the grass by eating them or drinking their milk. This gave humans access to stored energy that they previously could not tap. Also, the domestication of herd animals made it more energy efficient to take a sheep from the paddock than to send out a hunting party to catch a wildebeest.

An array of people, from revered academics such as Jared Diamond to Paleo-diet hippies, view the end of the foraging lifestyle as a tragedy. It was, they believe, a massive mistake from which humans will never recover. However, I think it's a stretch to argue that we'd all be happier if we were still hunter-gatherers. I, for one, would be absolutely miserable. Sleeping in a cave. Wearing animal skins. No Thai food or hot showers. I mean, *come on*. However, as we've seen, the paradigm shift to an agrarian lifestyle was not without its drawbacks.

Climate change may have inspired humans to give up the hunter-gatherer lifestyle and farm, but once the bugs were ironed out, there were benefits. It wasn't long before these people of the Neolithic Revolution began banding together in larger settlements. It used to take two hundred hectares of land to keep one forager alive, but in agrarian societies, the same area fed about *two hundred* people. The adoption of agriculture meant that crops and animals could be farmed to meet demand, and once it hit its stride, the human population skyrocketed.

It's clear that humanity's rise was related to the cultivation of crops, but if some researchers are to be believed, there may have been an even greater imperative that drove the development of civilization...

Inebriation.

Hold my Beer

As we saw in Chapter One with the vervet monkey, some primates appear to have a natural predilection for drinking alcohol. Although we have no way of knowing, it's a fair bet that our evolutionary predecessors also drank naturally occurring alcohol whenever the chance arose. However, at some stage, long before recorded history, humans developed the ability to make alcoholic beverages for themselves. We're not talking about a bottle of Veuve Clicquot or martinis 'shaken not stirred.' We are talking about the champagne of the proletariat: beer.

The oldest known evidence of the brewing of beer dates to the Natufian period around thirteen thousand years ago in what is now Israel. In their paper, *What was Brewing in the Natufian?*, authors Brian Hayden, Neil Canuel, and

Jennifer Shanse make the argument that agriculture may have developed not just because of humanity's need for bread, but because of humanity's need for booze. This is the so-called *Beer before Bread* hypothesis. It's simplifying, but not *totally* misrepresenting Hayden, Canuel, and Shanse's findings to suggest it's possible that humans invented agriculture so beer could be made reliably, which had the knock-on effect of bringing about a little thing called civilization. This wouldn't be the last time that men's (I use that gendered term advisedly) desire to get blotto would have an effect on history.

Fig. 2: Grog is horrified (Fotomolos, Jacoblund, EugeneTomeev and S.E.W.)

A Bunch of Prized tools II: Sharper is better

In the previous chapter, I noted that tools were a massive technological leap for humans. The problem with Palaeolithic implements was that they were mostly flaked from soft stone, and were therefore unsuitable for long-term use. In the Neolithic era, humans developed innovative manufacturing strategies, which enabled the creation of stronger, longer-lasting tools. Instead of chip, chip, chipping away at soft stones, Neolithic toolmakers flaked, ground, and polished harder stones. This improved the performance of classic tool designs and allowed for the invention of newer, advanced designs.

One such design was the polished stone axe. Axe-heads were initially shaped by flaking and then smoothed down by grinding and polishing. Often the axe-heads were attached to a wooden handle, which made them effective in clearing land for agriculture and fashioning building materials for permanent dwellings. Axes may have been the Neolithic version of the Swiss Army knife, as another of their uses was as a bludgeoning weapon. Other familiar tools invented or refined around this time include hammers, adzes, and scrapers.

The new toolmaking methods also made for breakthroughs in weapons manufacturing. Arrowheads and blades had been around since the Palaeolithic, but advanced Neolithic technology made them lighter and sharper, a lethal combination. This meant better hunting for hybrid hunter-gatherer/agricultural tribes, and a tactical advantage during tribal warfare.

This is when the arms race began, and it hasn't stopped.

Hairy Potter and the New Age of Stone

While humans had been using unfired clay for making pottery since the Palaeolithic era, anyone who's tried their hand at pottery will know that unfired pots are pretty useless. In the early stages of the Neolithic, humans had experimented with other materials such as wood, stone, and leather. Pottery was such a significant development that it is used to determine a line of demarcation: this Early Neolithic period before ceramics is known as the pre-pottery Neolithic.

It wasn't until well into the Neolithic period, around 7000 BC, that humans developed the ability to bake the clay at hot enough temperatures to make ceramics. This was no mean feat. Properly firing clay required the ability to make ovens that could reach temperatures upwards of 850 degrees Celsius. This isn't easy. In addition, making ceramics successfully requires a great deal of specialized knowledge, particularly in relation to the choice, preparation, and purification of clay.

In the later Neolithic period, the once utilitarian pottery was decorated with abstract geometric patterns and other designs. These pots were glazed with iron oxide mixed with various minerals to create different colors. There's evidence that these artisanal crafted pots became sought-after trade objects.

The craft of ceramics would be improved upon by subsequent civilizations, each putting their own stamp on the physical shaping and decoration of the pieces.

Fig. 3: The change from hunter-gathering didn't suit everyone, Part II (Archivist and S.E.W.)

The Birth of Cities

Despite some bumpy moments, humans survived their long and dangerous ascent to the top, and their tenacity and technology had made them undoubted masters of the planet. Their next move, banding together in towns and cities, was a big idea that was to have far-reaching ramifications.

The first archaeological evidence of a permanent human settlement was a village in the Czech Republic, which was built 25,000 years ago. It is now known as Dolní Věstonice, which comprised some small dwellings built of mammoth bones and rocks. It is also known as the home of the *Venus of Dolní Věstonice*, a pendulous Venus figure to rival the *Venus of Willendorf*. Such villages continued to grow into towns and, thousands of years later, in regions affording an abundance of domesticated grains, they would develop into cities, which took *Homo sapiens* to a new level.

The identity of the first known city varies depending on how one defines 'city.' Some of the criteria used to judge are the population of the settlement, the population density, the presence of walled fortifications, some form of sewerage system, and evidence of government. By these standards, most credit the city of Jericho in the Levant as numero uno, although some give it to Uruk in Mesopotamia.

But before we consider bigger cities, we need to look at a place that predates the likes of Jericho by over two thousand years.

Çatalhöyük

By the standards I've just outlined, Çatalhöyük, situated in southern Anatolia, Turkey, only rates as a proto-city. It is, nevertheless, an extremely significant site. It existed for around a thousand years, starting circa 7500 BC, with a population that archaeologists believe varied from 5,000 to 10,000 inhabitants. One way Çatalhöyük fails to satisfy the 'city' definition is that, to date, no public buildings have been found. As far as archaeologists have been able to determine, it was composed entirely of tightly clustered domestic buildings, and strangely to modern sensibilities, had no streets.

Due to the whole 'no streets' vibe, the main thoroughfare of the town was across the roofs of the buildings. Because of this peculiarity, the houses had no need for front doors, and were accessed via hatches in the ceiling and a ladder. I can't help imagining a trip to the Çatalhöyük 'shops' looking more like a James Bond chase scene.

Fig. 4: Çatalhöyük: the birthplace of parkour? (mbolina and S.E.W.)

Another aspect of Çatalhöyük that wouldn't pass public health and safety codes today was how dead bodies were disposed of. Excavations of the site have shown that bodies were routinely buried under the floor of the house. As I'm sure you've noticed, this is quite different from modern burial practices, unless Çatalhöyük was a society of serial killers.

These features of Çatalhöyük seem strange to us, but we must remember that the familiar hallmarks of urban living were yet to be invented. While the town successfully existed for just under a thousand years, its signature lack of ground-level thoroughfares was not repeated elsewhere. Once streets were invented, humankind never looked back.

Jericho: Before the Walls Went Up

As far as can be proven, Jericho is the site of the longest continuous human occupation. For a start, it had been an area frequented by hunter-gatherers. Then, around 9500 BC, a small, permanent settlement was established. This settlement appears to be transitional between foraging and farming lifestyles. The inhabitants cultivated a combination of wild and domestic crops, but still relied on hunting for meat. Unlike Çatalhöyük, this pre-Jericho consisted of small circular stone dwellings, but like Çatalhöyük, the dead were buried under the house.

A couple of thousand years later, these round huts were replaced by rectangular mud-brick buildings. However, this generation of Jericho residents still buried grandma under the floor. They also had a creepy new obsession: reconstructing the likenesses of loved ones by plastering their skulls and putting cowrie shells in their eye sockets. These macabre tributes were kept as keepsakes in the same home where the headless body was buried. In less disturbing news, it's believed that sheep were domesticated around this time.

By the time Biblical Joshua reputedly brought down the walls of Jericho by having his army march around it carrying the Ark of the Covenant and blowing their horns, it had already been a city for around 8,000 years.

Fig. 5: Years later, Joshua is about to learn where the bodies are buried (Public Domain and S.E.W.)

The Significance of Cities

The rise of the city during the Neolithic Revolution meant a lot of change for the man in the street (or rooftop). Once a few generations of Neolithic farmers ironed out the problems in the initial shift from a hunter-gathering lifestyle, positive change was possible. The cultivation of crops and domestication of animals allowed urban civilizations to sustain larger populations, experiment with systems of government, and establish a division of labor. Importantly, it also enabled the production of art and large-scale architecture.

The Massive Erections of the Neolithic Revolution

Throughout our history, humans have excelled in the art of constructing massive erections. Inspiration flashes in the mind of a visionary, who then persuades his people to commit to a construction project of breathtaking proportions. In subsequent chapters, we'll encounter pyramids, acropolises, forums, temples, and massive stadia—all of which, it seems, were designed to validate humanity's collective ego.

Perhaps we, as a species, are compensating for something?

It's hard to say, but whatever drives this constructive obsession, it was during the Neolithic Revolution that we saw evidence of its beginnings. Even before people began living in settled towns and cities or invented written language, it appears that loose confederations of hunter-gatherer tribes joined forces. These Neolithic people were of a higher caliber than Grog or Ugg, and could undertake the planning and execution of significant, long-term civil engineering projects, such as Stonehenge and Göbekli Tepe.

The Temples at Potbelly Hill

Göbekli Tepe (which translates to the decidedly less poetic 'Potbelly Hill') is an archaeological site in Anatolia, built around 9500 BC, making it the world's oldest known megalith. It's so old, it was ancient before Stonehenge was a fiery reflection in a druid's eye. This megalith comprises many large round structures and massive T-shaped stone uprights, and is believed to be the oldest place of worship ever constructed. Even by today's standards, Göbekli Tepe was a colossal construction project.

Given the scope of Göbekli Tepe, it seems certain that a number of foraging tribes must have co-operated on the project in order to assemble the extensive workforce required. This speaks to a level of social stability and organizational ability that well surpasses our traditionally low expectations of Neolithic people.

Fig. 6: The project managers of Göbekli Tepe would have been more sophisticated (He2, PeskyMonkey, Suzi, and S.E.W.)

Although Göbekli Tepe was initially thought to be a single (albeit massive) temple, over time, archaeologists uncovered a much larger complex composed of more than twenty individual sites of similar design. Whether this was the work of obsessive-compulsive builders, or whether there was a bigger picture in mind, we may never know.

Göbekli Tepe isn't notable just for its size and scope. It also incorporated interesting design features, with many of the T-shaped stone pillars being carved with impressive bas-reliefs of wild animals such as snakes, wild boars, brown bears, big cats, aurochs, and vultures. Other artifacts discovered on the site include stone face masks, human and animal figurines, and even what appears to be a totem pole. These provide archaeologists with intriguing, but sometimes difficult to interpret insights into the emergence of monumental building and life in the Neolithic era.

Of course, the fact that it was discovered twenty-five years after *Chariots of the Gods?* didn't stop the believers in ancient astronauts from claiming that humans couldn't possibly have created Göbekli Tepe in the Pre-Pottery Neolithic period. However, while 'Potbelly Hill' was a startling achievement for Neolithic humans, it rates as a pathetic effort from intergalactic space-faring aliens.

A Hollywood Legend's Last Resting Place?

Like the advent of farming, standing stones were ubiquitous throughout the Neolithic world, from England, Europe, Africa, and Asia, to South America. Sometimes they arose as circles of stones such as Stonehenge; sometimes as a large flat stone laid on upright ones, known as a dolmen; and sometimes as single stones, called menhirs.

The first time I saw a photograph of a menhir was in Year 9 art history. As usual, the class was discussing slides projected onto a screen by our teacher, Mrs Cowan. We'd been looking at some interesting cave art when the slide carousel whirred and the next image flashed up: a long, slim, obviously phallic stone, pointing proudly skywards from a green field. As a fifteen-year-old smartass in a world *before* the invention of Viagra, there was only one comment I could make—

"It's Errol Flynn's grave!" I announced, alluding to the reputedly well-endowed Hollywood icon. The class began to crack up, but Mrs Cowan stopped us all with a gimlet eye.

"It's a *menhir,*" she said through gritted teeth (although I flattered myself that she was trying not to laugh, as well). I was genuinely shocked. I was familiar with Obelix's cartoon menhir from the *Asterix* comics, but his menhir was more like an elongated egg than a massive stone dong.

Menhirs are human-made standing stones, usually found in France, Great Britain, or Ireland. Although difficult to date, they are believed to have been – ahem – *erected* at various times from the Neolithic era up to the Bronze Age. The purpose of menhirs has been hotly debated. Theories for their use include druidic religious ceremonies (possibly including human sacrifice), territorial markers, or as a type of calendar. That, or these massive stone phalluses were the ancient world's equivalent of 'dick pics.'

Fig. 7: Errol would've been proud (Михаил Решетников, Eugenesergeev, and S.E.W.)

Given the obvious sexual nature of many menhirs, it's tempting to believe the theory that they were used as a part of ancient fertility ceremonies. This wouldn't be far from the mark. In fact, their significance for fertility rites may have endured for thousands of years. As recently as the eighteenth century, an anatomically correct standing stone in a churchyard in County Cork was given a sledgehammer circumcision by the local priest. This was, ostensibly, to stop local villagers from using it as a venue for performing ancient healing and fertility rituals. Another menhir in Tara, Ireland was locally famous as the 'Phallus of Fergus' for obvious reasons.

It's quite possible menhirs were phallic symbols associated with Celtic sun worship. Evans Wentz observed in 1911 that this was "because among all ancient peoples where phallic worship has prevailed, the sun has been venerated as the supreme masculine force, [...] while the phallus has been venerated as the corresponding force in human nature."

Some things take a *long* time to change.

Like the much earlier Göbekli Tepe, many menhirs are engraved with bas-relief sculptures of animals, although farming implements such as plows and shepherds' crooks were also popular subjects. Sometimes, menhirs are grouped together in a circular earthwork known as a henge.

Which brings us to the most famous of these megaliths...

Stonehenge: If These Stones Could Speak

Stonehenge, situated on the Salisbury Plain in England, is a ring of massive standing stones topped with lintels, and is arguably the most famous ancient megalith. If its architects were endeavoring to create an iconic and enigmatic image to ring down the millennia, they succeeded beyond their wildest dreams.

Archaeologists believe construction of Stonehenge began around 3000 BC, and think it took almost 1,000 years to complete. These stones are aligned in such a way to mark the midsummer and midwinter solstices. Given the importance of Celtic sun worship, it's clear this seasonal cycle was the driving force behind the construction. However, the original builders, who just threw up a few astronomically aligned wooden posts, would have been surprised to see the monumental arrangement of standing stones that it eventually became.

Stonehenge is made up of two types of stone: the largest, most iconic stones are known as sarsen stones, and the inner ring of smaller stones are called bluestones. The sarsen stones are a type of sandstone found naturally across the south of England. Recent research has confirmed what has been believed for many years, that these stones were quarried in the Marlborough Downs and transported 32 kilometers to the Salisbury Plain. This was a

Herculean task, as sarsen stones weigh between 25 and 30 tons each. The bluestones are much smaller, weighing in around 2 to 5 tons apiece, and are believed to have originally come from the southwest of Wales. However, Stonehenge appears to be their second home since that journey, as they have been recycled from a previous stone circle just under two kilometers away.

Although little evidence of the building methods remains, conspiracy theorists have filled the void with crackpot theories of how these massive stones were moved and erected. As you might suspect, my friend Herr von Däniken had a particular opinion about Stonehenge. Although, the logic of advanced extraterrestrials crossing the galaxy to assist glorified chimps to arrange giant stones into a rough circle escapes me.

Fig. 8: Sorry Erich (by PikePicture, acrogame and S.E.W.)

Credit Where Credit is Due

Despite the attempts to discredit the Neolithic megalith makers, it's clear that these decidedly human builders had developed a significant suite of mathematical, engineering, and problem-solving knowledge. Along with this scientific and technical expertise, artisans and tradespeople also added to the collective learning of humanity.

Now that humans had developed more sophisticated technological, artistic, and higher-order thinking skills, they required a concrete way of ensuring that this intellectual capital would be transmitted to future generations. They needed to somehow permanently record their ideas, not just leave them to be recounted orally.

In the big scheme of things, the invention of the written word rivals agriculture as one of the biggest ideas of all. As far as we know, only four cultures in human history have invented writing: the Sumerians, the Egyptians, the Mesoamericans, and the Chinese. There are arguments that the scripts of the Indus Valley and Easter Island are potential examples of invented writing, but experts can't agree without a breakthrough in translation of these scripts. However, there is consensus that the development of the written word has had momentous and long-lasting ramifications.

One of these ramifications was the organization that allowed cities to increase in population. Among the first cities to house populations of tens of thousands or more were Memphis in Egypt and Uruk in Sumer. This happened around 3100 BC and equates timewise with the beginnings of written language in both cultures. In this new world of civilization, knowledge would be a saleable commodity. The big idea of collective learning was about to take on an even greater importance.

Let there be no doubt—whether it is writing, art, science, education, organized religion, and more—so much of what we value in the twenty-first century had its foundations in the ideas and discoveries of ancient civilizations from all over the world. We owe our forebears a great debt.

The End of Prehistory

The Neolithic Revolution changed the way humans survived, expressed themselves, used tools, worshipped, organized their lives, and got smashed. In fact, it fundamentally changed what it meant to be human. No longer were humans glorified animals. They were the lords of their domain.

The descendants of Grog and Ugg had taken on a measure of sophistication.

Lightbulb moments led to more lightbulb moments, and humans were now ready to take the next significant step. Having already begun to band together in towns and cities, these would eventually coalesce into sophisticated civilizations.

But before that, there was another humongous change on the horizon: metals and metalwork. Humans had been working with soft metals such as gold since the Palaeolithic, but stone as a material for tools was about to be superseded in a big way. The Bronze Age was emerging, and with it, a time when prehistory ends and recorded history begins.

This is when lightbulb moments took on even greater significance.

Chapter Three

By the Rivers of Babylon
Ancient Mesopotamia

Those Lazy-Hazy-Crazy Days Of Sumer

Ancient Mesopotamia is often referred to as 'the cradle of civilization.' However, current academic opinion is that there was no single place where civilization began. Rather, it appears that several significant civilizations developed simultaneously in different places: Egypt, China, and India. Nevertheless, many still consider the region in the Fertile Crescent to be the place where civilization began. The name 'Mesopotamia' is derived from a Greek word meaning 'between the rivers,' referring to the area between the Tigris and Euphrates rivers. However, Mesopotamia also includes eastern Syria, southeastern Turkey, and most of Iraq.

Mesopotamia was the home to several significant cultures, not least of which were the Sumerians, the Akkadians, and the Babylonians. The *Reader's Digest* version of their relationship is this: The Sumerians were the first literate culture in the region. Sumer was conquered by the Akkadian Empire, and when the Akkadian Empire collapsed, the Sumerian culture was resurgent. The Babylonians were a later civilization that took up residence in the same region of Mesopotamia as the Sumerians. In this chapter, in general, I might sometimes refer to them all as 'Mesopotamians,' even though this is not always technically correct.

While researching, I encountered at least three nineteenth-century histories whose authors believed it was only worth beginning their works with the Ancient Greeks. Elwood Cubberley, a nineteenth-century educational historian, sums up this attitude to pre-Hellenistic civilizations: "Our

Western civilization does not go back to these as sources, and consequently they need not concern us."

The Assyrian and Babylonian empires have been well-known for thousands of years, but due to their coverage in the Bible, these civilizations didn't get good press, and so were often viewed in a negative light. Added to this, it wasn't until the mid-nineteenth century that the Sumerian culture was discovered. All of this led to historians of Cubberley's era tending to ignore the achievements of the civilizations of Mesopotamia. This is despite the obvious fact that they had greatly contributed to the collective learning of all humanity. There's no way the Greeks or Romans could have done what they did in a vacuum. Their knowledge came from *somewhere*.

Of course, the later Persian Empire had long been known to historians due to its epic battles against the Greek city-states. Persians were often seen as the 'baddies' in a war of aggression, but we shall see that they were cultured and had big ideas of their own, not all of which are as well-known as they should be.

The succession of civilizations that fanned out from the Fertile Crescent were impressive and deserve the kudos for their many human firsts. Foremost among these was arguably one of the biggest human ideas: writing.

How Accountants Invented Writing

As we know, spoken language was the innovation that allowed humans to accumulate and transfer knowledge. But until the Sumerians invented writing, there was no way to preserve information other than oral history.

Fig. 1: Rough translation: 'This is one hell of a ziggurat'
(Morphart, homocosmicos, ZU_09 and S.E.W.)

Scholars believe that early Sumerian script was developed from a type of tally mark used in counting. Over time, such marks led to simple representations of cattle, sheep, and other counted commodities being etched onto wet clay tablets. Sad to say, but we have humanity's need to count wealth—and as a result, accountants, and bookkeepers—to thank for the genesis of writing.

Rather like our computer icons in the present day, these symbols bore only a passing resemblance to the objects they represented. This system of symbols is called archaic cuneiform and is the earliest known form of writing. The problem with such a system was that those symbols represented specific items but did not represent grammatical elements, so a new system needed to be developed. Those icons became more stylized strokes that represented the syllables of spoken language. The resulting chicken scratchings were the beginnings of cuneiform script.

Although it is possible that Sumerian script was the inspiration for Egyptian writing, the Egyptian hieroglyphs are very different to Sumerian cuneiform. Writing that used these pictorial figures signaled the beginning of Egyptian civilization. Although it is still image-based, Egyptian script was more than a sophisticated form of picture-writing. Each glyph served one of three functions: to represent the actual thing or action; to stand for a phoneme or phonemes, or to give the precise meaning of adjacent hieroglyphs.

Only a privileged few had the advanced levels of education to read hieroglyphs. Even fewer had the skill to write them, as it was taught to a limited number of artisans.

And so it came to be that after millions of years of the musclemen and knuckle-draggers of this world holding sway, the nerds and sensitive, artistic types were coming into their own. In this new world of civilization, *learning* was now a saleable commodity. Education was about to take on a new importance, and the need to pass on collective learning required teachers and schools to fill the growing need.

The Epic of Gilgamesh: Mesopotamian Iron Man?

When it comes to writing blockbuster stories, it seems like it's all been done before. This wasn't a problem faced by the author of *The Epic of Gilgamesh,* the epic Mesopotamian poem considered to be the world's earliest surviving written narrative. *The Epic of Gilgamesh* defies classification in any of today's conventional genres: Is it a superhero story? A fantasy? A buddy comedy? A porno? There are even aspects of science fiction, historical fiction, and horror. It's definitely both a comedy *and* a tragedy. It was even plagiarized by the Bible: particularly the story of Noah and the flood.

Our hero/anti-hero Gilgamesh begins the story as a tyrannical king ruling over the city of Uruk. To keep him under control, the gods of Mesopotamia created a rival for him, the barbarous Enkidu. However, the best-laid plans went astray and they became friends instead. For reasons best known to Gilgamesh, he decided to civilize Enkidu, and engaged the help of Shamhat, a sacred temple prostitute (of which, more later). She tamed the wild Enkidu through a fortnight of sacred shagging, after which Enkidu was miraculously transformed into the perfect gentleman.

Enkidu and Gilgamesh became even more inseparable pals, setting off on the first heroes' quest in recorded history. As a part of this quest, the Dynamic Duo slayed the Bull of Heaven and the monster Humbaba. This seriously pissed off the gods and they punished Enkidu by smiting him, which proved to be a turning point for Gilgamesh. It wasn't a positive outcome for Enkidu either.

Inconsolable after the loss of his hairy buddy, Gilgamesh became determined to find the secret of immortality. Dressed in a lion's skin and not much else, he set out on a quest to find the legendary and long-lived survivor of the Mesopotamian flood story, Utanapishtim (AKA the Bible's Noah), who Gilgamesh believed had the secret to cheating death. After surviving a long and perilous journey, Gilgamesh eventually located Utanapishtim, only to find he did *not* know the secret of immortality after all. Defeated, Gilgamesh returned home to the city of Uruk.

So, it's not a happy ending for the first written narrative. Luckily, it set the stage for millions more to come.

Fig. 2: Achmed had been trying to off-load the Gilgamesh garden sculpture for years (Archivist and S.E.W.)

Religion, Prostitution, and the World's First Named Author

The first writer whose name is known to history was a woman: Enheduanna, who did double-duty as a princess and High-priestess of the goddess Inanna. Inanna was the goddess of, among other things, love, sex, and the military, so one could be forgiven for thinking that her motto was 'make love *and* war.' She was a goddess with a lot on her mind, and being her high-priestess was an exalted role. Enheduanna lived in the Sumerian city-state of Ur in the twenty-third century BC. She wielded considerable clout, not least because her father was the first Akkadian king, Sargon the Great. She wrote the first known poetry by a named poet, *The Hymn to Inanna*;

> *Her wrath is a devastating flood which no one can withstand.*
> *A great watercourse, she abases those whom she despises.*
> Enheduanna

The hymn carries on in a similar vein. Inanna was a bit of a goth and was not to be trifled with, which makes sense considering she had dominion over sex and violence.

It is believed that the temples of Inanna were the hub of a 'sacred prostitution' ring. Inanna is often depicted as a prostitute, so it stands to reason that worshipping her would involve the temple being a holy knocking shop. Hymns to Inanna don't shy away from her whorishness: "The pearls of a prostitute are placed around your neck, and you are likely to snatch a man from the tavern." Inanna's genitals are often graphically portrayed and are also a common theme in Babylonian literature:

> *See now, my breasts stand out; see now, hair has grown on my genitals, signifying my progress to the embrace of a man. Let us be very glad! Dance, dance! O Bau, let us be very glad about my genitals!*
> Dumuzi-Inanna C, 42-48

Fig. 3: Inanna's hit 'My Genitals' [Parental Advisory - Explicit Content] (Osama Shukir Muhammed Amin and S.E.W.)

Now, please don't think I'm slut-shaming Inanna—she was just a goddess who had it all, knew what she wanted, and knew how to get it. However, I *am* saying that Enheduanna, the world's first named author, was educated in more than just reading and writing, if you get my drift.

Writing was the innovation that allowed Sumerians to develop the first known educational establishment, the temple-based 'edubba', or what we would later term in English: 'school.'

You Can't Beat School (But You Can Get Beaten at School)

School is a really big idea that was needed to ensure that scribes could be trained to cater to increasing demand. We get a glimpse into life in Ancient Mesopotamian schools through several surviving

Sumerian texts. These texts, known as Edubba-literature, are traditional pieces of literature that were copied out by would-be scribes over successive generations for over 1,000 years. One such piece, 'Schooldays' gives us an insight into what student scribes had to endure as a part of their training. Apart from learning how to write, it seemed to involve an awful lot of physical violence:

> *The door monitor (said), 'Why did you go out without my say-so?' He beat me.*
> *The jug monitor, 'Why did you take beer without my say-so?' He beat me.*
> *The Sumerian monitor, 'You spoke in Akkadian!' He beat me.*
> *My teacher, 'Your handwriting is not at all good!' He beat me.*

By today's standards, Sumer's teachers were incredibly strict. As we have seen, a student would be whipped simply for breaking a rule or making a mistake when copying onto a clay tablet. The school day lasted from sunrise to sunset, which was a long time to be closely watched by someone desperate to inflict a beating for the Sumerian equivalent of not dotting an 'i' or crossing a 't'. While the educator of today will, mostly, see the constant beatings as cruel and counterproductive, they may in their darkest moments admit to a wistful envy of the Sumerian teacher's ability to use summary justice as a classroom management tool.

Scribal education concentrated on learning to write Sumerian and Akkadian using cuneiform, and the conventions for writing letters, contracts, and accounts. It doesn't seem that the teaching methods were that sophisticated: Students learned the cuneiform script by continued copying and re-copying onto clay tablets until the text was error-free. Archeologists have found examples of these tablets covered with a student's work, which had been corrected by their teacher, presumably after they had committed verbal and physical assault on the errant student.

Records show that Mesopotamian scribal students were usually boys, although there is evidence for the existence of female scribes. These students had to undergo intensive training, which, when completed, would entitle them to describe themselves with the coveted title 'scribe.' At that point, they became part of an elite group of literati, who would look down upon lesser citizens. Of course, achieving this status wasn't fast or easy. It took twelve years to master cuneiform script and to gain the significant general knowledge required of a scribe. Originally, scribal schools were established in temples to educate their young students into either priests or scribes. However, over time, established scribes saw the potential for making some serious cash from tutoring the sons of the rich. These expensive, privately run schools eventually supplanted the temple schools and ensured that only the sons of the wealthy elite could afford to be educated. Few poor Sumerians were literate. Just like in America.

One of the elite private school students was Šulgi, a Mesopotamian scribe who, in the following text, boasts not only of his skills, but of his high birth:

When I was young, I learned at school
the scribal art on the tablets of Sumer and Akkad.
Among the highborn, no one could write like me.
Where people go for instruction in the scribal art
there I mastered completely subtraction, addition, calculating, and accounting.
The fair Nanibgal Nisaba
provided me lavishly with knowledge and understanding.
I am a meticulous scribe who does not miss a thing!

Although he finished by gloating about how meticulous and learned he was, Šulgi had the grace to credit 'the fair Nanibgal Nisaba,' the Sumerian goddess of scribes, for his abilities. Nisaba became the goddess of literacy after a long and distinguished career as the goddess of grain, and—given the origin of Sumerian writing—one can see the logic behind this transition. Šulgi is not the only scribe who honors her, as texts from many scribes often end with the phrase, 'Praise be to Nisaba!' Apart from her importance to scribes, Nisaba had an exalted position in the pantheon of Sumerian deities, as she was the scribe of the gods.

Being an educated person in Mesopotamia was a rare and significant thing. Despite the years of repetitive copying, as well as mental and physical abuse from teachers, survival from scribal school was a stellar addition to one's Mesopotamian CV. Newly graduated scribes were in high demand in the military, at the palace, in temples, or in business.

The average Sumerian learned a skill, art, trade, or craft from their parents or a close relative. However, from very early on, the powers-that-be regulated the training in skills to ensure that there were enough tradesmen in various trades. Later, in Babylon, the Code of Hammurabi required, by law, that an artisan pass the skills associated with his craft down to the next generation.

The Code of Hammurabi

Hammurabi (c. 1810 – c. 1750 BC) was a king of the First Babylonian dynasty. His eternal fame lies in having proclaimed the Code of Hammurabi, among the first known sets of written laws. Hammurabi was a stickler for good government and issued these laws because he wanted to standardize laws to create a universal sense of justice. He professed to have received the code directly from Shamash, the Babylonian god of justice.

Shamash (whose name sounds like Sean Connery doing an impersonation of the Hulk), was the sun god, and was also the god of truth, justice, and the Mesopotamian way. But here's where it gets creepy: he was the twin of our old friend, Inanna. And they were *close*. So close they would've made Jaime and Cersei Lannister blush.

So, surprisingly, considering Hammurabi's laws were derived from Shamash, they were strict on incest:

If a man be guilty of incest with his daughter, he shall be exiled.

If any one be guilty of incest with his mother, both shall be burned.

These laws go on *ad infinitum*, but you get the idea. However, none of them specifically precluded the bonking of twin brother and sister gods, so, without a word of innuendo, Shamash and Inanna enjoyed the loophole.

Hammurabi was all about letting the punishment fit the crime. Legal retribution focused on 'proportionate' physical punishment of the perpetrator—the 'eye for an eye' concept of justice. By modern standards, the penalties were severe, with many crimes resulting in physical disfigurement or death. Yet, despite its Draconian aspects, the code provides one of the first historical examples of a person being considered innocent until proven guilty. Of course, if you *were* proved guilty, you could have your eyes gouged out or your balls cut off, so it was more *Law and Order: Special Victims Unit* than *Ally McBeal*.

But laws weren't the only things the Mesopotamians invented.

Fig. 4: Hammurabi ponders proportionate justice (Nastasic and S.E.W.)

Big Wheels Keep on Turnin'

The Wheel is a big idea that rings down through the ages. As we know, the first wheel was not chiseled out of stone by a Neanderthal. It was invented in Mesopotamia around the fourth century BC. Although initially used as potter's wheels, the Sumerians' real brainchild was to insert an axle into two solid discs of wood, laying the groundwork for war chariots and carts.

The war chariot first appears in Mesopotamia around 3000 BC, when it is depicted on monuments from Ur. These show four solid-wheeled chariots pulled by a pair of oxen. These chariots were driven by a charioteer, but also accommodated a spearman. Given the plodding nature of oxen, these were unlikely to be swift enough to have been groundbreaking military vehicles. Later, a more maneuverable two-wheeled version of the chariot pulled by horses would revolutionize warfare.

Fig. 5: The groundbreaking two-wheeled chariot attacked by a groundbreaking lion (ZU_09 and S.E.W.)

Printing on Clay

The Mesopotamians then merged wheel technology and writing to create an early type of printing in the form of the cylinder seal. These small cylinders were engraved with cuneiform and/or illustrations. When rolled onto soft clay, they left an impression of the image. The clay would then be baked into permanence.

These seals were a form of signature, and because holes were drilled through them, it's believed they were worn as jewelry for convenience.

That, or Mesopotamians also invented the lanyard.

When one considers Mesopotamians wrote on wet clay, this method of engraving is analogous to modern-day printing on paper. The image to be 'printed' was engraved on the cylinder, leaving the negative space raised, making it an early form of intaglio printing. However, in some cylinder seals called roller stamps, the image was raised in a type of letterpress printing.

Fig. 6: Dad Joke + Sumerian Cylinder Seal (Steve Harris and S.E.W.)

Ninkasi: Goddess of Beer

As we saw in the previous chapter, brewing had been around for thousands of years, having likely been developed in the Natufian period. However, it was in Mesopotamia where the big idea of brewing beer and drinking to drown one's sorrows was first recorded. Specifically, it was about five thousand years ago in the Sumerian settlement of Godin Tepe.

By all accounts, Sumerians saw beer as a way of life. It turns up in the *Epic of Gilgamesh* and, somewhat unsurprisingly, the holy prostitute Inanna is also mythically associated with it. We are even gifted a recipe for the brewing of Sumerian beer through the *Hymn to Ninkasi*, with Ninkasi (literal translation: The Lady who Fills the Mouth) being the Goddess of Beer.

Of course, with Sumerian beer, we're not talking about anything approaching the craft beers that hipsters lovingly brew these days. Oh no. Sumerian beer was made from twice-baked barley bread that had been left to ferment in a vat. This created a grainy, glutenous drink, best consumed through a straw to filter out the sludge.

Fig. 7: Dashiell, the micro-brewer, contemplating his white whale (YakobchukOlena and S.E.W.)

In *A (Brief) History of Vice*, author Robert Evans details how he used instructions in the *Hymn to Ninkasi* to make a twenty-first century approximation of Sumerian beer. He then taste-tested his "much chunkier than you're used to" re-creation. His verdict? "It wasn't great, but it wasn't *bad*, either. It had a slightly sweet, slightly sour taste," and "packed a significant punch." For more details of Evans' experiment with Sumerian beer (and other historical vices), read his excellent book, *A (Brief) History of Vice.*

Although beer has been the downfall of many, Sumerian beer was, for one young woman, a stepping stone to greatness. Before becoming queen of the Sumerian state of Kish, Kubaba was a humble tavern-keeper. Through a mechanism lost to time, she ascended the throne of Kish around 2500 BC. She's the only woman on the Sumerian King List, in which she's referred to as 'Kubaba the Beer Woman.' The list also claims she reigned for 100 years.

Which just goes to show that beer can't be that bad for you.

The Library of Ashurbanipal

When it comes to big ideas, there are few more significant than the library. While somewhat eclipsed these days by the internet, for most of recorded history, libraries were the gateways to knowledge. Without them, much of the world's cumulative knowledge would likely have been lost. It's deeply ironic that the world's first known library was commissioned by Assyrian King Ashurbanipal, who was a strange blend of bloodthirsty conqueror and book nerd. This unique combination allowed him to build up his library by plundering texts from the cities he conquered.

The Library of Ashurbanipal was founded in the seventh century BC in the city of Nineveh (located in modern-day Iraq). It housed a collection of approximately 30,000 cuneiform tablets, which were cataloged by subject matter. The most famous text discovered in the Library of Ashurbanipal was the aforementioned *Epic of Gilgamesh,* although it held a great number of scholarly and religious texts as well.

The library was discovered by the Englishman Austen Henry Layard in 1849. After locating this amazing find, Layard took most of the tablets from Iraq to the British Museum. It seems somewhat appropriate that Ashurbanipal's ill-gotten treasure trove of books was, in turn, looted by the English.

Nevertheless, the establishment of the first library, by whatever means, was a significant step in ensuring that collective knowledge was safeguarded for posterity.

Fig. 8: Ashurbanipal explains his deep-seated need to loot books (rm8t and S.E.W.)

The Persian Empire: The World's First Superpower

After the fall of the Babylonian Empire in the fifth century BC, Cyrus (soon to be known as 'the Great') took control of a collection of semi-nomadic Iranian tribes. Forging these tribes into a formidable force, Cyrus defeated adjoining kingdoms, such as Lydia, Media, and Babylon, uniting them under his rule. This was the beginnings of the first Persian Empire, also known as the Achaemenid Empire. Eventually, it would unite three of the most important sites of ancient civilization: Mesopotamia, Egypt's Nile Valley, and the Indus Valley. If superpowers are a big idea (and the jury's still out), then Cyrus the Great's Persian Empire was the very first.

Rather than impose Persian culture on the peoples he

conquered, Cyrus practiced an early form of multiculturalism. He allowed them to continue their lives as before, with their customs and religions intact. All Cyrus asked was that they paid their taxes and obeyed his rule. All in all, Cyrus seemed like a pretty cool guy for a despot.

Cyrus had an inclusive management style. He involved conquered peoples, such as the Medes, in government. He returned religious icons looted by Babylon to their rightful place. He adopted the fashion sense of the Elamites, and in Babylon, he made a show of worshipping the god Marduk. This was a guy who knew how to schmooze.

One of Cyrus' most enlightened acts was to free the Jews, who had been forced into Babylonian exile by Nebuchadnezzar II. Upon defeating the Babylonians, Cyrus allowed the captives to return to Israel and rebuild their Temple. As a result, the Jews gave the Persian emperor five-star Yelp reviews.

Fig. 9: And they all lived happily ever after?

(Pavel Kusmartsev and S.E.W.)

It's arguable that this acceptance of diversity allowed the Persian Empire to become the epicenter of science and technology for the next two hundred years.

The Persian Wars

Over time, the Persian Empire continued to expand and eventually turned an eye towards Greece. The fourth Persian king, Darius, was a bloodthirsty fellow who had nefariously disposed of Cyrus' son Bardiya, and crushed all internal resistance to cement his position. Darius wanted to make an example of the Greeks, who had been actively fomenting a revolt against Persian domination in the Ionian islands.

Unfortunately for Darius, his 'punishment' of Greece didn't quite go according to plan. He began his campaign in 490 BC with some initial success, capturing a few Greek city-states. So far, so good. But when he attempted to take the city of Athens, the Persians got their asses kicked by the Athenians at the Battle of Marathon. Greece 1 - Persia 0.

Ten years later, Darius' barking mad son, Xerxes I, decided that he'd have a crack at conquering Greece. According to Herodotus, Xerxes successfully amassed one of the largest armies of ancient times. Things went a little south from there, as the bridges he had commissioned across the Hellespont were destroyed by a storm before the army had a chance to cross them. Xerxes absolutely lost it, and, like a totally sane person, had the engineers responsible for constructing the bridges beheaded. But that wasn't the end of his insanity. Xerxes had the sea given three hundred lashes and branded with red-hot irons to punish it for failing to comply with his will.

Fig. 10: It wasn't an auspicious start to the campaign
(Public domain and S.E.W.)

Despite this professional and psychological setback, Xerxes' Persians experienced success against the famous 300 Spartans and assorted other Greeks in the Battle of Thermopylae (Greece 1 - Persia 1). While the outcome was positive for the Persians, the bravery of the small contingent of Spartans and Thespians was heartening for the Greeks. When the Greek fleet smashed the Persian navy in the Battle of Salamis, Xerxes went home with his tail between his legs.

Final score: Greece 2 - Persia 1.

What began so promisingly with Cyrus the Great carried on for another 200 years. After Cyrus, Darius, and Xerxes, there followed a rag-tag group of other Dariuses, Xerxeses, and Artaxerxeses that seemed to make a sport of knocking each other off. Nevertheless, they managed to maintain control until, eventually, the First Persian Empire met its end when it clashed head-on with the armies of Alexander the Great.

It is difficult to overstate the importance of the civilizations that inhabited the fertile crescent. Thanks to the incredible durability of clay tablets (and the writing of Herodotus), we know quite a lot about the big ideas of the peoples of Mesopotamia. They were pioneers in law making, wheeled vehicles, fiction writing, beer drinking, and education. Other cultures would see what they produced and emulate it. Driven by their biggest idea, the written word, collective learning was taken to a whole new level.

The genie was well and truly out of the bottle.

A Brief Interlude II

Little Egypt

When I was a kid, I wanted to be an Egyptologist.

Admittedly, that was the third choice after paleontologist and astronaut, but it was close. My dad always read to me before bed, mostly non-fiction books about things that interested me: Dinosaurs and space were the most popular topics. As time went on, however, I expanded my repertoire. The local library was a great place to do this. One day, I borrowed a book about Egypt with a picture of Tutankhamen's gold death mask on the cover. I was fascinated. Tutankhamen's unblinking gaze regarded me through the millennia. I stared back. He won.

I couldn't get to sleep with it sitting on my bedhead. The book had to go face-down on the floor. Then I could sleep.

But I couldn't wait to read it in the morning.

It wasn't long after this that I discovered Erich von Däniken. His crackpot theories seriously skewed my view of Ancient Egypt. Suddenly this fascinating culture was at once devalued. Humans, Erich von Däniken claimed, couldn't possibly have constructed the pyramids without extraterrestrial assistance. However, he had other 'earthshaking' observations that he believed supported his idea that it must have been aliens:

> *How can we explain the fact that the Egyptians had a decimal system…? How did such a highly developed civilisation arise at such an early date? Where do the objects of copper and bronze originate as early as the beginning of the Egyptian culture? Who gave them their incredible knowledge of mathematics and a ready-made writing?*

While these Egyptian innovations were amazing, none of them were so inexplicable they required extraterrestrial visitors to explain their existence. The Egyptians invented a decimal system because we all have ten fingers and ten toes. Copper and bronze? Surely these aliens would've had more advanced metal hanging around. Von Däniken's claim about mathematics and writing is just ludicrous

Crazy Uncle Erich put paid to any ambition I had of being an Egyptologist.

Fig. 1: Von Däniken thought the Egyptians had the same contractors as Stonehenge (by PikePicture, wowinside and S.E.W.)

Chapter Four

Walk Like an Egyptian
Ancient Egypt

For over three thousand years, Ancient Egypt was the benchmark in ancient civilizations. It lasted from the unification of Upper and Lower Egypt around 3100 BC to its annexation by Rome in 30 BC. Ancient Egypt occupied the region along the lower reaches of the Nile River, not surprisingly, where the modern country of Egypt exists today.

What we blithely think of as 'Ancient Egypt' was not a coherent whole. Rather, it was a series of three politically stable kingdoms spaced out over three millennia: The Old Kingdom (3150-2686 BC), the Middle Kingdom (2055-1650 BC), and the New Kingdom (1550-1069 BC). These kingdoms were ruled over by thirty dynasties. Sandwiched between these kingdoms were the somewhat unstable Intermediate Periods.

Compared to the other major civilizations, the scope of Ancient Egypt is staggering. Let's put things in perspective. The Roman and British Empires each endured for less than 20% of Egypt's ancient ascendancy. America as a country has only been around a paltry 7.5% of that time. A generalized discussion about such an exceedingly long-lived civilization is an impossible task. Also, given the extreme longevity of Ancient Egypt, no single belief system lasted for the entire 3,000 years. Rather, they had a complex array of gods until the maverick pharaoh, Akhenaten, flirted with monotheism. Then, after his death, Egypt quickly reverted to the old gods.

Much of the durability of the Egyptian civilization is because its people harnessed the predictable flooding of the Nile River Valley. Irrigation and other agricultural practices enabled this valley to sustain a dense population. Unshackled from a subsistence lifestyle, the Egyptians were free to develop a unique culture. A culture that included big ideas such as distinctive religious beliefs (including the belief in an afterlife), writing, schooling, and monumental public works.

Life after Death

The Egyptians were not the first to conceive of an afterlife. However, their fanatical belief in this big idea drove virtually every aspect of their existence. Their pyramid building, as well as the practice of mummification, related directly to the big idea of cheating death. The Egyptian people were sticklers for religious rituals they believed ensured that life continued beyond the grave. They paid homage to the gods during their lives and made provision to continue that practice in the hereafter.

Those who know nothing else about Ancient Egypt have at least heard of mummies. This is probably thanks to horror movies, but there was more to mummification than wrapping bodies in Boris Karloff-like cloth bandages. Before any fancy wrapping could begin, the embalming process required numerous steps. Mummification was not for the poor or squeamish. But Egyptians considered it vitally important. They believed mummification preserved the body so the soul could return to it in the afterlife.

Mummification was also expensive and complex. The first step was ripping out the viscera, except for the heart, which was crucial for immortality. This included removing the brain by inserting a metal hook into a nostril, breaking through the skull, and then scraping out chunks of 'useless' grey matter. These organs were then sealed in canopic jars and buried with the body. Presumably on the off-chance they were required in the afterlife.

Icky stuff removed, the embalmers then packed the body cavities with natron, resin, preservatives and, understandably, perfumes. The natron dehydrated the corpse into human jerky. After forty days, this husk was cleaned and wrapped in linen strips. And voila! Our image of a mummy.

The quality of life for a soul resurrected into this brainless biltong? Sub-optimal, I'm guessing.

Fig. 1: Rameses II extolls the virtue of his extreme makeover (benoitb and S.E.W.)

At this point, the body was not fully prepared for the tomb. It could not progress any further until the 'opening of the mouth' ceremony took place. Priests performed this ritual, which included burning incense and anointing the body. It also included the all-important incantations to restore the mummy to its senses.

Then the mummy traveled to the afterlife, a journey fraught with danger. First, it passed through the underworld, a hell-scape inhabited by five-headed reptiles, knife-wielding serpents, and fire-breathing dragons. Assuming the mummy beat this first obstacle, there are seven more gates to negotiate. A successful mummy then arrives at the Hall of Osiris, where judgment is passed.

First, the jackal-headed god Anubis performed the 'weighing of the heart' ceremony. The probably decomposing heart was placed on a scale and weighed against a feather. If the heart and the feather counterbalanced each other, lights flashed, bells rang, balloons dropped from the ceiling, and the word IMMORTALITY flashed on the screen.

Second prize in this afterlife game show was less desirable. If Anubis judged the contestant to have been naughty, their heart was devoured by the goddess/demon Amemet. She had the head of a crocodile, the front half of a lion, and a hippo's backside.

You are the biggest loser. Goodbye.

Fig. 2: The weighing of the heart (Aloya3 and S.E.W.)

Writing and the Magic Word

By the emergence of the Egyptian state around 3200 B.C., the big idea of writing had become an essential aspect of its culture. The concept of using symbols to denote words was probably imported from Mesopotamia. Egyptians used writing for accounting and administrative purposes, but it had a far more critical role. Magic.

The persistent human belief in magic is an erroneous, yet pervasive idea. It began well before the Egyptians and was a mainstream belief until the Scientific Revolution. Given today's proliferation in 'Magic Happens' bumper stickers, it clearly still has some adherents. However, unlike now, magic in Ancient Egypt was considered a very real factor in everyday life and the afterlife.

Egyptians believed that writing had been invented by Thoth, the god of writing. He was an excellent multitasker who also moonlighted as the god of wisdom and magic. Thoth was an extremely powerful being. So powerful that, according to one legend, he willed himself into existence using the power of his own words.

However, Thoth also has a different and far more lurid origin story. In that tale, he was conceived when the god Horus 'accidentally' swallowed the god Set's semen during a struggle between them for supremacy. Somewhat taken aback, Horus lopped off Set's testicles and, tit-for-tat, Set ripped out one of Horus's eyes. Enter Thoth, who emerged fully formed from the disembodied Eye of Horus to mediate between the warring gods.

Yep. That was *some* fight.

Fig. 3: Horus and Set discuss the aftermath of their world title fight (Olga Che, Aksonov and S.E.W.)

Whatever Thoth's genesis, his god-job included setting down the deeds of every man brought to the Hall of the Dead. He didn't waste time on recording how many jars of grain were in the storehouse. Thoth was in the immortality business, and not the metaphorical kind that allows the names of pharaohs to ring down the millennia. His brand of immortality was more arcane and mystical. When the hieroglyph of a pharaoh's name was carved in stone, Thoth's power gave him literal life after death. However, simply chiseling away the pharaoh's name from a monument was to obliterate him for all eternity. A pretty lame way to subvert the will of a god.

Fig. 4: Thoth faces his greatest fear
(by BasPhoto, diephosi and S.E.W.)

Of course, behind every great god is a great goddess. Thoth's female counterpart, Seshat, was the goddess of the written word. She is depicted as either his wife or daughter—the Egyptians weren't too squeamish about these things. The literal meaning of the name 'Seshat' is 'female scribe' and she was popular with scribes because she granted them life everlasting through their works. Seshat's job was to add a copy of all writing into the library of the gods. This conferred immortality on the author. Thoth and Seshat were, without doubt, a power couple.

If you've seen any movie about a mummy's curse, you know that hieroglyphs were imbued with divine power. Some hieroglyphs were believed to be so powerful that scribes were nervous about carving them, in case dark forces were summoned. However, carving these symbols was cumbersome, so it wasn't useful for doing what cuneiform did so well: keeping accounts and records. The Egyptians got around this problem by creating a more accessible form of writing for daily use: Hieratic script. Thanks to this simplified style of hieroglyphics, content that would take hours to chisel into rock could be inked in a few lines. Not surprisingly, Hieratic script quickly became the preferred method of writing for business and the bureaucracy. However, this new form of writing's rise to prominence relied on an Egyptian innovation: papyrus.

Paperback Writer

Where the Mesopotamians used clay for writing accounts and records, the Egyptians used papyrus. Papyrus was the earliest paper-like material. It was made by cutting the fibrous stems of the papyrus plant into thin strips. These were then laid out in rows, then topped with a second, perpendicular layer of strips forming a kind of latticework. The lattice was dampened, pressed, and left to dry in the sun, a final process which adhered the layers together, creating a paper on which the scribes could write. For over three thousand years, papyrus was the ancient world's most significant writing material.

Egyptian scribes took to this next generation of technology with enthusiasm. While the magical hieroglyphs continued to be carved on the stone of tombs and statues, the humdrum writing that enabled the workings of daily life was inked in hieratic script on papyrus. From an historian's perspective, the major drawback of the papyrus revolution was its impermanence. Its transient nature accounts for the comparative lack of records from this era. Although in defense of papyrus, it was still more enduring than the ephemeral emails of today.

Of course, such a useful material was of no use without a method of marking its surface. The world needed ink, but it had to be invented. To do this, the Egyptians mixed soot, beeswax, and vegetable gum to make the world's first black ink. To make different colored inks, they removed the soot and substituted other materials such as ochre.

Leading the Way with Cosmetics

In all likelihood, the Egyptians were probably late to the cosmetics party. Face painting and body art had certainly played a role in the ceremonies for prehistoric peoples. Where the Egyptians *were* innovators was in using make-up for beauty enhancement. Thousands of years later, this big idea developed into a multi-billion-dollar industry.

In the same way, Egyptians used soot as a pigment for ink, they also used it to color eye makeup. Unfortunately, in creating the black eye make-up known as kohl, they combined the soot and other ingredients with lead. The Egyptians were unaware of lead's potential danger, and kohl eye make-up became a fashion item for women and men. The original smokey-eyed style was boosted by the Egyptians' belief it protected them from the evil eye. Maybe it did.

But unfortunately, it didn't protect the wearers from self-inflicted lead poisoning. The side effects of which included dried-out skin, grey hair, abdominal pain, and constipation. Oh, and death.

But seriously, why let carcinogens get in the way of true beauty?

Fig. 5: Maybe she's born with it. Maybe she died from it.
(Andrey_Arkusha and S.E.W.)

Egyptians also employed other cosmetics, most of which weren't lethal. Just like modern people, they fought a desperate and futile battle against 'the seven signs of aging.' Egyptians used various lotions, creams, and oils made of ingredients such as crushed lotus flowers, papyrus oil, and honey. These were smeared on by hand or, more daintily, applied with brushes.

Egyptians valued paler complexions. This was largely class-based, because white skin was proof that one was rich and didn't work outside. As a result, white face make-up was fashionable—let's face it, not everyone can stay out of the sun all day. Nevertheless, it wasn't all about beauty. Thickly applied foundation would have protected the skin as a primitive sunscreen. Unfortunately, any health benefits which may have accrued were disastrously offset by the probability that lead was a key ingredient in this face goop.

The social stigma of B.O. was not lost on the people of the Nile. To combat this, an expensive perfume called *kyphi* was used. It was made from ingredients such as saffron, frankincense, myrrh, mint, juniper, cinnamon, and pine resin. If you were stinking rich, it was a pungent and highly effective solution. Poorer people had to use a cheaper, less effective methods. Or they just ponged like a camel's rear end.

Clearly, living Egyptians cared about how they looked and smelled. They must also have cared about their appearance in the afterlife. This accounts for the plethora of mirrors, hairbrushes, hairpins, and cosmetic containers that archaeologists have uncovered in tombs.

When it came to beauty, the unofficial Egyptian ethos was *Live fast, die young, and leave a good-looking (and smelling) corpse.*

Hogwarts with Hieroglyphs

Like Mesopotamia, Egypt developed schools to educate the scribes it needed to record knowledge. However, the schools of the Nile delta weren't just places where marketable skills could be gained; they were places one could learn to wield magical power (think Hogwarts, if the teachers had the heads of animals). Of course, such otherworldly power wasn't meant for your average Ptolemy, Dick, or Harry. The overwhelming majority of people remained illiterate and magic-less. High-born male children or those from scribal families were believed to have a great destiny. They began their school career around age five and continued until their early to mid-teens. Just in time for their transition to adulthood.

Fig. 6: On the way to Hogwarts with Hieroglyphs
(code6d, Olga Che and S.E.W.)

The fathers of peasant boys taught them the skills of their

vocation. Most girls, peasant or otherwise, were trained by their mothers in home duties. Despite this, women in Ancient Egypt enjoyed an equality unparalleled in the ancient world. Female scribes occupied important religious posts and were part of the entourage of several queens. This suggests that some girls took their place in school. More likely, women who were literate had been taught at home by family members.

Scribal training was a pathway to a high-status position. Short of being a high priest or adviser of the pharaoh, the profession of the scribe was the pinnacle of Egyptian vocations. Unfortunately, there is little reliable information about the organization of Egyptian schools before the Middle Kingdom. What we know is that schools were in religious temples or government buildings. This explains why teachers were drawn from the priesthood or were scribes.

The priests instructed their students in writing and religion, and this was where the magic literally happened. On the other hand, the instruction passed on by the scribes in government buildings was secular. Either way, education was controlled by, and under the surveillance of, the Egyptian powers-that-be.

Add this to the frustrating lack of information about how Egyptian scribal schools worked, and our brief snapshot of Egyptian education is based on supposition. Although some recent discoveries include images that show, in at least some eras, there were similarities to modern education: children are shown seated at desks in a classroom, with a teacher sitting at the front at a larger desk. Also familiar are the examples of scribal students' written work that still exist, with the teacher's corrections marked in red.

Like the brutal teaching methods of the Mesopotamians, the Egyptian educators also displayed a psychopathic streak. The Papyrus Lansing, a document from the late Twentieth Dynasty (1189–1077 BC), appears to be writing exercises set by a teacher for his student, incorporating a number of sections of text reminding the pupil of his master's dominance, threatening him with whippings should he fall short of expectations. "I grew into a youth at your side," the text relates, "You beat my back; your teaching entered my ear." A straightforward case of identifying with the abuser if ever there was one.

Like a primary school teacher of today, the Egyptian scribe-pedagogues were generalists, teaching all the subjects. However, in later years, specialist teachers could be found in schools that taught specific subjects such as ethics, engineering, medicine, and mathematics. Some educators even took their students on field trips. There is ancient graffiti in a New Kingdom tomb, left by teachers and students who scrawled literary quotes and artwork on the walls, behavior frowned upon during modern-day school excursions.

Flirting with Monotheism

Religion was a big idea that was constantly evolving. For the overwhelming bulk of their history, Egyptians worshipped a pantheon of gods. Mostly, these gods seemed to be bizarre, animal-headed humanoids, although notably Osiris and Isis were depicted as more-or-less fully human. This traditional way of worship was shattered for a time under the heretical kingship of Akhenaten.

If we think of Akhenaten today, it is by association with the famous bust of his wife Nefertiti, still an icon of beauty, and the treasures of his son, Tutankhamen. However, at the time, it was Akhenaten who was Number One. In later years, he would be *Public Enemy* Number One, infamous for his sacrilege. Future generations of Egyptians would dismantle his monuments and destroy his statues. In a form of proto-Soviet revisionist history, his name would be left off lists of past pharaohs.

So, why were the haters hating?

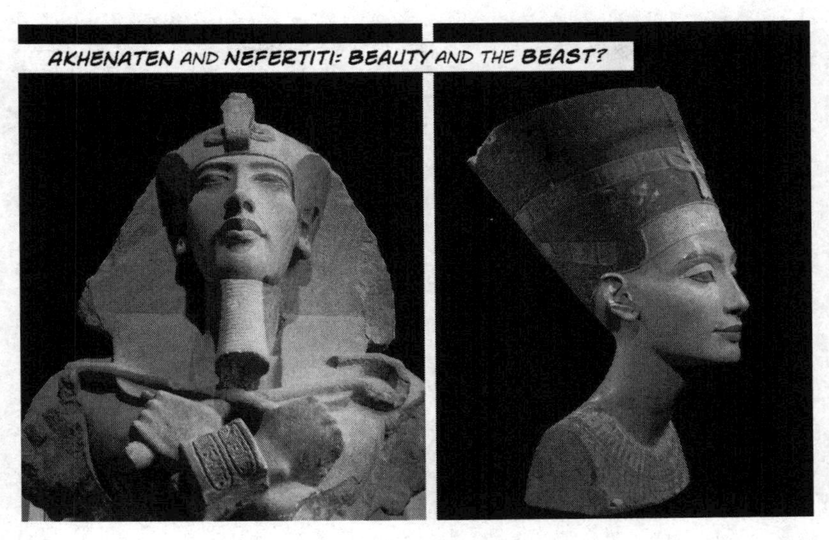

Fig. 7: The Odd Couple
(Tamer Hassan Ahmed Hassan, Wrangel and S.E.W.)

Akhenaten is known for setting Egypt's traditional polytheism aside and introducing worship centered on a new sun god named Aten. Replacing Ra as the sun god would have been provocative enough. Controversially, Akhenaten revealed that Aten was, in fact, the *only* god. This change did not go over well with vested interests, such as the powerful priesthood. However, this wasn't the only change that Akhenaten made that irked his people.

Akhenaten moved the Egyptian capital from Thebes to a newly built city called Akhetaten. Today, we know the area as Amarna. No one knows why Akhenaten made this change. Unfortunately, the inscription explaining the foundation of Akhetaten is damaged in the place where historians believe Akhenaten's reasons might be outlined.

Depictions of Akhenaten are very different from previous portrayals of pharaohs. The Amarna style of art was, let's say, a little odd. For instance, bodies were not treated realistically. Either that, or the royal family looked *extremely* strange. Their faces were pinched with pronounced jaws, bee-stung lips, and narrow, slitted eyes. The bodies were even weirder, featuring skinny necks, sloping shoulders, pot bellies, pear-shaped hips and thighs, and gangly legs. The 'lovely' little princesses were usually depicted with elongated skulls like cliché aliens.

Quite how Nefertiti's famously beautiful visage was sculpted at this time defies explanation.

Was Akhenaten mad? Deformed? A cult-leader? We can't say for sure. We know that the changes he wrought on Egyptian society did not last long after his death. The world wasn't quite ready for the big idea of monotheism. Tutankhamen, his son and successor, moved the capital to Memphis in the third year of his reign and began restoring the old gods. Before long, Aten was a distant memory, although Tutankhamen achieved very little else in his short life, dying at nineteen. Despite his relative obscurity in ancient times, the discovery of his tomb by Howard Carter in 1922 ensured Tutankhamen is now one of the most well-known pharaohs.

Public works mega-projects

Despite Mr von Däniken's beliefs, the pyramids were not project managed by E.T. They were literally the biggest of Egyptian big ideas. Their construction relied upon the massive egos of the pharaohs, as well as boundless determination and a vast number of artisans and laborers. Despite many years in which scholars believed these laborers were slaves, they now think the pyramid builders were free men. There are almost as many estimates of the number of workers used at Giza as there are Egyptologists, but most reliable sources agree that the Great Pyramid required around four thousand quarry workers, hauliers, and masons. These workers were bolstered by up to twenty thousand ramp builders, mortar mixers, tool-makers, and ancillary workers. Most of these were skilled trades, and it would be surprising if these workers were taught by their fathers in the traditional way.

In fact, many Egyptologists agree that the pyramids were not only a massive public works project, but they were a training exercise to create thousands of skilled workers. The theory is that workers from all over Egypt were drafted to help in the construction. Once these workers' 'tour of duty' was complete, they would take these news skills back to their provinces. They also took with them an expanded worldview and loyalty to the state. They'd teach others their skills, resulting in an exponential increase in the size of the skilled workforce.

Quite apart from the hard-to-ignore pyramids, the Ancient Egyptians had many other engineering achievements. They pioneered surveying and construction techniques that allowed the construction of not only the pyramids but also of temples (including the temple and monumental sculptures at Abu Simbel), underground tombs, obelisks, and of course the Sphinx.

More Beer and the Egyptian Binge Drinking Culture

Egyptian legend has it that the god Osiris gifted humanity the art of brewing beer. However, as we've already seen, beer predates Egypt. Humans had been making it for thousands of years. What the Egyptians did was take beer drinking to the next level: chronic binge drinking. According to Mark Forsyth's *A Short History of Drunkenness,* Egyptians only drank to get smashed. Forsyth describes a tomb painting of a banquet where a woman is copiously spewing. Nearby, a kindly slave holds her cup, waiting to hand it back so the drinking could continue. Such representations were not uncommon.

So popular was it, that Egyptians had a regular Festival of Drunkenness, under the auspices of the goddess Hathor. Its concurrence with the flooding of the Nile likely made it a celebration of fertility. Or just a reason for Egyptians to get smashed. The thing was, Egyptians didn't need an excuse, as there was no shame associated with drunkenness. Zilch. Nada. Just an odd sense of pride associated with getting shitfaced.

The tradition of binge drinking is still current in some circles today. However, unless you're in your late teens, there's no pride attached to vomiting your guts up. That's a 'big' idea best left in the past.

Calendars and Clocks

The Egyptians devised a calendar that had 365 days and twelve months. They standardized the number of days in a month to thirty, with an extra five days at the end of the year when festivals were held. The basis of this calendar was the yearly appearance of the star Sirius in the eastern sky, which was significant because, by chance, it coincided with the Nile's yearly flooding. However, the Egyptian calendar only allowed for 365 days and did not account for the additional 0.256th of a day it takes for the Earth to orbit the Sun. Because of this, the Egyptian civil calendar cycled slowly through the seasons.

Clocks were another brainchild of the Egyptians. In fact, they invented two kinds of clocks. They used obelisks as massive sundials, observing the movement of the obelisk's shadow during the day. However, water clocks were also used in Egypt. Such clocks were made from stone bowls with a hole at the bottom that dripped water at a predictable rate. The passing of time was measured from differently spaced marks.

Can I Get a Second Opinion?

It was in Egypt that the first dedicated surgical instruments were found. The Cairo Museum displays a collection of ancient surgical instruments, including needles, scalpels, scissors, forceps, lancets, hooks, spoons, and pincers. Given that several of these were also used in extracting the organs of the dead for mummification, the existence of these tools should not come as a surprise.

In fact, the Egyptian obsession with pulling bodies apart before embalming meant they were pioneers in many areas of surgery. Much of what we know about anatomy and surgical techniques had its foundation in the observations of Egyptian physicians and embalmers. They were the first to observe the role of the spinal cord in transmitting signals from the brain to the limbs. They were also trailblazers in surgical techniques such as stitching and trepanning.

Egyptians weren't the first ancient people to attempt trepanning. However, due to the magic of writing, they were the first to explain *why* they had chipped holes in the heads of living people. Inscriptions survive, recommending this radical treatment in certain cases. Unfortunately, these cases were the expulsion of demons. Still, some patients survived the procedure, so kudos to Egyptian surgeons.

I guess.

Heavy Petting

While humans had shared their hearths with animal companions for some time, these beasts usually occupied an important role in the tribe. Dogs, for example, were working animals, valued for their utility as protectors and hunting companions. Cats were kept for their prowess at keeping the rodent population at bay. For ancient peoples, keeping animals just as cuddly pets was an unaffordable luxury. Such useless creatures were merely another mouth to feed with no worthwhile purpose.

Civilization, with its accompanying reliability of food sources, made the big idea of animal companions possible. However, when it came to keeping pets, no one took up the practice with more gusto than the Egyptians.

The Ancient Egyptians loved their pets. They kept some animals as pets we would recognize today, such as cats, dogs, fish, and birds. However Egyptian pet shops also carried more exotic fare, such as monkeys, baboons, lions, gazelles, lions, and hippos. Pets were considered divine gifts to be cared for until they died, and then even beyond death. There was a reason for this unusual devotion.

For a start, the Ancient Egyptians were all about animal worship. Many of their pantheon of gods, such as Set, Thoth, and Hathor, were animal/human hybrids, after all. Even if these gods weren't part animal, most still had the power to shape-shift into animals. Egyptians revered animals for all different reasons, often ascribing them certain magical qualities. While they loved their dogs, there was one animal that occupied an even more revered place in the Egyptian world. The cat.

Yes, the Egyptians were smitten by the humble house cat. To get an accurate picture of this obsession, one need only imagine a civilization of crazy cat ladies who sidelined in mummification. Of course, cats were more than mere pets to the Egyptians. They believed their feline friends were magical creatures who brought good fortune to their homes. The fact that Egyptians believed cats to be the physical manifestation of the goddess Bastet didn't hurt either.

Bastet was the cat-headed goddess of pleasure and protection. She was also the bringer of good health. This goes some way to explain why Egyptian cats were treated like gods. Today, only the most deranged pet owners spoil their pets to the same degree as Egyptian cats. The rich and powerful bedecked their moggies in jewels and fed them far better food than their servants received. In the tragic event of Mr Tibbles' demise, he would be mummified to ensure a place for him in the afterlife. But that was only the beginning. Bereaved cat owners would shave their eyebrows and remain in official mourning until they could regrow.

If Mr Tibbles' death was not of natural causes, the shit would hit the fan. Punishment was swift and permanent. The penalty for cat killing, be it intentional or accidental, was death. Certainly, if the Egyptians had heard of Herr Schrödinger's thought experiment, they would have executed him merely for putting his hypothetical cat in quantum danger.

Fig. 8: Imhotep about to feel the wrath of Mr Tibbles (Kalifer, Cristiansavin2, and S.E.W.)

So Strange yet so Familiar

There's a reason I was fascinated by Ancient Egypt as a child, and it wasn't all about mummification and pyramids. It's the same thing about Egyptians that has fascinated people throughout the ages. They're so strange and yet so *familiar* to us. One minute they were eviscerating a body or pulling brains out through a nasal passage, next they were patting their pets or creating timeless works of art.

Even after thousands of years, their artistic, medical, technological, and engineering feats still have the power to amaze us. So much of what we do today was set in motion by this astounding civilization. If not directly, then through the collective learning that was passed on to the Greeks and Romans.

For the time being, however, we leave the shores of the Mediterranean. Now we move on to an ancient culture that the West has not appreciated as much as it should. You see, the Chinese are the originators of big ideas aplenty.

Chapter Five

Another Brick in the Wall
Ancient China

Is it any wonder why today's China has little love for the West?

To say Westerners have not always given China its due would be a massive understatement. Some of this lack of recognition results from ignorance and some from racism. Levi Seeley in his *History of Education* (1904) managed both in one paragraph:

> *The civilization of the 'Celestial Empire' has certainly contributed but little to the advancement of the world. Were it not that this nation furnishes a most striking illustration of false methods, the study of Chinese education might be omitted without loss.*

For some reason, Seeley then saw the need to illustrate these 'false methods' and so he devotes a full nine uncomplimentary pages to the 'Celestial Empire.' However, over the centuries, China has been the wellspring of big ideas, many of which the West claims as its own. Other Chinese breakthroughs may have happened concurrently with other early civilizations.

(Rather Complicated) Writing begins

The earliest beginnings of Chinese writing were a mystery until 1899, when the Yüan River flooded. The floodwaters receded, revealing animal bones bearing inscriptions etched in ancient Chinese characters. Study of these 'oracle bone inscriptions' has shed new light on China's ancient history, revealing the development of writing in China around 1200 BC, during the Shang Dynasty. While the possibility exists that writing in Sumeria and Egypt influenced the Chinese invention, there is no support for such a hypothesis. There is some evidence to suggest that writing in China began even earlier than 1200 BC, as pottery exists from an earlier period bearing writing-like marks. However, the evidence is inconclusive.

As the name suggests, oracle bones were bones used for predicting the future, and the script engraved on them is the precursor to modern Chinese script. In fact, they provide the first mention of 'school' in Chinese literature:

"Is it auspicious for the children to go to school? Will it rain on their way home?"

Definitive proof that even in 1200 BC, fretting, overprotective parents would use the latest technology to protect their poor little darlings. Of course, not all uses of the oracle bone ritual were so frivolous, and the royal court became a virtual post office for divine revelations from the honored ancestors.

The gatekeeper for these messages from beyond was, of course, the Shang emperor.

Word of Mouth

The origin story of the Shang Dynasty will sound somewhat familiar to fans of Thoth. Legend has it that the wife of Emperor Ku somehow contrived to swallow an egg that was dropped by a blackbird, resulting in the miraculous birth of her son Xie. This singled out Xie as someone special. For his role in helping Yu the Great control a flood, he was given control of the region of Shang, and the Shang Dynasty was born. Perhaps there was an ancient meme that required legendary characters to have their parents impregnated by random things being introduced into their mouths. The idea that at least two mythical characters were inseminated in this way displays something of an oral fixation. That, and a woeful ignorance of human reproductive biology.

In 1112 BC, the emperor Wu-yi made the mistake of mocking the gods and not long after was killed by a bolt of lightning. It was all downhill for the Shang Dynasty from there. A succession of Wu-yi's descendants showed their ineptitude as emperors by increasing their levels of cruelty and injustice, sending the dynasty into a dangerous tailspin. Legend has it that the Shang Dynasty's downfall in 1050 B.C. was because of drunk and disorderly behavior from the last emperor, Wu-yi's great-grandson, Chou. Chou was a sadist who enjoyed the use of a red-hot rack and flayed alive those he felt didn't pass the loyalty test. He also made a habit of doing the backstroke in a swimming pool brimming with wine, no doubt imbibing the 'poolwater' along the way, like an alcoholic Scrooge McDuck.

Chou's end didn't come from drowning in wine, but rather from the invading Zhou army torching his imperial palace. Given his love of roasting people on the rack, Chou suffered an appropriate death—burning alive in the inferno. The combination of poor government, lightning strikes, and fire-bombing attacks put paid to the Shang dynasty.

Education in the Barnyard

Education was of paramount importance in early civilizations, and China was no exception. The Chinese god of literature and culture, Wenchang Wang, is popular among students, particularly when they're swotting for exams. He is depicted as a kind, larger-than-life, older man. However, his miracles started at a young age, when Wenchang Wang displayed both supernatural power and an uncanny talent for self-butchery: after his birth, he cured his sick and malnourished mother by slicing off a chunk of his own thigh and feeding it to her.

The oldest word in Chinese for "school" is *xiang*, the literal meaning of which is a building where elderly people cared for sheep, pigs, or cattle and taught the village children. Anyone who has taught young students will recognize how appropriate the word *xiang* is for describing a classroom: kids are impossible to herd, and they leave crap everywhere. Although there are claims that schools were established during the Xia dynasty 2070 BC-1600 BC, this is unverified because, as we have seen, there are no known written records in China before 1200 BC.

Confucius and Self-Cultivation

The year 551 BC saw the birth of Confucius, acknowledged as China's greatest teacher and philosopher, in what is now Shandong province. His family name was Kong, and throughout his life, he was called 'Kongfuzi,' meaning Master Kong, which was later Latinised to Confucius. He ran a private school that catered for over three thousand students, educating them in the so-called 'six arts': rites, music, archery, charioteering, calligraphy, and mathematics. Confucius was instrumental in the promotion of teaching as a profession and committed his life to societal transformation. He saw education as a path to the training of 'junzi' or exemplary persons.

Confucius believed all people could benefit from 'self-cultivation,' which isn't the ancient Chinese art of self-abuse, but rather the development of a person's mind and character through their own efforts. To promote this goal, he instituted a humanities program for leaders of the future, which was open to all. It is believed that Confucius was chief minister to King Lu on diplomatic missions; however, his moral rectitude was at odds with the king's love of a good, old-fashioned debauch. So, as you can imagine, this partnership didn't last long. Confucius spent many years in politics and public service, but towards the end of his life, he returned to his home province to his first love, teaching. He died in 479 BC, at age 73.

Given the amazing contribution Confucius made to humanity, it is sad that so many only know about him for off-color, but let's face it, often amusing dad jokes couched as his sayings. Although, I'm sure that Kongfuzi would not think these 'comedians' were even close to being junzi.

Fig. 1: The author chose to avoid controversy here
(By philipus and S.E.W.)

Here Comes the Sun

Whether you're in the military, a professional sports coach, or just like playing *Call of Duty* on your Xbox, there's one historical Chinese figure you'd revere above all others: General Sun Tzu. Sun Tzu's lightbulb moment was to record the military tactics and advice for which he is known, in *The Art of War*, a text that's still the go-to guide on military strategy after 2,500 years. The book outlines the General's deeply philosophical view of war, with keen observations such as:

> *Be extremely subtle even to the point of formlessness. Be extremely mysterious even to the point of soundlessness. Thereby you can be the director of the opponent's fate.*
> *Let your plans be dark and impenetrable as night, and when you move, fall like a thunderbolt.*

Supreme excellence consists of breaking the enemy's resistance without fighting.

Gems of philosophy these may be, but there is a problem: historians disagree as to whether the man Sun Tzu actually existed. Some early records appear to indicate that Sun Tzu served the King of Wu as general and strategist in the late sixth century BC. His subsequent success on the battlefield inspired him to write his magnum opus. Later, *The Art of War* was a bestseller among generals during the Warring States period. However, by the twelfth century AD, Chinese historians had grown to doubt the existence of an historical Sun Tzu. They suspected *The Art of War* was not written by one person but was instead a composite of the sayings of a range of military strategists. That may well be. However, there *was* an historical figure known as Sun Bin, who was a military genius and may have served as the basis for the myth of Sun Tzu. But it's likely we'll never know.

However, if Sun Tzu *was* a real person, he was quite the uncompromising taskmaster. One (most likely apocryphal) story has the great general challenged by a warlord to use his military expertise to train one-hundred-and-eighty women from the royal court to respond to orders like a well-trained army. Sun Tzu separated the women into two companies, putting one of the warlord's favorite concubines in charge of each. He then trained these two 'armies' to perform a simple military drill. Training complete, he ordered the concubines to lead their troops in the drill, and both groups broke up laughing. Somewhat miffed, Sun Tzu ordered his concubine commanders to try again. Again, the two courtesans giggled and failed to successfully lead their 'troops.' This seriously pissed-off Sun Tzu, who declared that the failure of the female troops was due to poor leadership, and to the warlord's dismay, General Sun Tzu promptly had the concubines beheaded for incompetence.

Something of an overreaction? Perhaps. But decapitating the

king's favorite doxies worked like a charm. Sun Tzu appointed new commanders who, unsurprisingly, were extremely careful not to make the same mistakes as their predecessors. When Sun Tzu ordered his new 'officers' to execute the drill for a third time, the companies performed perfectly. The lesson for the shocked onlookers was that an army is only as good as its commanders.

It also goes to show that *The Art of War* works extremely well if you're prepared to chop off the heads of high-class prostitutes to make a point.

Fig. 2: The concubines were definitely in the dark about Sun Tzu's intentions (Public Domain and S.E.W.)

The First Emperor of China

Qin Shi Huang (259 BC–210 BC) unified China after the Warring States period and became its First Emperor in 221 BC. However, although he believed that his Qin Dynasty would last ten thousand years, it disintegrated quickly after his death. Even so, his 11-year reign as First Emperor was consequential. So consequential that his name has lived on for two thousand years. It may even last eight thousand more.

In many ways, Qin Shi Huang set the scene for generations of Chinese leaders to follow: he was an innovator who brought an intellectual and cultural revolution, but was also a tyrant who oppressed his people. He made a concerted effort to erase China's disunited past, using the time-honored way of despots: he destroyed any information he didn't like. "I have collected all the writings of the Empire," he wrote, "and burnt those which were of no use." Qin Shi Huang also outlawed private schools of any form, so he could ensure his control over the populace. He was certainly no fan of Confucius. Qin's desire to destroy the famous philosopher's liberal influence was so great, he had Confucian scholars buried alive.

Obviously, the need to silence dissent is an ancient Chinese tradition.

Like many tyrants before and after, Qin Shi Huang made his empire run like a well-oiled machine. He divided up the newly unified country into administrative districts, making it easier to rule. He established a common currency. He standardized the units of weights and measures. In addition, he standardized the written Chinese language across the empire.

If there'd been trains in Qin China, they would definitely have run on time.

Although these changes were important, these were not what secured Qin Shi Huang's lasting fame. The First Emperor might go unremarked were it not for two major projects: the building of the Great Wall of China, and his own spectacular tomb. A tomb that is home to a vast terracotta army.

An Army Made of Terracotta

Qin Shi Huang was obsessively fearful of his own mortality and had sent emissaries far and wide searching for the elixir of life. Alas, this quest was a failure, but the wily emperor had instigated a backup plan. What better way to secure his place in the afterlife than build the most imposing mausoleum imaginable? With that in mind, he had already begun constructing his final resting place soon after he took the throne. As far as human megastructures go, it was very impressive.

There are wildly varying estimates of the number of workers it took to construct Emperor Qin's tomb. They range between 12,000 and 720,000 men, although both figures seem either side of implausible. But no matter how many workers it took, Qin already had a dire track record with workplace safety, which guaranteed it was a dangerous job.

Talking about dangerous, it is rumored that Emperor Qin's yet-to-be-opened burial chamber is booby-trapped with crossbows primed to target would-be grave-robbers. It's a pity that Indiana Jones is a fictional character, because this seems right in his wheelhouse. The unopened chamber is also reputed to contain, among other treasures, over one hundred rivers of mercury. Whatever is inside, none of the workers used to construct the burial chamber lived to tell the tale: they were put to death to keep the First Emperor's secrets.

Of course, the section of the mausoleum that *has* been opened is impressive. In 1978, former French president Jacques Chirac said that "on top of the seven wonders of the world, the terracotta army should be deemed to be the eighth." The tomb housing the terracotta army houses 8,000 soldiers, as well as many horses and chariots. The attention to detail in these terracotta figures is remarkable. They are life-sized, but not uniform in appearance or height, and each warrior has different facial features. Like the ushabti figures in an Egyptian Pharaoh's tomb, these warriors were meant to come to life to protect and serve Emperor Qin in the afterlife. To supplement this manpower, we might have thought that there would be terracotta weapons supplied, but no, the warriors are armed with 40,000 bronze weapons.

Fig. 3: Perhaps some of the Terracotta Warriors had a run-in with Sun Tzu? (alantobey and S.E.W.)

The Great Wall

While the Great Wall of China was not Qin Shi Huang's brainchild, he is closely connected to its construction. The reason for this association isn't immediately clear, although his sections plugged gaps between the older walls. The big idea of creating a long wall on the border had been conceived seven centuries before. In fact, very little of the Qin's work on the wall still stands. The parts of the Great Wall we see in tourist brochures were built during the Ming Dynasty, between 370 to 650 years ago.

Therefore, Qin Shi Huang's close association with the Great Wall has nothing to do with the structure we see today. It has rather more to do with the vast numbers of workers who died during construction of the now eroded rammed-earth walls he created. Let's be clear, Qin's Great Wall was an unmitigated occupational health and safety disaster. It is estimated that somewhere between a hundred thousand and a million workers lost their lives on Qin's sections of the Great Wall.

The main purpose of the Great Wall was to repel nomads from the Eurasian steppes. The nomads were 'horse people,' basically the equivalent of the Dothraki in *Game of Thrones*, so they were *not* to be trifled with. The other benefit of the Great Wall was that it also allowed the government to collect import duties from traders of the Silk Road, which was a nice little earner.

So, China built a wall, but the nomads didn't pay for it. Taxes did.

Han Dynasty Jade Burial Suits

The imperial dynasty immediately following the Qin was the Han Dynasty (202 BC–220 AD). The Han dynasty oversaw an age of prosperity and significant economic growth. Collective learning also prospered. There were marked advances in science and technology, with innovations like paper-making, the invention of ship rudders, the use of negative numbers, the first relief maps, and a type of seismometer. The Hans are rightly acknowledged for their contributions to Chinese society, but they may be best known for something completely different.

The Han created amazing, hand-crafted jade burial suits. These were used for the burial of royalty and aristocrats, the Han equivalent of Egyptian sarcophaguses. Jade has been valued by the Chinese for thousands of years. They believed that it could preserve the body and soul after death. So, on their death, those who could afford it were stitched into burial suits made of pieces of polished jade, sewn together with thread. They look a bit like human-shaped disco balls, or flamboyant robots.

The type of thread used to sew up the deceased's burial suit said everything about their status. Silk was used as the thread for aristocrats of lower rank. Royals of lesser significance had their suits threaded with silver. As you might imagine, the emperor's jade suit was sewn with gold thread. Some jade suits leave the viewer in no doubt of the owner's gender.

I guess these were the deluxe models.

Fig. 4: Liu Xiu, King of Zhongshan State, obviously needed extra room... ahem... down there (Gary Todd and S.E.W.)

Gunpowder Plot?

In 142 AD, alchemist Wei Boyang described a new, chemically explosive substance. In his *The Book of the Kinship of Three,* he wrote of a combination of three powders that reacted violently together. Although unnamed, these were believed to be charcoal, saltpeter, and sulfur, the ingredients of gunpowder.

Contrary to some reports, it's untrue that the Chinese only used gunpowder for fireworks. In 904 AD, during the Song dynasty, the Mongols learned this the hard way, as they were at the receiving end of the world's first rocket barrage. These 'fire arrows' comprised a tube containing gunpowder, sealed at one end, with the other end remaining open, which was then fastened to a long stick. When lit, the burning of the powder produced a thrust that sent the fire arrow fizzing at the enemy, frightening the Mongols and setting their horses to flight.

Fig. 5: China, world leaders in rocket warfare
(By Marina and S.E.W.)

Fire arrows were not the only gunpowder weapons that the Song dynasty devised. Others included flamethrowers, primitive cannon-like weapons, poisonous gas shells, and hand grenades. The effect of these technological advances continues to be felt today, but fire arrows were more than weapons technology.

One Small Step for Wan-Hu

According to some tales, the Chinese use of gunpowder wasn't limited to fireworks and warfare. Legend has it that a minor functionary named Wan-Hu saw the potential for rocket-powered flight. So sure of success was he, that he volunteered for the inaugural journey. Strapping himself to a chair powered by forty-seven fire arrows, he then had forty-seven assistants simultaneously light the fuses.

I think you can see where this is heading.

When the smoke cleared and the dust settled, there was no chair and no Wan-Hu. Whether he ended up in orbit or blown to bits was anyone's guess. At least until 2004, when Jamie and Adam from TV's *MythBusters* attempted to replicate Wan-Hu's 'flight.' They strapped Buster the crash test dummy to a chair surrounded with forty-seven rockets, then took cover. When they remotely ignited the rockets, the chair simply exploded, leaving Buster a flaming wreck only salvageable because of Adam's quick work with a fire extinguisher.

A real-life Wan-Hu would probably have faced a similar fate. Minus the extinguisher.

Fig. 6: NOT an accurate representation of Wan-Hu's flight (Erica Guilane-Nachez, OrthsMedien and S.E.W.)

Chinese Naval Gazing

Inventors of the Han Dynasty (202 BC–220 AD) used lodestones to create north-south oriented compasses which they used solely for divination. It took nearly a thousand years for people to work out that compasses could also be vital pieces of maritime hardware. Without this game-changer, the later Age of Discovery wouldn't have been possible.

Yet, well before the compass was used for navigation, China had a significant naval presence. In 221–206 BC, the Qin dynasty used its navy to invade Guangzhou and the northern part of Vietnam. There is evidence they could construct ships up to 30 meters long, with a beam of 8 meters. These vessels dwarf the Portuguese caravels of the fourteenth century, which had an average length of around 19 meters and beam of 5.5 meters.

China's formidable fleet sailed into the Indian Ocean and there is some evidence they reached as far as Ethiopia. By the fifth century AD, they had traded with India via sea routes, and this appears to have expedited the spread of Buddhism to China and the *I Ching* to India. Collective learning was on the move.

Throughout the Middle Ages, Chinese merchants and diplomats continued to sail into the Indian Ocean after visiting Southeast Asian ports such as Malaya. These travels took them to India, Sri Lanka, into the Persian Gulf, trading to the Arabian Peninsula and the east coast of Africa. The Song dynasty developed the first junks based on vessels they had encountered in Southeast Asia, including the adoption of the classic, fully battened junk sail from the Malay. This ship design was the basis of Chinese naval power for centuries to come.

Admiral Zheng's Lost Kangaroos

One may well think it took balls to be a sailor in the fifteenth century. Well, as one of history's most famous eunuchs, Admiral Zheng would have begged to differ. Between 1405 and 1433, fleets under the testicularly challenged Zheng traveled to the Indian Ocean many times. Despite this, China was only interested in 'treasure voyages' and trade, rather than engaging in the colonial expansion which obsessed the western powers of the time.

However, Gavin Menzies in his book *1421*, theorized the Admiral's fleets landed in Australia 200 years before the Dutch, and even ranged as far as America. Regarding the potential Australia visit, Menzies believes that "there's stacks of evidence that they were there." He even claims that kangaroos were taken back to China for display in the emperor's zoo. Given the lack of evidence for Gavin Menzies' claims about Zheng He, most serious historians believe that he's one of the Admiral's long-lost nuts.

Fig. 7: Zhang He is distraught when the 'evidence' he discovered is lost overboard (acrogame and S.E.W.)

Later, in a time roughly equating to the western Age of Exploration (between the fifteenth and eighteenth centuries), Southeast Asia was a continuous target for Chinese trade and settlement. However, in the late eighteenth century, the navy was rundown and declined in importance. This neglect left China virtually helpless in the face of British naval superiority and was one of the keys to their defeat in the opium wars. That, and the British drug cartel making sure they were all stoned.

The Invention of Paper and Printing

The printing press was the big idea that enabled the mass production of printed material and, in time, revolutionized society. For all the hoo-ha about Johannes Gutenberg, the real story of the invention of printing is a lot older and a lot less Western. Even so, some relatively well-known websites still list 'printing' as a European invention. It was not.

It was invented in China.

In the past, there were two main ways of mechanically reproducing images. The first was woodblock printing, with which the Chinese had always been credited. The other was moveable type. Until recently, Western histories acclaimed Gutenberg for this latter invention. Yes, he worked hard to refine and popularise this process, but giving him full credit for inventing printing with moveable type is demonstrably untrue. The explanation for this historical inaccuracy is that Gutenberg had an amazing PR machine driven by Western cultural biases.

Let's examine these two methods. Woodblock printing is exactly what one might expect: Letters or symbols are carved into a block of wood. This created raised images that were coated in ink and pressed onto paper, working like a Mesopotamian cylinder seal, only using ink and a different print stock. China justly gets the credit, as they invented the first woodblock printing press in the first century AD.

To back up a step, artisanal block-making had been practiced in China since around the sixth century BC, but did not result in mainstream printing. However, printing got a boost in 105 AD, when the Chinese learned how to make paper (another big idea) from organic fibers. Compared to parchment or papyrus, this new-fangled paper was much cheaper to manufacture. The marriage of printing presses and paper made printing economically viable on a larger scale.

Once widespread printing got started, the Chinese put it to many uses. Soon, they elevated printing to an art. Illustrations and calligraphic symbols were expertly cut into woodblocks, printed, then pasted together to make scrolls. By the ninth century, printed books superseded scrolls. Around 868 AD, during the Tang Dynasty, a Buddhist book called *The Diamond Sutra* was printed. It is the oldest known printed book. But it wasn't only books: Printed playing cards and paper money also made their appearance around this time.

So far, so good. Unfortunately, this is the point where traditional European history diverges from *actual* history. Just after the turn of the first millennium, Chinese inventor, engineer, and alchemist Bi Sheng invented moveable type, nearly *five hundred years before* Gutenberg. Unlike Gutenberg's lead type, Bi Sheng's system used characters made of porcelain. With moveable type, the mechanical process of impressing the image onto paper is the same. The difference is that instead of a single, carved woodblock, the image to be printed is made using smaller, individual letter or word blocks. These can then be reassembled according to the page to be printed.

Despite the obvious potential in this method (on which Gutenberg would later capitalize), moveable type didn't catch on in China. This was likely because of the large number of characters they used, compared to the 26 phonetic letters in Gutenberg's native German alphabet.

Fig. 8: Age-old Chinese printing methods still practiced today (Erica Guilane-Nachez and S.E.W.)

Letters vs Characters

How far might China have advanced had they used phonetic letters to *spell* words rather than individual characters to *represent* words? There are over fifty thousand characters in their written language, although most modern dictionaries list around twenty thousand at most. A well-educated person might know around eight thousand characters. However, to be functionally literate, one 'only' needs to know three to four thousand characters.

For hundreds of years, Chinese technology and learning were more advanced than those of Western civilization, particularly during the Middle Ages. They possessed game-changing technologies such as the printing press, paper, and gunpowder well before the West.

So, what happened? Why didn't China capitalize and extend its technological advantage?

While literacy was taking off in Europe after Gutenberg's reinterpretation of moveable type, Chinese public servants were still required to memorize thousands of individual characters, just to do their jobs. It took many years of study to be a part of the scholar-bureaucracy, and learners had to be from wealthy families to support themselves during the time it took to gain that knowledge. There was little time to be creative. Small wonder that Chinese literacy rates didn't catch up to those in the West until the last couple of decades.

Would China have continued its technological advantage over the West if its system of writing had been easier to learn? One can only speculate, because there is no data for Chinese literacy rates prior to 1982. Their 1982 starting point was 66%, compared to 97–99% in western countries at the same time, although there are many variables that could account for that difference.

One thing is undoubtedly true: Mandarin is consistently featured in lists of the most difficult languages to learn to write and speak. This, coupled with the historically low literacy rate, must have had a detrimental effect on collective learning, probably ensuring that the West caught up with and then surpassed Chinese technology. Nowadays, however, with its massive population, 96% literacy rate, and single-minded determination to be the predominant global superpower, expect China to again accelerate past the West.

Not bad for a country that in 1904 was considered to have 'contributed but little to the advancement of the world.'

Chapter Six

While My Sitar Gently Weeps
Ancient India

We owe a lot to the Indians, who taught us how to count, without which no worthwhile scientific discovery could have been made.
Albert Einstein

Situated in the South Asian subcontinent, today's India has the second largest population of any country on Earth. It has a rich cultural heritage, being the birthplace of three of the world's top five religions: Hinduism, Buddhism, and Sikhism. While it continues to face significant challenges dealing with endemic poverty, its economy is modern and fast-growing. However, its origins are ancient indeed.

It is believed that humans have lived on the Indian subcontinent for at least 55,000 years, having migrated out of Africa. They initially lived in hunter-gatherer bands, but around 9,000 years ago they settled in small settlements in the Indus River basin. Over time, these settlements coalesced into the Indus Valley Civilisation.

Indus Valley Civilisation

The Indus Valley Civilisation (or the Harappan Civilisation), developed during the Bronze Age around 3000 BC, and is the last 'cradle of civilization' we will examine. Compared to the Mesopotamian and Egyptian civilizations, the Indus Valley Civilisation spanned a much larger area, from the northwest of India all the way up into Pakistan, ranging as far as Afghanistan. It's thought to have been home to as many as five million people.

The Indo-European-speaking peoples arrived there around 2000 BC, establishing large-scale settlements centered around the Indus River. Cities such as Harappa and Mohenjo-daro were believed to have been home to as many as 60,000 people. While no Harappan DNA samples have been analyzed, samples from skeletons found close by indicate a genetic relationship with modern Indians.

These cities weren't just ramshackle collections of rude huts either. Harappa and Mohenjo-daro featured baked brick houses, and are renowned for their urban planning, with sophisticated water and drainage supply systems. They even had flush toilets. Over one thousand Indus Valley Civilisation sites have been identified, although less than ten percent of them have been excavated.

The Harappan people could accurately measure length, mass, and time. They are even believed by some to have developed a uniform system of weights and measures. They created artistic goods, some with only aesthetic uses. Items excavated in Harappan sites include sculptures created with sophisticated carving techniques, gold jewelry, bronze vessels, and pottery. In addition to these manufactured goods, thousands of seals have been found. They are flat, but otherwise similar in nature to Mesopotamian cylinder seals. The combination of standardized weights and measures, seals, and trade goods suggests that these Indus Valley settlements constituted an extensive trade network, and it is believed they traded as far afield as Egypt, Mesopotamia, and Central Asia.

Between 2600 and 1900 BC, the Harappan civilization used a kind of writing now referred to as the Indus script.

Indus script

Indus script comprises short strings of symbols, and experts believe it was written from right to left. Despite many attempts to decipher it, it remains a mystery. Most known examples of this script are extremely short, and it is not categorically known whether these symbols even constituted a complete writing system. Some scholars believe that the Indus script is associated with various other scripts and languages in the region, but so far, there is no concrete evidence of any relationship.

A typical inscription in Indus script was a mere five characters long, and the most verbose inscription was only 26 characters. So, it's clear that the people of the Indus Valley hadn't recorded the collected works of Shakespeare. However, there's still hope that one day the script will be translated and we will know whether it was 'real' writing or not.

End of the Harappans

There's no archaeological evidence that the demise of the Harappan civilization was caused by invasion. Instead, some scholars believe that climate change eventually brought about its collapse. The onset of intense heat and drought conditions not only affected the Harappans but also impacted Egypt and Mesopotamia. As climate change progressed, it is theorized the Indus River flooded less reliably. Rather than a cataclysmic end to the Harappan Civilisation, it may have slowly fallen apart as its people moved on to greener pastures.

Ancient India

As the Harappan Civilisation declined, its Dravidian people began to move into India, establishing themselves throughout the subcontinent. So did the Indo-Europeans from the Eurasian Steppe (modern-day Ukraine, Russia, and Kazakhstan). This influx of people mixed with the indigenous Indian people, creating the modern genetic mix of the Indian people. This also partially accounts for the large diversity in languages spoken on the subcontinent.

Sanskrit is one of the oldest documented Indo-European languages that emerged from this time. Sanskrit is thought to have been the main language of Ancient India. It is the sacred language of Hinduism and is still used today in Buddhist hymns and chants.

Although Sanskrit had been a spoken language for 2,000 years, the earliest written texts were Vedas, which appeared around 300 BC. The Rigveda, the oldest sacred book of Hinduism, dates back to around 1500 BC, and was preserved as an oral text before being recorded in the written word.

Hinduism

When it comes to religion-as-big-idea, Hinduism is in a league of its own. It is the oldest major religion on the planet, and its roots go back more than four millennia. Even today, only Christianity and Islam have more adherents. However, unlike these other religions, Hinduism's origins are so lost in time that it has no known founder.

Hinduism is unique in a couple of ways: It is henotheistic, meaning while Hindus worship a single god, Brahman, they also believe in other gods and goddesses, and it combines many traditions and philosophies. For this reason, there are many ways to worship as a Hindu. It's sometimes considered more a way of life rather than a religion.

Hindus believe in a continuous cycle of life, death, and rebirth, known as samsara. This is a big idea also adopted by Buddhism and Jainism. The body dies, but the soul is everlasting and indestructible. This soul is called *Atman* and is unchangeable, cycling through different bodies over time. This is the eternal journey of the soul.

In contrast, the body and personality are changeable. The body is born, grows old, and dies. A person with good intentions and actions reincarnates to a better future. A person whose intents and actions are malign—well, you get the picture. In this way, a person's state of karma (another big idea of Hinduism) affects not only this life, but future lives as well.

There is no single text holy to Hindus. Rather, there are a number of texts that Hindus regard as sacred. Arguably the primary texts are the Vedas. They are a collection of verses, and comprise the Rig Veda, the Samaveda, the Yajurveda, and the Atharva-Veda. These texts transcend traditional timelines and are not considered to have a beginning or an end. Other texts that Hindus consider sacred are the Bhagavad Gita, the Upanishads, 18 Puranas, the Ramayana, and the Mahabharata.

Good luck with the Swastikas

In the 1930s and 40s, the world had a gut-full of the symbol of Nazi hate: the Swastika. It was the flag under which Germans had marched into World War II. It waved proudly over the death camps. It is a symbol so reviled that there is still a ban on its use in Germany. But before its heinous misuse by Hitler and his minions, it had a totally different meaning.

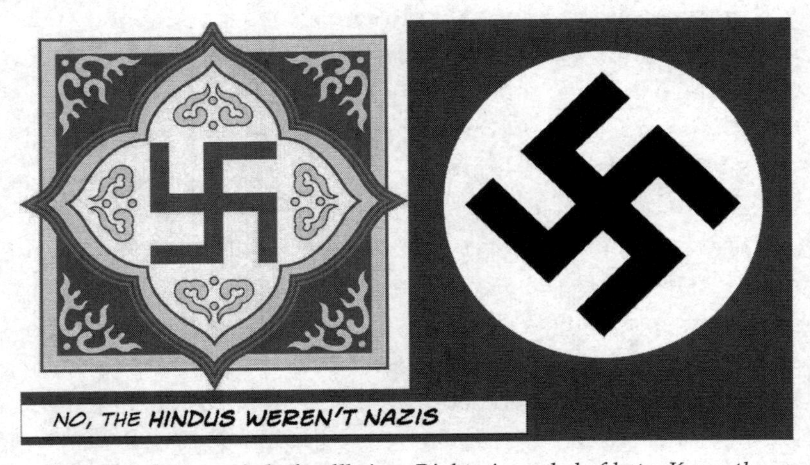

Fig. 1: Left: A symbol of wellbeing. Right: A symbol of hate. Know the difference (Public Domain and S.E.W.)

In Sanskrit, swastika means 'wellbeing', and has been used by Hindus and Buddhists for hundreds of years. It is a symbol of the spiritual and divine in religions such as Hinduism, Buddhism, and Jainism. Even in the West, before the swastika was perverted by the Nazis, its Indian connotation followed it, and it was considered to be lucky.

In Hinduism, there are two types of swastikas. The one that faces right (卐) is called swastika, and symbolizes the sun and good luck. The left-facing symbol (卍) is called sauwastika, and symbolizes the night. In Buddhism, it symbolizes the Buddha's footprints. Swastikas have been uncovered by archeologists during digs in the Harappan Civilisation, and they are found on artwork all over the world.

Mukti Jain Campion's BBC article, *How the world loved the swastika - until Hitler stole it*, quotes Peter Madsen, founder of 'Learn to Love the Swastika Day': "The swastika is a symbol of love and Hitler abused it. We're not trying to reclaim (it). That would be impossible."

He's not wrong.

Education

Independent of other cultures, the Indians saw the need to preserve and interpret these sacred texts, and an intellectual, priestly class arose: the Brahmins. Their rise ensured that formal education in Ancient India was—like much else, including law, government, and philosophy—associated with religion and class. While education was not denied to women, mothers still instructed their daughters at home.

During the third century BC, there were two periods of schooling, equating to elementary and secondary education. Children received elementary education in the home. Formal schooling, which was restricted to males and compulsory for members of the three highest classes (the Brahmins, Kshatriyas, and Vaishyas), began at the secondary stage and was heralded by the *upanayana* or thread ceremony. The student would leave his childhood home to enter his teacher's ashram, something between a private residence and a boarding school, where he would get board, lodging, and education. If this deal sounds too good to be true, one must factor in that in return, the student did the teacher's housework and tended his cattle.

Studying was no picnic, either. Besides chanting the Vedas, students memorized rituals and studied literature and astronomy. The Brahmin, Kshatriya, and Vaishya boys underwent differentiated types of schooling applicable to their stations in life. It required a Brahmin boy to follow a particular curriculum to suit his religious role, including an intimate knowledge of the three Vedas. While attending school, students lived on basic foods, slept on hard beds, and committed to a celibate life. And celibacy was a solid commitment from the civilization that brought us the *Kama Sutra*.

The Hindu goddess of learning and wisdom is Saraswati. In later religious texts, she is identified as the inventor of Sanskrit and said to have presented a gift of pen and ink to Ganesha. Ganesha emerged as a deity around the first century AD. He's relatively easy to identify because he has four arms and the head of an elephant. But it could have been a lot worse.

Seriously, what is it with impregnation by mouth?

In yet *another* origin story that relates to impregnation-by-mouth, the goddess Parvarti's dirty bath water was thrown into the river Ganges and drunk by the goddess Malini (who had an elephant's head and dubious taste in liquid refreshment). As a result, she gave birth to baby Ganesha, who had the misfortune of being born with an extra couple of arms and five elephant heads. As luck would have it, the god Shiva cured Ganesha of some of this congenital birth defect by reducing his number of elephant heads to one.

It was better than nothing.

Fig. 2: The God Ganesha (MoreVector and S.E.W.)

Despite, or perhaps, *because* of his appearance, Ganesha became one of the best-loved and most worshipped of the Hindu deities. He is revered as the god of wisdom and education, the remover of obstacles, and as the patron of arts and sciences. Given these attributes, it is fitting he is associated with the many big ideas of the Indian people.

Animals are revered in Hinduism. They are believed to have a secret spiritual importance, given to them by Brahma at their creation. It is the job of humans to uncover the animals' spiritual meanings. Hindus also believe that animals may house the souls of dead friends and family members, making 'knowledge of animals' an important area of study. Perhaps for this reason, Hindus believe some animals enjoy a higher status. We've all heard of the way cows are venerated in India, but animals such as elephants, horses, boars, tigers, and lions are also believed to be spiritually evolved and sacred.

Fig. 3: Enunciation is everything (Radiokukka and S.E.W.)

The above image is one of a number of sexually explicit images from the Khajuraho UNESCO World Heritage Site, a group of Hindu and Jain temples in Madhya Pradesh, India. They were constructed during the Chandela dynasty between 885 AD and 1050 AD. No one quite knows the meaning of this sculpture, but one interpretation is it was simply meant to be humorous. Another possibility is it's a depiction of soldiers on the march taking their pleasures where they could get them. Yet, despite this graphic depiction of bestiality in a holy place, it is at odds with the beliefs of Hinduism and Jainism. In fact, India has always been one of the few countries on Earth where life has been universally respected and revered.

Well, the guys in the sculpture had a funny way of showing it.

Yep, one thing you can say about the Ancient Indians is they weren't prudes. One of the most famous Hindu texts is closely related to the images carved into the Khajuraho site. The *Kama Sutra*, which literally translates as the 'Principles of Lust,' is an ancient Sanskrit text on sexuality. Most people hearing the words *Kama Sutra* immediately think of sexual positions, but there's a lot more to it than that. Sure, the text is big on desire and sexuality, but it also lists one of the goals of life as emotional fulfillment. It has chapters on finding a partner and courtship. It also has a chapter on how to flirt, and a chapter on the art of sociability. The chapters that took the West by storm in the Swinging Sixties were, of course, the ones on sexual positions. The *Kama Sutra* shows an enlightenment towards same-sex relationships and even addresses sadomasochism. Given the carvings at Khajuraho, group sex was clearly not an issue either.

While sexuality as a means of procreation has been around for two billion years, the *Kama Sutra* codified it as a pleasurable activity. This brainchild of the Ancient Indians has come down to us through the centuries, past the censors, fundamentalists, and puritans. Collective learning can be fun.

Fig. 4: Thanks to Ancient India, Ken and Barbie were almost paralyzed by choice (Kaspars Grinvalds and S.E.W.)

Yoga: Mastering the Roaming Tendencies of the Mind

The origins of the practice of yoga lie before the beginning of recorded history. Around the second century BC, the scholar Patanjali is reputed to have collected the known writings, theories, and practices of yoga into a text, the *Yoga Sutras* (not as popular as the *Kama Sutra* but providing the flexibility necessary for many of the positions). The term *yoga* is taken from the Sanskrit word *yuj*, which means "to yoke, unite, or bring together." Yoga is the effort to restore harmony in the mind-body complex and an attempt to reunite an individual's spirit with their essential nature. It is both a process towards achieving a goal, and a goal in itself. The *Yoga Sutras* regard it as a way of mastering the "roaming tendencies of the mind." Deep.

But how is this achieved?

Yoga attempts to unite the body, breath, and mind through a system of techniques that help achieve oneness of being, peacefulness, and mental clarity. Ultimately it leads to self-awareness and higher consciousness. This is done through a combination of breathing exercises, postures and movement, relaxation and concentration, and meditation.

Yoga does not exclude any religion or belief system. However, in recent years, it has been co-opted by woo-woo New Age spiritualism. It bears repeating that yoga is an ancient practice based on the Vedic traditions of India.

Fig. 5: Mastering the roaming tendencies of the mind isn't always easy (quickshooting and S.E.W.)

Buddhism

Around the fifth century BC, Gautama Siddhārtha, better known as the Buddha (Sanskrit for 'enlightened one' or 'awakened one'), turned heads in India. He was a philosopher and religious leader and became celebrated as the founder of Buddhism. He is still revered by Buddhists as one who has transcended Karma, escaping the cycle of suffering and rebirth, which is the ultimate goal of Buddhist practice. His ministry lasted for around forty-five years, and he built a large following for his movement, which is now considered both a philosophy and a religion. This historical Buddha is portrayed in art as skinny, serene, and peaceful. But there are also iconic fat and jolly depictions of Buddha.

So, did 'the Enlightened One' develop a thyroid problem?

The short answer is 'no.' In Buddhism, anyone who has achieved enlightenment and transcended Karma is considered a Buddha. That means there is more than one. Many more. There are the Seven Buddhas of Antiquity, the 29 Buddhas of Theravada, and the Mahayana Buddhas, to name but a few. In the surviving visual representations, most of these Buddhas are almost indistinguishable from Gautama.

With one obvious exception.

The Laughing or Fat Buddha (I don't mean to be fat-shaming an enlightened one, but I didn't make up the name) is often pictured laughing and open-shirted, his gut cascading onto his lap. However, this Buddha is most definitely not the original guiding light of Buddhism. This jovial, rotund fellow was a Zen monk named Budai, who lived in tenth-century China, well over fifteen hundred years after Gautama Siddhārtha roamed the Earth, dispensing wisdom.

To say Budai had a distinctive look would be an understatement. Apart from his expansive, exposed belly and beaming smile, he had a shaved head and massive earlobes. He also carried a large sack bearing all his possessions. This large, cheerful apparition shuffled across China, unsurprisingly grabbing the attention of the people he encountered. Children were particularly taken with him. He was fond of kids as well, supplying them with sweets from his sack.

Fig. 6: Gautama vs Budai: Who would you back in a fight?
(Public domain, phonghuynh and S.E.W.)

Let me be clear: there is NO suggestion that Budai was anything other than a jolly, kind-hearted, and spiritual soul. He *was* an enlightened one, after all. However, these days, if a laughing, half-naked stranger wobbled barefoot into town and handed out candy to children, it would attract attention for all the wrong reasons.

But I digress. Back to Gautama Siddhārtha.

Gautama displayed many superhuman characteristics. He was considered a perfect, transcendent being. The Buddha was conceived without intercourse (sound familiar?) and caused his mother no pain in childbirth. He didn't need rest, nourishment, or medication. He didn't need to wash and, it is not written but

I assume, his feces smelled like a fresh summer breeze. The Enlightened One's lifetime could be as long or short as he wanted.

While this may sound too good to be true, we are pretty confident that Gautama Siddhārtha actually existed. Whether or not he was super-powered, his teachings challenged the exclusive religious claims of the Brahmin. Buddhist temples often had monasteries attached and imparted education, specializing in religious education. However, around 100 AD, Buddhist monasteries also began to provide secular education. This popularised elementary education and allowed for growth in collective learning.

A Golden Age

Then, beginning around 300 BC, the stars aligned and India underwent a golden age. It saw the rise of universities and exponential growth in the study of mathematics, astronomy, and the sciences. The fame of the university at Nalanda was such that it attracted students from all over India and Asia. It offered courses in grammar, logic, Buddhist and Hindu philosophy, the Vedas, medicine, and the sciences.

Heroes for Zero

Indian mathematicians had been using a place value system since the third century AD, as seen in the Bakhshali Manuscript. In the fifth century AD, Aryabhata the Elder, an astronomer and arguably the most influential mathematician of the age, proposed the idea of the number zero and decimals. However, he still didn't use Hindu-Arabic numerals. Instead, he used an alphabetic system to denote numbers. Even though Aryabhata invented the concept of zero, he didn't denote it with a symbol.

Then, in the sixth century, Indian mathematician and astronomer Brahmagupta (598–668 AD) became the first person to provide the rules to perform calculations using zero. Although still not using the Hindu-Arabic numeral system, Brahmagupta composed his magnum opus, the *Brāhmasphuṭasiddhānta,* commonly (and understandably) abbreviated to *BSS*, around 628 AD. The *BSS* combines mathematics and astronomy, and contains significant mathematical content, including his method of using zero in calculations, rules for using negative and positive numbers, ways of solving linear and quadratic equations, and a method for deriving square roots. As usual for the time, Brahmagupta wrote the *BSS* in Sanskrit verse.

As you do.

Hindu–Arabic Numerals

The positional decimal system of numerals, that would become the Hindu–Arabic system we use today, had been evolving for a few hundred years in India. It was formalized around 700 AD, likely because Brahmagupta's work on zero made a new system a necessity. The digits they used at the time looked quite different and were later changed into the more familiar Arabic numerals in North Africa. As we will see in a later chapter, Arab mathematicians adopted, then developed this system in the ninth century AD. Despite this, it's only from the fifteenth century onwards that we could read numerals the way we can today.

If you've ever tried to do even a simple calculation using Roman numerals, you'll know why the invention of the Hindu-Arabic system was so important. Which is easier to understand and calculate: 10 x 9 = 90 *or* X x IX = XC?

For that, we must thank the early Indian mathematicians.

Medicine

Medical science has a long history in Ancient India, with therapeutic ideas set out in the sacred Vedas around four thousand years ago. Hindu surgery was quite advanced, even though they had limited knowledge of human anatomy because they were prohibited from dissecting dead bodies using knives. However, ingenuity found a way around this ban. Some bright spark discovered that if a body was immersed in water for seven days, it could be *peeled* apart and examined. This wasn't ideal and was more than a little icky, but it beat the 'no cutting' ban and got the job done.

Luckily for doctors and patients alike, there was no such prohibition about cutting *living* humans. Hindu surgeons were skilled in excising tumors, performing cesarean sections, stitching wounds, dealing with fractures and amputations—and the procedure you were wondering about, repairing anal fistulas. Compare this to the filthy barber-surgeons of the European Middle Ages, and I know who I'd prefer dealing with *my* anus.

Fig. 7: Doctor Sushruta seeing patients (Wellcome and S.E.W.)

Hindu surgeons also excelled in treating bladder stones with surgery. In 600 BC, the famed physician Shushruta gave the first description of surgery to treat such stones, known as a perineal lithotomy. I would describe the operation here, but for the likelihood I'd faint at the keyboard. Suffice to say, a man with a very sharp knife, and no anesthetic, cuts into one's nether regions.

Indian surgeons also pioneered plastic surgery, particularly a primitive form of rhinoplasty. Extreme nose jobs were often required because a common punishment for adultery was amputation of the nose. A new nose would be fashioned with skin taken from the patient's cheek or forehead. The result? Let's just say it wasn't pretty, but it was a damn sight better than going through life with a gaping hole in the face.

Shushruta believed a well-equipped surgeon should have twenty sharp and one hundred and ten blunt surgical instruments. These instruments were usually made of steel. As in the American Wild West, alcohol was used to make the patient insensible for operations. I might even have signed up for the beer anesthetic, but there could never be enough beer for the perineal lithotomy. Or cataract surgery.

Nevertheless, Shushruta is credited with being the first known cataract surgeon. One of his twenty sharp surgical instruments was especially designed to enter the eye and push the cataract aside. This, with no anesthesia other than getting the blind man blind drunk. It was, however, effective. As long as the patient didn't develop an infection, their vision recovered enough to count fingers and see to eat food. Not bad for 600 BC.

This Indian enlightenment made Indian culture highly influential across Central and Southeast Asia. Buddhism had already begun to spread throughout Asia as early as the first century AD. Indian scholars were also invited to teach in China. In exchange, a steady stream of Chinese and Tibetan monks came to India to study in Buddhist monasteries.

From the beginning, India had a strong tradition of creating big ideas. Their tradition for collective learning meant that many ideas were conceived and developed over hundreds of years. Like in Egypt, schooling was primarily driven by religious belief and the desire for religious scholarship. However, there was also a strong tradition in secular education. Much that had been learned in India made its way around the world. As a result, the collective learning and big ideas of India greatly influenced both the European Renaissance and Enlightenment.

A Brief Interlude III

(It's No) Sacrifice

Fig. 1: It just doesn't add up… (PikePicture, artbalitskiy and S.E.W.)

Even More Ancient Astronauts?

Earlier in the book, I mentioned my lifelong dread of the Great God Mars from Tassili n'Ajjer. Well, there was one other ancient image that spooked me from *Chariots of the Gods?* Admittedly, not as much as the Great God Mars, but it was a close-run thing. The image came from a tomb in Palenque, Mexico.

When King Pakal of the Mayan state of Palenque died in 683 AD, his people thought they'd do something nice in gratitude for his successful 70-year reign. His jade-encrusted body was interred, with all pomp and ceremony, into a pyramid known today as the Temple of Inscriptions. His sarcophagus was then covered with a massive stone that was, archaeologists assure us, carved with an image of Pakal's rebirth as a deity. This bas relief image is an acknowledged masterpiece of Mayan art.

Fig. 2: You decide (Archivist and S.E.W.)

However, to our old friend Erich von Däniken, this was yet more compelling evidence for ancient astronauts: "Could primitive imagination have produced anything so remarkably similar to a modern astronaut in his rocket?" he wrote. "Those strange markings at the foot of the drawing can only be an indication of the flames and gases coming from the propulsion unit."

Doubtless, it's an intriguing and somewhat puzzling picture. One could be forgiven for questioning that it depicted Pakal's ascension to godhead. It irks me to write this, but it *does* rather look like a cut-away view of a vehicle with a flaming exhaust, and a pilot at the controls. But is there *really* no other explanation, Herr von Däniken?

Well, as it happens, there are many more logical explanations. In fact, virtually *any* explanation is more logical.

Using the principle of Occam's Razor (a shortened and overly simplified definition: the idea with the least assumptions is most likely correct), we have to wonder: *is* this a cross-section of an extra-terrestrial flying machine? Or is this merely a weird artwork that we can't quite understand?

For the extra-terrestrial flying machine, our assumptions are:

1. Extraterrestrials exist;
2. They have mastered faster-than-light, dimensional, or wormhole travel;
3. They visited Mesoamerica over a thousand years ago; *and*—
4. They let a Mayan king take their rocket ship for a burn.

For the weird artwork, we merely:

1. Admit our ignorance.

Admitting ignorance isn't sexy, but it's not rocket science either. Or is it?

Chapter Seven

I Left my Heart In Chichén Itzá
Ancient Mesoamerica

Coming to America

The continents of America were inhabited by humans between 16,500 years and 23,000 years ago. These Paleo-Americans originated from Central Asia, in small hunter-gatherer groups which followed herds of megafauna across what was then the Beringia land bridge between eastern Siberia and Alaska. At that time, the Asian and North American continents were joined due to a drop in global sea levels caused by glaciation. From Beringia, these hunter-gatherer groups gradually migrated south into North America and South America. By around 10,000 years ago, there were a number of Paleo-American settlements in Mexico.

One of the most ancient human skeletons found in the Americas was discovered in the Quintana Roo region of Mexico in 2016. It was located in a submerged cavern and belonged to a woman who had died 9,900 years before. The poor woman clearly hadn't had a long or pleasant life. Analysis of her skeleton showed she was around 30 years of age. It also showed signs of syphilis. Given the way her skull had been stoved in, it doesn't take *CSI: Ancient Mexico* to ascertain that she had been murdered. Possibly as a sacrifice.

If true, she probably wasn't the first person sacrificed in Mesoamerica. And she certainly wouldn't be the last.

The Olmec

The Olmec were the earliest major Mesoamerican civilization. They appeared around 1600 BC, and their heyday was between 1200 BC and 400 BC. They are often considered to be the mother culture that provided the template for future civilizations such as the Mayans and, much later, the Aztec. There are several reasons for this belief.

It was the Olmec who began the craze for pyramid building that so obsessed subsequent Pre-Columbian cultures. The Olmec also used hieroglyphs which were possibly writing or an embryonic form of writing. This text has not been deciphered, but if true, then they join an exclusive group of cultures who created verified written text. This was almost certainly an influence on the Mayans.

It is highly likely that the Olmec created the Mesoamerican ballgame (more on that soon), which was hugely influential for over 1,000 years. They inhabited a region known for the production of latex, and rubber balls of the type used for the ballgame were found at an Olmec site. Other implements potentially associated with the ballgame have been found at other sites. Given the significance of the ballgame in Mesoamerican life, this is a major influence.

However, there were other Olmec ideas that didn't seem to catch on.

Olmec Stone Heads

One of these was the creation of Olmec trademark giant stone heads. There have been 17 stone heads found so far, the smallest being about 1.5 meters tall, and the largest just under 3.5 meters tall. They have flat faces, lips a supermodel would die for, and are wearing what appear to be helmets. No one really knows who they portray, but the consensus is they are representations of Olmec rulers. Were they a big idea, who can say? But they certainly were big.

Fig. 1: An Olmec Stone Head (Alexandersr and S.E.W.)

Were-Jaguars

We're all aware of the legend of werewolves: humans who transform into human/wolf hybrids during the full moon. Well, the Olmec had the were-jaguar. These beasts were a common motif in Olmec art and are identified by their human-like bodies combined with down-turned mouths, feline noses, and (cherry on the cake) a cleft head. It is believed the were-jaguar played a role in the Olmec religion, possibly as a god. Were-jaguar babies were common on Olmec iconography.

Originally, archaeologists believed the were-jaguar was part of an Olmec myth that involved a human woman mating with a jaguar. This belief arose because some Olmec carvings looked rather a lot like a jaguar and a woman having sex. This was patently ridiculous. Can you imagine what would happen to a woman who offered herself to a jaguar? Sex wouldn't be on the menu.

She would.

It is now believed that the sculpture that was initially seen as human/jaguar copulation was, in fact, depicting a shaman morphing into a jaguar. It's all a bit confusing. The idea of a baby were-jaguar seems cute though…

Fig. 2: A rare portrait of a were-jaguar baby
(Famveldman, Meunierd and S.E.W.)

Were-jaguars or not, the Mesoamericans really had a thing for jaguars. They saw the jaguar as a strong and powerful creature. Jaguars became a part of Mayan mythology, with many gods portrayed with jaguar-like characteristics. This reverence was reflected in the names of some of their kings, such as Great Jaguar Paw, Bird Jaguar, Shield Jaguar, and the delightfully named Jaguar Penis. One has to wonder: how did Jaguar Penis earn his nickname?

As with much Mesoamerican culture, the true significance of the jaguar (other than it was a powerful, dangerous animal) is still the subject of debate.

The Mayans

While the Olmec may have set certain Mesoamerican cultural norms in train, the Mayans really took these concepts and built upon them. Of course, there wasn't a distinct line of demarcation between the Olmec and the Mayan civilizations. In the Preclassic period, there was another significant culture that overlapped both.

They were the Zapotec who inhabited the region around Oaxaca from around 600 BC-800 AD. The Olmec influence on the Zapotec was also significant. They used Olmec style 'writing' and followed Olmec innovations such as pre-writing, mathematics, and of course, pyramid building.

The city of Teotihuacan existed from 200 to 900 BC. During this period, it grew from a village to a powerful city. The name Teotihuacan has been interpreted as 'birthplace of the gods' and archaeological evidence bears this out. It was a city devoted to the veneration of the Great Mother Goddess and her husband—the Plumed Serpent, Kukulcan. Teotihuacan is the site of the famous Pyramid of the Sun, the third largest pyramid on Earth.

However, while these societies left their mark, it was the Mayans who created a civilization for the ages. They created a true system of writing that we can still interpret today. They developed a base 20 number system far superior to Roman numerals. They also devised a sophisticated calendar, which famously ended in 2012, sparking some people to think the end of the world was nigh. They were enthusiastic practitioners of human sacrifice, and they loved body modification.

Above all, they, like Mesoamerican civilizations before and after, enthusiastically played the Mesoamerican ballgame.

Mesoamerican Ballgame

> *Some people think football is a matter of life and death. I assure you, it's much more serious than that.*
> Bill Shankly, Liverpool FC

While he was referring to soccer, Bill Shankly could easily have been talking about the Mesoamerican ballgame. Shanks was speaking metaphorically, but the game invented by the Olmec and played by successive cultures up until the Spanish conquest in 1521 sometimes had actual life-or-death consequences for the players.

Today, nobody has a complete understanding of how the ballgame was played. Although the modern sport of ulama, played in parts of Mexico, is considered to be descended from the much later Aztec version of the ballgame. There are three versions of the ulama: one played by bouncing the ball off the hip, with a ball weighing up to 4 kilograms; a version played with the forearm, which uses a lighter ball; and one played with a bat and a still lighter ball. The rules of ulama are quite complex, but all we really need to understand is that the aim was to keep the ball in play. As far as anyone can tell at this remove, this is similar to how some versions of the original ballgame were played.

Fig. 3: Surely the headdresses would've gotten in the way…
(V. Korostyshevskiy, artbalitskiy and and S.E.W.)

However, one must remember that the Mesoamerican ballgame was played by many Mesoamerican cultures for over 3,000 years. Variations inevitably arose. One clear example of changes in the ballgame was how ball courts vary markedly in shape and size in different areas. Some ball courts also have circular goals, but this seems to be a later innovation. When one considers that the modern version of soccer has been popular for only two hundred years and has undergone hundreds of rule changes, it's obvious why the ballgame has had so many incarnations.

It appears there was also a ritual, almost religious dimension to the ballgame, possibly because it was integral to the Mayan creation story. There is also a persistent modern-day belief that the losing team in a ballgame would be executed. Given the bloodthirsty nature of Mesoamerican sacrifice, it's easy to see how this belief might have begun. While it is possible that competitions were combined with human sacrifice in some areas (there *are* carvings of ballplayers being beheaded), that was not believed to have been commonplace. To make a modern sporting analogy, it would be like Novak Djokovic being put to death after losing the final of Wimbledon. Like him or not, nobody wants to see him literally sacrificed on Center Court.

Well, almost nobody.

Fig. 4: But perhaps the stadium decorations tell a different story (Tandemich and S.E.W.)

Writing: Sacrificing for Your Art

The Mesoamerican development of writing was a significant achievement. Prior to the discovery of Mayan writing, the theory of monogenesis suggested that writing had been discovered by the Sumerians and disseminated by traders to the Egyptians and Chinese. It is now believed that writing was invented independently four times: by the Sumerians, Egyptians, Chinese, and the Mayans.

The Mayans wrote in hieroglyphics. But unlike Egyptian hieroglyphics, the Mayan system used symbols to represent words, or could combine phonemes to 'sound out' new words. Because of this flexibility, the Mayans could combine several symbols to construct new words or sentences.

Like in so many other civilizations, only the wealthy Mayans became priests and learned to read and write. Even though there were inscriptions carved on Mayan buildings, the average Mayan-in-the-street couldn't have read them. Most of these inscriptions were in 'elites only' areas of temples. Given the carnage that regularly happened in the temples, the Mayan peasant probably stayed as far away as possible. No point being in the wrong place at the wrong time.

The elites who could write inked their glyphs on sheets made from bark or leather. These were folded up like an old-fashioned road map to make books. This form of Mayan book is called a codex. Unfortunately, most of the Mayan books were burned by Spanish conquistadors and Catholic priests in the sixteenth century.

There are three Mayan codices that have survived: the Dresden Codex, the Madrid Codex, and the Paris Codex. It wasn't until 1962 that the first Mayan hieroglyphs were deciphered. Work is still ongoing, but there's hope the records of the Mayans will eventually be fully understood.

Fig. 5: It's difficult to see how this wasn't immediately interpreted (Heritage Pictures and S.E.W.)

Mathematics: Heroes for Zero II

The Mayans invented an ingenious base 20 positional numeral system to represent numbers and calendar dates. Significantly, they invented the concept of zero without input from any other civilization. As seen below, their numerals were symbolized by a combination of three symbols: zero (a turtle shell), one (a dot), and five (a bar).

Fig. 6: The Mayan Base 20 Number System (drutska, Nailotl Mendez and S.E.W.)

The Mayans believed some numbers were sacred. Twenty was considered special, as it represented the number of human fingers and toes available for counting, and this was, perhaps, the reason for a Base 20 system. Five was also considered significant, as it represented the number of digits on a hand or foot. Thirteen was special because it was the number of original Mayan gods. Four hundred was sacred to the Mayan gods, possibly because as 20^2, it was as significant to the Mayans base 20 system as 10^2 is for us with our Base 10 system.

The Mayan mathematical system allowed mathematicians, astronomers, and engineers to carry out complex calculations. The enduring nature of their engineering feats speaks volumes for their mathematical ability. Nevertheless, their system was simple enough that the largely illiterate population could trade and do business. The Mayans understood square numbers, and this shape was the base shape of many of their pyramids.

It probably helped them calculate the number of hearts they cut out of chests as well.

Advanced Astronomy

Astronomy was really the Mayans' thing. They believed that the will of the gods could be interpreted through the movements of celestial bodies, and this made meticulous astronomical record keeping essential. They even constructed their most impressive structures with built-in astronomical features.

During equinoxes, sunshine on the terraces of the Temple of Kukulcan pyramid in Chichén Itzá causes the shadow of a 'serpent' to wriggle across its northern staircase. El Caracol at Chichén Itzá was built with links to the Sun's position at the solstices.

By the eighth century AD, the Mayans created astronomical tables tracking the movements of the Sun, Moon, and planets. These tables were carved into a temple wall, but are also found in the Dresden Codex. There were specialist astronomical observers whose job it was to maintain and correct the Mayan calendars, which were both complex and of great importance.

Calendars: Down for the Long Count

One calendar just wasn't enough for the Mayans. They used a complex system consisting of *three* calendars: the Long Count (an astronomical calendar with a cycle lasting 2,880,000 days); the Tzolkin (the 260-day sacred calendar used for religious events); and the Haab (a secular calendar, which lasted 365 days). The Long Count gave the year, and the Tzolkin and the Haab identify the days. Together these calendars triangulated the date.

As you can imagine, it took complex calculations to figure things out, which is probably why the Mayans invented such an advanced system of mathematics. Yes, their calendar system is intimidating and difficult, but luckily for our purposes, we don't need to understand how it worked. All we need to know is that it worked and worked well. However, the Mayans weren't totally responsible for the system. Rather, like many aspects of their culture, they inherited some of it from the earlier Mesoamericans, who devised it around 1500 BC.

Fig. 7: The Mayan Calendar

(Maria Egupova, Nailotl Mendez and S.E.W.)

Most of us would have been blissfully ignorant of the Mayan calendar until the years leading up to 2012. A 'great cycle' of the Long Count calendar was drawing to an end, which inspired doomsayers to predict the end of the Earth on December 21, 2012. It also inspired (for want of a better word) a disaster movie named *2012*.

Considering the accuracy and complexity of the Mayan system of calendars, it really deserved a better movie than one that scored a paltry 39% on RottenTomatoes.com.

And, spoiler alert: the world didn't end in 2012.

The Mayans ❤ Human Sacrifice

Like it or not, the ritual slaughter of humans to appease angry gods is a big idea that predates recorded history, as there is evidence of it in the Palaeolithic period. It didn't stop when humans could write, either. History records the Mesopotamians, Egyptians, Greeks, Romans, Celts, Germans, Chinese, Indians, Africans, and Pacific Islanders (among others) all had a crack at human sacrifice. So did Muslims, and Jews. The very basis of Christianity was God offering His son as a human sacrifice in a paradoxical attempt to appease Himself (see Chapter 8).

These civilizations used varied methods: People were beheaded, drowned, garrotted, burned at the stake, poisoned, crucified, and buried alive. I'm sure there were other gruesome practices as well. We can all agree that none of these were very pleasant. I want you to bear this in mind, as we're about to examine the Mesoamerican penchant for human sacrifice and we're in no position to get judgemental.

However, it is notable that the Mayans practiced a particularly graphic and cruel form of human sacrifice. First, a victim (or insane volunteer) would be dragged to the summit of a pyramid and held down on an altar. Then, after a brief struggle, a lot of screaming, and (hopefully) a quick bit of thoracic surgery, the throbbing heart of the victim/volunteer was ripped from their chest and held aloft.

Fig. 8: When a Mayan priest stole your heart, he really stole your heart (Public domain and S.E.W.)

However, the ever-inventive Mayans didn't limit themselves to the mere excision of hearts. They liked to sacrifice people by decapitation, which usually took place after the victim had been beaten, burnt, scalped, and disemboweled. They also threw young people to their deaths in a sinkhole to appease Chaac the water god, because why the hell not? I'm sure if they had a convenient volcano, they'd have enthusiastically pushed virgins into that as well.

Yet, even state-sanctioned murder and butchery weren't enough. The Mayans' religiously driven blood lust seemed to know no bounds. One could be forgiven for thinking the Mayans were the source for several serial killer tropes: They took heads for trophies two millennia before Ted Bundy. Even Jeffery Dahmer would have been gobsmacked at how they cannibalized their victims. And Mayan priests danced in the flayed skins of their victims well before the fictional Buffalo Bill wanted Clarice to "Rub the lotion on the skin."

Are these lightbulb moments? The Mayans certainly thought so.

Body Piercing and Modification

The twenty-first century is rife with the big idea of body modification. Cosmetic surgery, tattoos, and body piercings are very common ways that people alter the bodies they were born with. A brief Google search showed me some other, thankfully less common practices, such as cutting a tongue so it becomes forked, or implanting horns in the forehead. Nevertheless, even the most extreme of today's body modifications pale by comparison to the gruesome Mayan body mods.

The Mayans did fun stuff like intentionally re-shaping and elongating the heads of infants, inducing crossed-eyes, and performing horrific dental work. Flattened skulls were a sign of high social status. It was common to bind boards to newborn babies' heads to train their skulls to conform to the preferred flattened style. The elongated skulls that resulted looked like those of aliens, but they were actually those of kids whose heads had been squashed by mom.

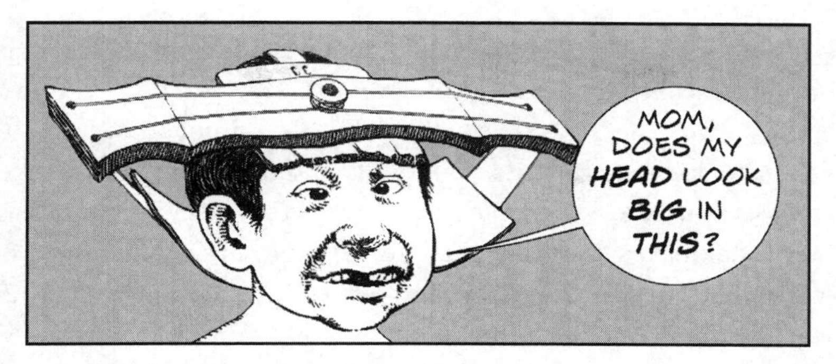

Fig. 9:"No darling, it's beautiful and flat. And what lovely crossed eyes!" (Fruitpunchline and S.E.W.)

Similarly, while crossed eyes are routinely corrected today, Mayans considered them as signs of intelligence and breeding. So, of course, parents did their darndest to encourage their children's eyes to be crossed. But it didn't stop with the skulls and the eyes. Mayan dentists performed such essential work as grinding teeth into points and inlaying precious gems. Jeweled teeth were a real status symbol. Pointy teeth were just scary.

Both Mayan men and women were tattooed and scarified, but this is hardly worthy of note in the face of their other extreme bodywork. This kind of human panel beating must have been excruciating, but enduring the pain of the piercings, tattoos, and dental work was considered a sign of bravery by the Mayans. For Mayans, perhaps more than any society in history, true beauty was born of suffering.

But it wasn't just beauty for which they suffered.

It stands to reason that people capable of sacrificing innocent people by cutting out their hearts would be into some other weird stuff. The good news was Mayan kings didn't get away scot-free. They too were expected to take one for the team, and while that didn't include having their hearts ripped out, it wasn't exactly pleasant. Their blood would be used in rituals to sanctify events such as choosing a successor or beseeching the rain god for precipitation. How was this blood extracted? Well,

I'm glad you asked. Kings would be cut or pierced with sharp implements like obsidian blades and, I kid you not, stingray spines. And where were these implements employed? Why, the ears, cheeks, lips, nostrils, tongue, and (gulp) the penis. There were various ways their blood was collected, but in the version that's making me cross my legs while I'm typing, a piece of rope was pulled through the wound to become soaked in blood. This was then burned as an offering to the gods.

All I can say is, I hope the gods bloody well appreciated it.

Tobacco and Chocolate

The Mayans weren't the first people to use tobacco. There's evidence humans have been using it for about 18,000 years. However, the Mayans were likely to have been the first to cultivate the tobacco plants, and there was a religious connotation to its use. It was common for the priests to offer tobacco as a sacrifice to the gods. This was done by burning it on the altar as an incense, but also by the smoky exhalations of the priests. It is believed that Mayan tobacco was stronger than the modern version, and this would account for the priests' hallucinations during worship.

When you think about it, that might explain a lot.

Tobacco also appears in a story in the Mayan sacred text, the *Popol Vuh*. In the tale, the semi-divine Hero Twins travel to the Underworld and are given a series of tests by the Lords of Death. The cheating Lords of Death lock the twins in a house and set them the impossible task of keeping their cigars alight all night but then presenting them unsmoked in the morning. The Hero Twins are too clever for the lords, pretending to smoke, but simulating lit cigars with fireflies. The twins easily fool the Lords of Death and eventually return to the land of the living.

The Mayans not only smoked cigars, but they took tobacco as a kind of snuff, too. Not content with those methods, they also made it into a paste to smear all over their bodies and even had tobacco enemas. I'm not sure if this last method was just an effective way of getting high, but it would certainly have stimulated an interesting offertory to the gods.

Now, in arguably the grossest segue of all time, I turn to the Mayans' use of chocolate.

The history of chocolate begins with Olmec, who first cultivated cacao beans around 1750 BC. As we already know, the Olmec were Mesoamerican trendsetters. They started the cacao ball rolling by using the plants for medicinal purposes and religious rituals. However, it was the Mayans who first used cacao as a beverage. But they weren't drinking sugary Milo or Ovaltine. Their unsweetened concoction was made from crushed cocoa beans, chili peppers, and water. It's no coincidence that the etymology of the word 'chocolate' from the Mayan word *xocolatl* meaning 'bitter water.' Nevertheless, the Mayans believed this drink was the food of the gods.

Mayan farmers would transport baskets of cacao beans and tobacco to trade with other city-states. This led to these trade goods being used as a type of currency. Historians believe that profits from inter-city-state trading led to a redistribution of wealth and resulted in a wealthy Mayan merchant class. So, the big idea of capitalism arose independently in Mesoamerica as well.

The Kingdom of the Crystal Skull? Not so much.

One of the big ideas of current New Age types is the supposed spiritual/paranormal/healing nature of the famous Mesoamerican crystal skulls. These skulls were purported to be pre-Columbian, probably Mayan, and therefore hundreds, if not thousands of years old. They also intrigued the ancient astronauts crowd because of claims they were made to a precision impossible using Mayan era tools.

"We believe the Crystal Skulls are a form of computer which are able to record energy and vibration that occur around them," claimed Joshua Shapiro, co-author of the 1989 classic of pseudo-archaeology, *Mysteries of the Crystal Skulls*

Revealed. I admit not having read this book, so I am ignorant of the arcane mysteries revealed within. However, I'm confident there's one thing Mr Shapiro's book doesn't reveal about the Crystal Skulls: they're fakes.

These large chunks of clear quartz, carved to resemble human skulls, were 'discovered' by bogus archaeologists in the nineteenth century, and passed off as Mesoamerican artifacts. *The Journal of Archaeological Science* published an article by Sax *et al*, 'The origin of two purportedly pre-Columbian Mexican crystal skulls,' which outlined the results of their study. They examined two skulls using electron microscopy and X-ray crystallography and found they had been carved using a rotary disc tool and polished with corundum or diamond. So, the 'ancient aliens' people were partially right: these tools *weren't* unavailable to the Ancient Mayans. They were, however, readily available in mid-nineteenth-century Europe, which is when and where they were made.

Fig. 10: Mediums the world over weren't too concerned (Innovatedcaptures and S.E.W.)

The Decline of the Mayan Civilisation.

The Mayan civilization dominated Mesoamerica for a thousand years, but their decline in the eighth to ninth century AD defies easy explanation. A highly developed culture encompassing agriculture, mathematics, literacy, and the ability to create significant megastructures, went into sharp decay.

There are various theories about overpopulation, depleted soil, and climate change. Some suggest the possibility of wars between the Mayan city-states. Maybe it was just that the priests had finally managed to sacrifice everyone.

However, despite the fall of the empire, the Mayans did not disappear as a people. To this day in Guatemala, 40% of the population is ethnically Mayan. However, in an echo of the problems facing indigenous peoples all over the world, the Maya face discrimination and marginalization. Many live in extreme poverty. One can only hope the descendants of one of the world's most advanced ancient cultures have a brighter future.

In my next book, I will examine the Aztec civilization of Mesoamerica and the Incan civilization of Peru, the pinnacles of which fit into the next period human big ideas.

The human sacrifices were only just beginning.

A Brief Interlude IV

Personal Jesus

Like many Australians in the 1960s, I was sentenced to partial weekend detention in Sunday School. It was a bit of a bummer really. The people there were lovely and good-hearted, but like most little kids, I'd rather have been anywhere than church on a Sunday morning.

What made it worse was that my parents would drop and run, craftily using Sunday School as free weekend daycare. I really don't want to speculate on what they did with their free time. But whatever happened, Dad still managed to pick me up promptly at 10 a.m.

In Sunday School, we learned that Jesus loved us, which I found comforting. We were told the story of Shadrach, Meshach, and Abednego, who survived being roasted in the fiery furnace by King Nebuchadnezzar, which I thought was kind of cool. We also learned how the God of the Old Testament decided to drown everyone except Noah and his family, which I found disturbing and quite at odds with the whole Jesus-loves-you vibe. We even learned a religious song sung to the tune of 'House of the Rising Sun.' Years later, I would learn that the original lyrics were about a brothel.

So, let's say Sunday School was a mixed bag.

My first ever day of Sunday School was memorable. I walked in to find long queues of small children forming up in front of four desks. At each desk was perched a kindly Sunday schoolmarm type. Mrs Camroux, the minister's wife, expertly corralled a feral mob of four-year-olds so their names and ages could be recorded. It got old pretty quickly for a little kid. After what seemed an interminable wait (but was probably only a matter of minutes), I decided to speed the process. Marching to the front of the line, I announced to all assembled: "I'm Scott Williams, I'm four, and I'm tired of waiting!"

That little anecdote made Mrs Camroux's column in the Church paper.

It signaled both the beginning of my love/hate relationship with religion and my career as a precocious smartass.

Fig. 1: Shadrach, Meshach, and Abednego are led out of the furnace by an Angel (Morphart and S.E.W.)

Chapter Eight

My Sweet Lord? The Biblical World

The Bible is a triple threat, doing duty as a Holy text for three major religions.

The Bible is also, without doubt, one of the most influential books ever written. It is the brainchild of numerous unknown authors, and well over half the world's population lives in societies based on its teachings. Even Sunday school dropouts can tell you that the Christian Bible comprises two parts: the Old Testament and the New Testament.

To say these books are uneven in tone is an understatement. The Old Testament spits fire and brimstone; the New Testament is all peace, love, and mung beans. Of course, this inconsistent tone is because both the Old Testament and the New Testament are a collection of books written, some literalists believe, over the course of approximately 4000 years. Apart from being a religious text, it is considered a somewhat unreliable history of the Levant region. However, despite the differing tones, both books contain big ideas that still resonate today.

As mentioned in the Introduction, the biggest idea of 'the Good Book' is that humans should do as they are bloody well told:

And I will put enmity between thee and the woman, and between thy seed and her seed; it shall bruise thy head, and thou shalt bruise his heel.
Unto the woman he said, I will greatly multiply thy sorrow and thy conception; in sorrow thou shalt bring forth children; and thy desire shall be to thy husband, and he shall rule over thee.
And unto Adam he said, Because thou hast hearkened unto the voice of thy wife, and hast eaten of the tree, of which I commanded thee,

saying, Thou shalt not eat of it: cursed is the ground for thy sake; in sorrow shalt thou eat of it all the days of thy life;
Thorns also and thistles shall it bring forth to thee; and thou shalt eat the herb of the field;
In the sweat of thy face shalt thou eat bread, till thou return unto the ground; for out of it wast thou taken: for dust thou art, and unto dust shalt thou return.
Genesis 3, 15-19

Let's get this straight: Adam and Eve made *one mistake,* and their petulant God cursed their relationship and the relationship between their children. He promised to cause them sorrow. He decreed that henceforth, all women will give birth in agony and gave men dominion over them. He tore away the human race's immortality, thus condemning them to eventual death. Then, as a grand finale, He kicked Adam and Eve out of the Garden of Eden, employing cherubic bouncers to ensure they never darkened His doorstep again.

Talk about an over-reaction.

Fig. 1: Adam and Eve get their marching orders (Morphart and S.E.W.)

If there was a positive in this incident, it was that Adam and Eve's loss of innocence led to the invention of clothing. This was a big idea that would eventually lead to the birth of fashion. Although, from Adam and Eve's clothing in the picture above, the only way was up.

A Cruel Master

It's fair to say that the God of the Old Testament, whom I will call 'Old Testament God' to differentiate Him from the kinder, gentler God of the New Testament, was not a warm and fuzzy guy (and from his bloodthirsty behavior, it is clear He was male). I bring this up because Adam and Eve's punishment was the first in a long line of harsh lessons that Old Testament God taught His people.

Not content with making all human lives miserable in perpetuity, Old Testament God's next big idea was positively psychopathic:

> *And God said unto Noah, 'The end of all flesh is come before me; for the earth is filled with violence through them; and behold, I will destroy them with the earth.'*
> Genesis 6: 13

However, before the Old Testament God taught the extreme swimming lesson that was the Great Flood, He gave Noah a quick tutorial in shipbuilding and an impossible job to accomplish: to rescue a breeding pair of every animal in creation. The story claims Noah had success in this hopeless venture, but how he managed to get the polar bears, kangaroos, and komodo dragons (among many others) is unknown.

Old Testament God just *loved* teaching people hard lessons. He obliterated the cities of Sodom and Gomorrah because they were naughty in His eyes, turning Lot's poor wife into a pillar of salt as collateral damage:

Fig. 2: Lot's wife makes a fatal mistake
(Public domain and S.E.W.)

He made a deal with Abram (whom he renamed Abraham on a whim) that if he and his descendants ritually cut off a part of their penises, that He would look upon them with favor.

Who does that?

But slicing off part of his todger wasn't even the worst thing that Old Testament God demanded of Abraham. The Lord commanded him to offer his only son, Isaac, as a burnt sacrifice. Having endured the forced name change and genital mutilation, Abraham had been so thoroughly gaslit he'd do just about anything. So the next thing Isaac knew, he was trussed up on an altar with dear old dad poised to cut his throat. Then, at the last possible moment, Old Testament God let Abraham (and most importantly Isaac) off the hook.

Fig. 3: I mean, what a jerk! (Public domain and S.E.W.)

Yet even with the bowing, scraping, sacrificing, and dick-snipping, the Hebrews *still* ended up as slaves in Egypt. Thanks, Old Testament God. And that's where they stayed for 430 years until He concluded that His Chosen People had finally learned their lesson. So He freaked out Moses (a new guy He'd decided to torment) by appearing to him as a burning bush, and assigning him the thankless task of leading the Hebrews out of Egypt. Old Testament God then gave Moses some stone tablets full of rules (some of which—Thou Shalt Not Kill, for one—He clearly didn't adhere to himself). To be fair, Old Testament God's Commandments were laws, and written laws were a big idea at this early time, quite likely owing a lot to the Code of Hammurabi.

Of course, the Ten Commandments were kept in the Ark of the Covenant, which Moses had specially constructed from Old Testament God's instructions. Now anyone who's seen George Lucas' documentary *Raiders of the Lost Ark* knows that the Ark of the Covenant crackles with power. It melts a Nazi's face-off, after all.

In the Bible, a man who grabs the Ark to stop it toppling over is struck dead as if by a flash. This news gave Erich von Däniken, who'd combed the Bible for ancient aliens and knew a good thing when he saw it, an *Aha!* moment: "Undoubtedly the Ark was electrically charged!" Von Däniken asserted (with zero evidence, as usual) that if the Ark were constructed today to Old Testament God's specs, it would automatically generate several hundred volts. He thought this charge ran a device that facilitated "communication between Moses and the space-ship."

The man was incorrigible.

Fig. 4: The Ark of the Covenant was so dangerous, it had to be covered like a sleeping budgie (ruskpp and S.E.W.)

Then, after all this drama, Old Testament God neglected to give Moses the Heavenly GPS. This meant the Hebrews had to wander aimlessly in the desert for forty years. *Forty bloody years*. Then finally, after everything Moses had done for him, Old Testament God didn't have the compassion to let him enter the Promised Land. He just let him keel over and die on its doorstep.

To this point, all the genocidal dictators in the history of this planet would collectively have less blood on their hands than Old Testament God. And we're still only in the second book of the Bible.

Unfortunately, according to the Bible, Old Testament God taught humans the big, bad idea of abusive relationships. If you vehemently disagree with that definition, here is what *Relationships Australia* has to say about abusive relationships: "Psychological and physical safety are a human right. Coercion, intimidation, [and] demeaning, threatening, and frightening behaviour is unacceptable and has no place in a relationship." I believe most thinking people would acknowledge that Old Testament God did indeed do all of those things to his 'children.'

All of which makes one wonder about Old Testament God's psychological profile. We've already seen His fits of murderous rage and so would be forgiven for thinking Him something of a psychopath. Considering His mania for being praised (and having His personal pronouns capitalized), He's definitely narcissistic. Woe betide those who don't praise Him long or loud enough. Or who disrespected his sycophants.

The prophet Elisha was a terrible suck-up to Old Testament God. He was also a little touchy about being follicularly challenged and didn't mind calling in his tough mate to defend him. Let's let the Bible tell the story:

Elisha went up from there to Bethel. As he was going up the road, some young people came out of the city. They mocked him: "Get going, Baldy! Get going, Baldy!" Turning around, Elisha looked at them and cursed them in the Lord's name. Then two bears came out of the woods and mangled forty-two of the youths.

2 Kings 2:23-24, Common English Bible

If the Bible wasn't already clear enough, let's break it down: A group of kids was making fun of Elisha's male pattern baldness, and his ego was so fragile that he cursed the boys in the name of the Lord. Old Testament God then caused two passing bears to maul *forty-two* boys. Fatalities almost certainly ensued. It seems that He encouraged and assisted his prophets to also abuse the people He was ostensibly supposed to protect.

Given this rich vein of craziness, it was only fitting that Erich von Däniken raised his ugly head yet again. The Book of Ezekiel is particularly bizarre, and there is enough ambiguity to fuel all sorts of conspiracy theories. In the book, the prophet Ezekiel has a vision, and his description of what he saw got Erich all hot and bothered:

And I looked, and, behold, a whirlwind came out of the north, a great cloud, and a fire infolding itself, and a brightness was about it, and out of the midst thereof as the colour of amber, out of the midst of the fire.

Also out of the midst thereof came the likeness of four living creatures. And this was their appearance; they had the likeness of a man.

And every one had four faces, and every one had four wings.

And their feet were straight feet; and the sole of their feet was like the sole of a calf's foot: and they sparkled like the colour of burnished brass.

Ezekiel 1: 4-7

You guessed it, this is perfect ancient astronauts 'proof' of an extra-terrestrial visit. "Ezekiel," von Däniken breathlessly claims, "gives precise details of the landing of this vehicle. He describes a craft that comes from the north, emitting rays and gleaming and raising a gigantic cloud of desert sand."

Precise details? Oh, *come on*, Erich. I don't think Ezekiel saw a UFO landing—or Old Testament God. Best case scenario, poor old Ezekiel was suffering psychosis. Worst case scenario...

Fig. 5: I wouldn't put it past Old Testament God messing with Ezekiel's mind on purpose (Public domain and S.E.W.)

Old Testament God was a racist, playing favorites with the Hebrews and being complicit with the ethnic cleansing of races who did not pay Him due obeisance. For thousands of years, He was a raging fanboy of human sacrifice. Last, but not least, His parting act was to knock up a nice young Hebrew girl, leaving her and her *very* understanding fiancé to deal with the consequences.

In fairness, like all the other gods and goddesses we have seen in our romp through ancient times, Old Testament God's psychology tells us a lot more about the society that venerated Him rather than being a damning indictment of the Lord Himself.

To paraphrase Jessica Rabbit: He's not bad, He's just worshipped that way.

Transmission of Knowledge: Old Testament Style

Since the days of Abraham, the transmission of knowledge was a big idea integral to the Jewish faith. This religion is based on the Hebrew Bible, known to Christians as the Old Testament. Being a religious text, a 'teacher' in the Biblical sense is a teacher of religion. The prophets of the Old Testament, such as Isaiah, Jeremiah, and Ezekiel, were teachers who had the challenging job of explaining their boss's cruelty to his 'Chosen People.'

It was Old Testament God Himself who taught the prophets, and judging on His performance, there's no way He'd get a job in any Western education system. For a start, He'd never pass the criminal background check. His might find work in a hyper-fundamentalist school, but given His rap sheet, He'd freak out even the most hardcore zealot. Little Jedediah might be annoying, but he doesn't deserve to spontaneously combust.

But lest I spend this entire section trawling through the Old Testament looking for more instances of O.T. God's cruel and unusual ways (and believe me, I could with very little effort), I will move on.

In the New Testament, the teacher was Jesus, and he was a whole different kettle of loaves and fishes.

Fig. 6: Sometimes the business opportunities were tempting
(Tony Baggett and S.E.W.)

Bad God/Good God

One could be forgiven for thinking that Jesus, being God in human form, would be like a Palestinian Jack the Ripper. Thankfully, this was not the case. Instead, Jesus brought love, rationality, and forgiveness to His role as Son of God. It is difficult to overstate how different this new paradigm was from before. Even today, there are 'Christians' who can't reconcile themselves to the big idea of love and kindness.

The gentle teacher of the Sermon on the Mount is about as far away from O.T. God as one can get:

> *And he opened his mouth and taught them, saying,*
> *Blessed are the poor in spirit: for theirs is the kingdom of heaven.*
> *Blessed are they that mourn: for they shall be comforted.*
> *Blessed are the meek: for they shall inherit the earth.*
> *Blessed are they which do hunger and thirst after righteousness: for they shall be filled.*
> *Blessed are the merciful: for they shall obtain mercy.*
> *Blessed are the pure in heart: for they shall see God.*
> *Blessed are the peacemakers: for they shall be called the children of God.*
> *Blessed are they which are persecuted for righteousness' sake: for theirs is the kingdom of heaven.*
> Matthew 5: 2-10

The God of the New Testament had undergone a complete metamorphosis. His tenure as homicidal maniac was over, and it appeared that He was trying to make up for thousands of years of torturing and killing humans. Perhaps He realized that His abusive relationship with humanity was a massive P.R. problem and He needed someone a little closer to His people to interpret His message.

> *For there is one God, and one mediator between God and men, the man Christ Jesus;*
> 1 Timothy 2:5

It appears that O.T. God knew the adage: 'If you want a job done right, do it yourself', because his chosen mediator was the human aspect of his own tripartite Godhead. And once there was a human in charge of this task, things got a lot better. Gone were the days of the extravagantly orchestrated sacrifices that

O.T. God required, as outlined in Leviticus:

> *And he shall kill the bullock before the Lord: and the priests, Aaron's sons, shall bring the blood, and sprinkle the blood round about upon the altar that is by the door of the tabernacle of the congregation.*
> *[Loads of gory stuff edited out here]*
> *... and the priest shall burn all on the altar, to be a burnt sacrifice, an offering made by fire, of a sweet savour unto the Lord.*
> Leviticus 1: 5-9

Instead, we have:

> *For God so loved the world, that he gave his only begotten Son, that whosoever believeth in him should not perish, but have everlasting life.*
> John 3:16

Fig. 7: How to rebrand a Deity (Leo Lintang, bowie15 and S.E.W)

The big idea of God sacrificing *for* His people was both new and refreshing. Instead of God demanding that humans suffer for His sake, in this new world order, He was demonstrating the desire to suffer for His people. I'm not saying that the New Testament is all rainbows and puppies— the bizarre ayahuasca dream that is the *Book of Revelation* remains disorienting and impenetrable. But I think that most of Jesus' reported words are of kindness and love, which are antithetical to the crazier pronouncements of O.T. God.

Of course, this loving, caring Jesus could also be the product of selective editing, as we'll see a little later.

Transmission of Knowledge: New Testament Style

Let's look at how big ideas were communicated to the masses at the time of the New Testament. The focus of formal education in the Hebrew tradition was to teach moral and religious discipline; for a start, the word 'rabbi' literally means 'teacher.' However, as in all societies we have looked at, education began at home with parents teaching their children. The *Torah* instructed parents to teach their children about the Hebraic covenant with God. The *Talmud*, considered by many the central text of Jewish religious law and theology, states:

> *Just as a man is bound to have his son instructed in the Law, so also should he have his son taught some handicraft or profession. Whosoever does not teach his son a handicraft teaches him to be a thief.*

And so, the girls learned 'women's work' from their mothers, and boys learned their father's trade and the religious laws taught in the synagogue.

Elementary school learning was believed to be compulsory by as early as 75 BC. Boys began schooling at age five in a local synagogue that served as both primary and secondary schools. Religious education was considered so important that students even attended school rather than the synagogue on the Sabbath.

At ten, some boys were promoted to the secondary level. Here they studied oral *Torah,* and during the Roman occupation, learned Greek, which was the language of business in the Roman world. Around this time, students would find a particular rabbi to follow and learn from in a kind of apprenticeship.

Jesus' education most likely followed the course set out above; he was taught a trade by his father (as we will later see, he was excellent at wood-stretching) and went to the synagogue school, where he picked up his knowledge of the scriptures. At some point, Jesus took an interest in the teachings of John the Baptist and was baptized by him.

That's how Jesus started hanging out with his cool older cousin.

The First Council of Nicea, The Apocryphal Gospels and Delinquent Jesus

In 325 AD, Emperor Constantine I convened a meeting of Christian bishops in the city of Nicaea. His brainchild became known as the First Council of Nicaea, and it codified many Christian beliefs. Constantine's bishops had a lot to discuss. First, there was the little problem among early Christians about the relationship between God and Jesus. Was Jesus a man or God? Or something else?

They just couldn't agree on the big idea that would be the basis of Christianity. Some early Christians believed Jesus was just an ordinary guy who had been miraculously adopted by God in the moment of his baptism…or maybe after his Resurrection—they couldn't quite make up their minds. Gnostics taught that Jesus's body was not corporeal, but merely an illusion, and so could rise above the sins of the flesh. Still others thought Jesus was a direct physical manifestation of God. There were many other similar 'heretical' ideas, and there was certainly some sorting out to do. In the spirit of compromise, the Council struck on the novel idea of the Holy Trinity: God the Father, God the Son, and God the

Holy Spirit.

That sorted, they then had to deal with some problematic Jesus fan-fiction.

All Christian sects at the time accepted the canonical Gospels: Matthew, Mark, Luke, and John. But there were many other accounts of the life of J.C. which were considered non-canonical: the Gospels of Mary, Peter, James, and Thomas, to name a few. Collectively, these are known as The Apocryphal Gospels. One imagines a spirited debate on the Council floor, deciding which of these might be the Word of the Lord, and which were the product of seriously troubled minds (although, given what we know of Old Testament God, how could one tell?).

However, a legend arose about how the books of the Bible were chosen at the Council of Nicaea. It has been claimed that canon was derived by dumping all the gospels on an altar during the Council and then waiting to see which ones just fell off onto the floor. The ones that stayed on the altar made the cut. In this way, God Himself decided which gospels were kosher and which weren't.

Of course, it's far more likely that the bishops made the choice through political machinations, negotiation, and horse-trading. Some gospels would have been rejected because they didn't match up with the newly minted Father/Son/Holy Spirit schtick. Some for other assorted heresies. And some were probably chucked out because they just made Jesus look like a bit of a dickhead.

None more so than *The Infancy Gospel of Thomas*.

The Infancy Gospel of Thomas purportedly depicts the life of Jesus up to the age of twelve. So far, so good: Other than the nativity, we haven't seen Jesus's backstory. *The Infancy Gospel* shows Jesus struggling to be a combination human kid/all-powerful super-being. It was clearly a difficult balancing act.

Normal human children aren't perfect and neither is the child Jesus in this account. For a start, Jesus curses a boy, just because he felt like it, causing the boy to shrivel into a desiccated corpse. He then kills another boy who was bullying him. When the dead boy's parents subsequently complain to Joseph and Mary about Jesus murdering their son, the little bugger strikes the couple blind. While there may be stylistic similarities, there is no truth to the rumor that Stephen King was the ghost writer of *The Infancy Gospel of Thomas*.

After other wacky hijinks, such as Jesus humiliating his teachers and being insufferably arrogant, he begins to get the hang of his powers. He heals his brother James from a snake bite. He resurrects a guy killed in a building accident. He even helps Joseph build furniture, magically stretching a miss-cut piece of wood to fit. Finally, the young Jesus learns the same lesson that Uncle Ben taught Peter Parker: 'With great power comes great responsibility.' He resurrects the boys he's killed and restores the sight of the blinded parents. No harm, no foul.

Fig. 8: He ***IS*** *the messiah, and he was a very naughty boy (inhauscreative and S.E.W.)*

The members of the First Council of Nicaea weren't massive fans of *The Infancy Gospel of Thomas,* probably because the idea of a murderous, magic-wielding Dennis the Menace didn't fit in with the 'Prince of Peace' vibe they were going for. *The Infancy Gospel* got the heave-ho. The bad boy of the Bible would have to be someone else.

Luckily, there was a ready-made candidate.

The Ultimate Antagonist?

Starting in the Old Testament, the Bible introduced the big idea of the ultimate antagonist. Satan. The Devil. Lucifer. Beelzebub. The Prince of Darkness. Spanky. Call him what you will, you've all seen his likeness: red scaly skin, horns, the legs of a goat, a pointed tail—and sporting a devilish look on his face and a pitchfork in his hand.

Would it surprise you that this description of Satan never appears in the Bible?

Sure, Satan is the serpent that encouraged Eve to eat the forbidden fruit, thus dooming humans forever. He also puts in an appearance tempting Jesus in the desert. And, of course, he is prophesied to lead the demonic battalions in the Battle of Armageddon. But he's not the horny red devil to which we've become accustomed—that's a purely medieval creation.

The Biblical Satan is traditionally depicted as a beautiful ex-angel who led a rebellion of fallen angels against God. Defeated, Satan and his buddies were cast out of Heaven before the creation of the Earth. To say this left Lucifer with a bit of a chip in his shoulder is an understatement. However, in the big scheme of things, Satan seems more of a Loki-like trickster than a destroyer of worlds.

Even so, I wouldn't cross Spanky. He must have been a pretty bad dude for a nutjob like O.T. God to kick him out. And, of course, there's that whole 'leading the forces of darkness in the final battle between Good and Evil' thing.

Fig. 9: No one is happy about this (Marcduf, D-Keine and S.E.W.)

The Ultimate Protagonist?

As we have seen, the big idea that God could take human form and walk among us was not initially accepted by all early Christian sects. It took a bit of tweaking and cultural appropriation to get some people to warm up to the Son of God. Some of this meant rebranding. Early pictorial representations of Jesus show him as beardless and decidedly Middle Eastern in appearance. This image bears little resemblance to the bearded, robed, and unapologetically Caucasian Jesus we have been conditioned to seeing for at least 1,500 years. The reason this depiction of Jesus became the norm is likely because it matched the signature appearance of a Greek philosopher. Why would a man from the Middle East be shown in such a way? Putting aside endemic racism, which I'm sure played a huge part, there were other reasons.

Rebranding Jesus like this legitimized him for a Roman audience who were used to Greek philosopher-types, who also paraded around wrapped in bedsheets. Of course, there is another potential explanation: Philosopher Jesus bears more than a passing resemblance to a young Zeus (see below). The benefit of associating Jesus with the appearance of other known deities is obvious: it was shorthand for 'Jesus is a god.'

Fig. 10: Give Jesus a perm and they'd be identical
(by Dallas and Ruslan Gilmanshin)

Jesus certainly had some big ideas: 'Love one another,' 'Turn the other cheek,' and 'Love your neighbor as yourself' are some of his greatest hits. However, for some inexplicable reason (probably to do with money, power, and self-interest) many Christians over the last 2,000 years have conveniently forgotten these warm and fuzzy, feel-good ideas. Instead, we've had Holy Wars, sectarian violence, religious persecutions, Papal Indulgences, Republican politicians, and the list goes on. I guess Jesus is just too much of a hippie and socialist for these people.

Jesus taught his big ideas through the use of parables, stories about daily life which illustrated the lessons he was trying to teach. Because he was a kind, caring person/God, and an effective educator, Jesus would, with the proper academic qualification, get a teaching gig in a Western school. His criminal background check would come back clean, and he would be highly unlikely to immolate Little Jedediah on a whim.

At least now that he's all grown up.

All things considered, it's rather sad that Jesus ended up nailed to a cross; he seemed like a nice guy with great ideas.

Fig. 11: It was a rotten way to spend the Easter break (Renata Sedmakova and S.E.W.)

Chapter Nine

Greece is the Word
Ancient Greece

The Ancient Greeks were the wellspring of big ideas in a large array of fields. They were leaders in education, art, government, philosophy, science, and sport. Their culture influenced all subsequent Western cultures and is still venerated for its enlightened attitudes. Yet, despite its profound influence, Greek culture is deeply weird and alien to modern eyes. Spoiler alert: You wouldn't want any Ancient Greek man near your impressionable adolescent son.

It began with several successful cultures in Bronze Age Greece (around 3200-1100 BC), both in Crete and on the mainland. Mycenaean culture flourished from about 1600 to 1100 BC and was viewed by the Greeks as the 'age of heroes' perhaps because it provided the source material for Greek mythology. The fall of Mycenae around 1100 BC precipitated a period of isolation known as a Dark Age (not to be confused with *the* Dark Ages). By around 800 BC, Greece was trading with the outside world, and this triggered a renewed interest in arts, crafts, and writing. Historians dubbed this era the Archaic Period, and it lasted up to Solon's introduction of democracy to Athens in 508 BC. The Olympic Games also began during this time. Homer (if he existed) reputedly wrote the *Odyssey* and the *Iliad* around then.

The Classical era of Greece was characterized by a burst of political, artistic, scientific, educational, and philosophical achievements. Indeed, the culture of Ancient Greece was so significant that it forms much of the basis of Western civilization. The English language features many words derived from ancient Greek dialects: cemetery, democracy, and narcissism, to name but a few. Also, the literature, art, and architecture of

Ancient Greece remain influential, and its rediscovery instigated the cultural, scientific, and intellectual orgasm that was the Renaissance.

Ancient Greece was a collection of autonomous city-states that governed themselves using very different organizing principles. The most notable of these *poleis* were Athens and Sparta, although there were many others, including Corinth, Thebes, and Syracuse. Athens is famous as the birthplace of democracy, and it granted all male citizens the right to vote. It also had a long tradition in philosophy and art. By comparison, Sparta was a militaristic society ruled over by two kings and a council of elders. The Spartans became the dominant land power in Ancient Greece by focusing their education on physical development and martial training. In *Star Trek* parlance, the Athenians were the Federation, and the Spartans were the Klingons.

Fig. 1: It's amazing what you can get away with
(Tugay Aydin, Luca Oleastri and S.E.W.)

Greece lies at the junction of Europe, Asia, and Africa, and this location doubtless influenced the region's turbulent history. It hangs into the Mediterranean Sea like the scrotum of Europe and is surrounded by fractal peninsulas and islands. Its maritime location made powerful navies a necessity. Greece also has mountainous terrain, which, if you have ever seen the movie *300*, makes for easily defensible locations. It enjoyed a Mediterranean climate with hot, dry summers and mild winters. It would have been a nice place for a leisurely vacation when it wasn't being invaded by Persians.

History in the making

Recorded history is a big idea, and it would be remiss not to acknowledge the first known historian and teacher of history, Herodotus. His book, *The Histories*, is considered the first work of history in the Western tradition. Despite this, history remembers him as both the Father of History and the Father of Lies, so he may have been doing this history thing all wrong.

Nevertheless, Herodotus influenced the subsequent historian, Thucydides, whom he met when the latter was a youth. An apocryphal account has a young Thucydides attending one of Herodotus' lectures and weeping. Whether they were tears of joy at meeting his hero or tears of frustration at the great man's mangling of history is unknown. At any rate, Thucydides grew up to be a much more reliable historian and became known as the Father of *Scientific* History.

Not only did Herodotus and Thucydides 'invent' the concept of historical research, their histories were also integral to securing Greece's ongoing place in the world.

And when most people think about Ancient Greece, it's Athens they picture.

Athens: A City-State of Big Ideas

Yes, Athens, with its Parthenon crowning the Acropolis: serene, white-bearded men strolling around pointing their index fingers to the sky and shouting "Eureka!"—and lots of headless and/or armless marble statuary, that kind of thing. Ancient Athens stood where modern Athens stands today, on the central plain of Attica and bounded by four mountains. While it is famous for being the home of people power, there is a catch: Despite the legendary and influential nature of Athenian democracy, this system of government only remained stable for about 180 years. Athens had three classes of residents: Athenians, *metics* (free foreign nationals), and slaves. The big bonus of Athenian citizenship was that you could not be sold into slavery. The unfortunate *metics* did not enjoy the same right. Splendid news for Athenians, not so great for foreigners.

Mr and Mrs Athenian's love for slavery is problematic and calls into question the basis of the big idea of democracy. Slaves were Athens' must-have labor-saving device, performing all the domestic chores and other menial work Some historians believe that Athenian democracy was only possible because of the leisure time this gave citizens.

Schools of thought

Athens is also famous for its commitment to the big idea of education. This is perhaps because of its philosophical traditions, but is also because of the type of education that young Athenian males received. Unlike many other Greek city-states (Sparta springs to mind), Athenian education had moved from a martial focus and looked to more cerebral pursuits:

> *So far has Athens left the rest of humanity behind in thought and expression that her pupils have become the teachers of the world, and she has made the name of Hellas distinctive no longer of race but of intellect, and the title of Hellene a badge of education rather than of common descent.*
>
> Isocrates

The reason that Isocrates (no relation to Socrates the philosopher or the 1970s Brazilian footballer) was so enthusiastic about Athenian education was because of the *paideia.* Around the fifth century BC, *paideia,* which Google translates as 'education' although some other translations prefer 'training' or 'culture,' was the system of education in Classical and Hellenistic Greece. In *paideia,* teaching for male students included subjects such as grammar, rhetoric, natural history, gymnastics, music, mathematics, geography, and philosophy. However, *paideia* did not spring fully formed into the Athenian world; it had been developed over time as scholars formulated more complex ideas around education.

The heroes of Homeric literature, sporting boundless *aretê* (a quality considered an amalgamation of military excellence and moral virtue), were role models for young Athenian men. Around 500 BC, a new type of professional teacher arose in Athens, the Sophist. Through instructing their students in philosophy and rhetoric, Sophists worked to inculcate the traditional values of *aretê* with an added fervor for intellectual inquiry. The word *paideia* is first found in Greek literature of this period. The education in humanities and virtue that *paideia* afforded was useful to the Athenian state because it produced men of the highest intellectual and moral caliber, well-prepared to take on the weight of citizenship in a democracy.

However, education, as we have seen in our studies of previous civilizations, was not for females. Only Athenian men took part in public life, so no one felt the need to educate women. Even the daughters of the most well-off citizens only received an informal education at home, their mothers teaching them the domestic skills necessary for running a household. You know, like ordering slaves to do everything.

Here's how it worked: Both the sons and daughters of wealthy Athenians would spend their early years at home. In this scenario, Mr Athenian spent most of his time on public or military life, and so the kids were cared for by Mrs Athenian and/or her house slaves.

Then, around the age of six, the boys went off to private school, which was a simple choice, as there was no public education. Then young Master Athenian was presented with his own personal slave. Cool, right? Wrong. This slave was the *paidagogos*—often an older, illiterate male family slave, who would go to school with the boy. While the *paidagogos* had a responsibility to ensure the little guy's safety, he also had a couple of other jobs. The first was to ensure that Master Athenian worked hard in class and displayed excellent manners. The *paidagogos* would do this by giving his young master a good flogging if he stepped out of line. With the *paidagogos* keeping tabs on Master Athenian, the schoolmaster's job must have been quite a lot easier. However, the *paidagogos* also had certain other responsibilities unrelated to schooling. But before we get there, we must go back a few steps.

We need to address the normalisation of pederasty in Ancient Greece.

During the Classical period, it was acceptable that an intimate relationship could exist between an adult male, known as the *erastes*, and a younger male, often a boy in his teens, known as the *eromenos*. Most of Greece's most famous heroes, including but not limited to, Achilles, Heracles, and the golden boy, Apollo, were active on both sides of such relationships. The comic playwright Aristophanes believed that hot man-on-boy action was a natural part of a *paideia* education. And yet, as transgressive as this seems to us today, the literal bromance between *erastes* and *eromenos* played an integral part in the social and educational system of Classical Greece. This mentor/mentee connection was taken to extremes: The older man had the responsibility for teaching the boy about his future role in society, politics, and the military. Such a relationship was romantic, consensual, and seen as a rite of passage, so to speak, for an upper-class Greek male. Upper-class Greek girls were married off at the onset of puberty, and despite what we might believe about women from the Isle of Lesbos (more about this later), there was no equivalent tradition of older female/young girls' relationships.

It was for these reasons that Mr Athenian encouraged his son, young Master Athenian, to take an older male lover. No big deal: It was both hoped for and expected. But pederastic relationships had their own complicated social-sexual etiquette. What Mr Athenian was worried about was that some pervy old bloke who was not *erastes* material would seduce his son before he could meet Mr Right. This is when the *paidagogos* came into his own. He chaperoned his young master, keeping the less desirable men at bay.

Fig. 2: This is when a young guy really needs his paidagogos (Public domain and S.E.W.)

Here I pause for a moment for a community service announcement: While I make light of the pederastic *erastes* and *eromenos* relationship and acknowledge that it was acceptable for the Ancient Greeks, there is nothing acceptable or funny about pedophilia. These days, an adult engaging in sexual activity with a minor (and many *eromenoi* would have been under the age of consent) would be guilty of child sexual abuse or statutory rape. Laws that govern this exist to protect children from abuse, because minors are not considered capable of consenting to sexual activity. This is because the effects of child sexual abuse are devastating and can include depression, PTSD, anxiety, and physical injury. Now, back to our tale.

There were three main types of teachers: *paidotribes*, *grammatistes*, and *kitharistes*. *Paedotribes* were PE teachers, instructing the boys in running, wrestling, javelin, and discus-throwing, the aim being to produce fit and attractive young men. *Grammatistes* taught their students arithmetic, ethics, and literature, with an emphasis on the work of poets such as Homer. *Kitharistes* taught singing, playing the flute and the lyre, and reciting poetry to music.

Around the age of sixteen, Athenians could choose to enroll their sons in further schooling. Rhetoric was a popular area of study, especially for those young Athenians who wanted to be active in public life. Of course, only the rich could afford to provide their sons with the full range of educational opportunities available, such as private lessons from an expensive Sophist academy. Following the completion of this liberal arts education, young men took military training for the army or the navy from the ages of eighteen to twenty. Through this emphasis on mentoring, schooling, and military training, Athenians could ensure their sons received a well-rounded education, fitting them for citizenship.

Of course, the Athenians' great frenemies, the Spartans, looked at the world in a totally different manner.

This is Sparta!

> *(The Spartans) are so far behind in general culture and study that they do not even learn their letters.*
> Isocrates

As you can see, Isocrates had very little regard for the standard of Spartan education. Unlike the liberal Athenians, the citizens of Sparta were dedicated to the big ideas of lifelong military discipline, service, and precision. Despite Isocrates' disdain, literacy wasn't unknown in Sparta, but it was less common. This was because of the Spartans' belief that if education didn't enhance one's physical preparation for the life of a soldier, then it was worthless. The Spartans were just a barrel of laughs.

Not all Athenian philosophers had such a low opinion of Spartan education. Both Plato and Aristotle admired the Spartan model of public education as opposed to the expensive private Athenian system.

> *One might well praise the Spartans for this: they most of all pay serious attention to their children and do so in common.*
> Aristotle

To be fair, Aristotle also regarded Spartans as the "least literary of men," so it wasn't all upside. This was not without reason: Almost from the moment they were born, Spartan boys underwent extreme physical and mental training for their inevitable military service. They stayed in the family home until age seven, when they were sent to military school. Once taken from their families, these young recruits were then brought up by the state.

> *[T]heir training was calculated to make them obey commands well, endure hardships, and conquer in battle ... When they were 12 years old, they no longer had tunics to wear, received one cloak a*

year, had hard flesh, and knew little of baths. They slept together ... on pallet-beds which they collected for themselves, breaking off with their hands—no knives allowed—the tops of the rushes which grew along the river Eurotas.
Plutarch

Spartan boys were subjected to a ruthless training and discipline regime known as the *agoge*, the purpose of which was to ensure military preparation and loyalty to the state. To harden them up for a life of pain and hardship, the students weren't allowed shoes or much in the way of clothing. Throughout their training, they received a high level of instruction in a wide range of militaristic activities, including boxing, wrestling, and the obligatory javelin and discus-throwing. Spartan boys were played off against each other. They were taught how to kill opponents. The harshness of their training fortified them against all number of potential physical privations. Spartan boys were encouraged to steal the food they needed to survive, and if they were careless enough to be caught thieving, they would be flogged. Not for the theft, but because they were caught.

Fig. 3: Agog at the Agoge (Nastasic and S.E.W.)

However, all this hyper-butch behavior didn't seem to stop the Spartans from pursuing *erastes* and *eromenos* relationships with equal enthusiasm to the Athenians. In fact, some historians consider the Spartans as being at the cutting edge of formalizing this form of pederasty. However, others believe that the Spartan attitude towards same-sex mentoring relationships was less exuberant. Still, Sparta had the distinction of being the first to practice athletic nudity, and lubed-up nude wrestling really can't have helped matters.

Fig. 4: Priapus always had an unfair advantage at the Olympic Games (By Ivan-96 and S.E.W.)

Like Athenian girls, Spartan girls took their education at home by their mothers. But in stark contrast to Athenian girls, Spartan girls went to school to learn physical education. While the girls' school was not as bloodthirsty as the boys' institution, the instruction they received made sure that Spartan females were fit and could handle themselves in a fight. It was a common belief in Sparta that robust women gave birth to robust babies, something that was of vital importance in a world where the weak were exposed on a hillside at birth.

Doctor, Doctor Give Me the News
Hippocrates

Most of what we know about Hippocrates (c. 469 BC-c. 375 BC), arguably the most famous ancient physician, is questionable or downright wrong. The high level of medical ethics he was supposed to have pioneered is also somewhat of a sham. It turns out that all the medical texts attributed to him were written by others. Yet, he is held up as the avatar of the perfect physician, and universally revered as the 'Father of Medicine.'

None of this was Hippocrates' fault. It was well after his death that the myths about his life began to take hold. As far as we can tell from this remove, all medical works from the Classical period were compiled and attributed to Hippocrates, becoming known as the *Corpus Hippocraticum*. He probably even wrote some of them, but there's no way of knowing.

The good news is that Hippocrates wasn't a total fraud. We know he achieved fame as a doctor and teacher during his lifetime. Plato referred to him as a well-known physician who taught paying students. Aristotle wrote that Hippocrates was 'the Great Physician,' but immediately undercut that by making the observation that he was on the diminutive side.

Hippocrates is best known today due to the Hippocratic Oath. This is an oath taken by new doctors and is a promise to follow a code of ethics for the practice of medicine. By now, it should come as no surprise to hear that the Hippocratic Oath was written well after Hippocrates' death. The Oath has changed a bit over the years, to suit the era (for instance, the healer no longer swears the Oath to Apollo Healer, by Asclepius, by Hygieia, by Panacea, and by all the gods and goddesses'). However, it is still the foundation for similar oaths to engage in ethical medical practices.

Given all that, what's the big idea with Hippocrates? Probably marketing.

Fig. 5: There's a reason the Hippocratic oath was amended (Gordon Johnson and S.E.W.)

Agnodice: A Legendary Feminist

The lot of a Greek woman was nothing to write home about. Assuming they were allowed to leave home. Or had been taught to write. It's a bit depressing, but by way of mitigation, I offer the story of Agnodice, which comes via Gaius Julius Hyginus, a Roman writer of the late first century BC. If Hyginus is to be believed (and let's be clear, most historians don't credit this story at all), Agnodice was an Athenian woman of the fourth century BC, who was Greece's first female physician.

Given the low status of women in the Greek states, a medical career was most definitely off the table. Not to be deterred, Agnodice had a solution. She cut her hair and did some cheeky cross-dressing to fool the famed physician Herophilus of Alexandria into teaching her/him. Perhaps Herophilus wasn't particularly observant, but that's another story. Once trained, Agnodice returned to Athens, where she began a career in medicine. As a drag king.

According to Hyginus, Agnodice soon built up a large and satisfied female patient base. Greek women were often ashamed to ask male doctors for help with certain maladies, and in such cases, Agnodice would lift her tunic, revealing her femininity, after which the patient allowed her to treat them. Unfortunately, some male physicians, jealous of her success, accused her of seducing patients. Given that she was exposing herself to them, it's easy to see how this idea took hold.

In the ensuing trial, she even flashed the jury, leaving them with no doubts about her gender. Initially, this did not go well, as she was then accused of breaking the law against women practicing medicine. Apparently, many of her patients were *the Real Housewives of Athens* and testified to Agnodice's medical ability. She was acquitted. Hyginus then claims that the upshot was that Athenian women were granted the right to practice medicine.

Fig. 6: Agnodice rests her case (zatletic and S.E.W.)

While there are historical inaccuracies that make Hygnus's story suspect, there *is* evidence for female midwives and physicians in Ancient Greece. There are inscriptions that refer to female physicians who treated all patients, and the Hippocratic treatises make mention of 'female healers' (*iatrinai*). Certainly, one can take comfort from Cambridge University's Dr Rebecca Flemming, who asserts it was a "well-established fact that women practised medicine in the ancient world."

Science and Mathematics: It's all Greek to me

The big ideas of Greek science and mathematics are inarguably the most consequential of the ancient world. Giants such as Pythagoras, Euclid, Archimedes, and Eratosthenes, built on Babylonian and Egyptian knowledge, developing new and exciting concepts. These big ideas influenced humanity's views in mathematics, science, and logic for over a thousand years.

Fig. 7: L-R Euclid, Pythagoras and Eratosthenes (GDJ, tzaralunga and S.E.W.)

Pythagoras

We all suffered through $a^2 + b^2 = c^2$ in high school, so for better or worse, Pythagoras (c. 571-c. 497 BC) has impacted all our lives. Yet, over and above his seminal contribution to mathematics, there was far more to this Greek philosopher. Pythagoras believed in immortality through reincarnation. He taught that all living things should be treated respectfully and humanely. He believed that contemplating the idea of 'number' as truth in mathematics cleared the mind, opening it to the comprehension of reality, man. All things considered, Pythagoras was a bit of a hippie.

Although he's best known these days for his brainchild, the Pythagorean Theorem, this may be a misattribution. Modern scholars have uncovered evidence from Babylonian texts, predating Pythagoras by hundreds of years, which outline very similar ideas.

Euclid

Despite his enduring fame, little is known about the life of Euclid (c. 325 BC-c. 270 BC). What we do know is that this Greek mathematician was highly influential and has been lauded as the 'father of geometry.' His most famous work, *Elements,* outlined his big idea, Euclidean geometry, which was used as a geometry textbook until the early twentieth century. Euclid also wrote works on conic sections, spherical geometry, number theory, and perspective.

Archimedes

Archimedes of Syracuse (c. 287-c. 212 BC) was one of the leading scientists and mathematicians of antiquity. He was also an inventor, astronomer, and engineer. One of his most significant achievements was an accurate approximate value of pi. Among Archimedes' contributions to geometry were the method of calculating the area of a circle, the surface area and volume of a sphere.

The best-known tale about Archimedes was his epic streak through the streets of Syracuse yelling "Eureka! Eureka!" However, there was a good reason for this overenthusiastic, overexposed celebration. After the great man stepped into his evening bath, he noticed the rising water level. The excitement came from Archimedes' realization that the volume of water displaced *must* equate to the volume of his submerged body parts. In one flash of brilliance, the once seemingly impossible problem of measuring the volume of irregular objects was solved.

Archimedes also pioneered the use of mathematics to describe physical phenomena. He explained the principle of the lever. He designed novel machines, such as the screw pump and compound pulleys. Archimedes designed ingenious war machines to protect Syracuse. One reported device was the 'Claw of Archimedes,' which was a crane with a mechanical claw used to capsize ships. Contemporary tests have shown the device to have been within the realm of possibility. Another invention was supposedly a series of mirrors that focused the Sun's rays like a laser. These mirrors could reputedly set enemy ships on fire. However, as no one has replicated this weapon, Archimedes' 'laser' was probably mythical.

Unfortunately, Archimedes' creativity and innovation couldn't save him. During the siege of Syracuse, an invading Roman soldier, who had presumably evaded the mechanical claws and lasers, ran him through with his sword. Archimedes' (probably apocryphal) last words were "Do not disturb my circles," referring to circles in a drawing on which he was working when he was murdered.

Even in death, Archimedes needed to get a life.

Fig. 8: Archimedes had some problems with priorities (Grafissimo and S.E.W.)

Eratosthenes

Today, in a world with GPS satellites, we take the Earth's circumference as a given. Well, 2000 years ago, Eratosthenes of Cyrene (c. 276 BC-c. 194 BC), measured it without the need of GPS or any other fancy technology. All he needed was his brains and a stick. By measuring the angle of the stick's shadow at two locations in Egypt, Eratosthenes was able to deduce that measurement with accuracy.

Eratosthenes also calculated the angle of the Earth's tilt on its axis. He drew an improved map of the world, which was the first to include parallels and meridians within his cartography. In the realm of mathematics, he devised an efficient method of identifying prime numbers: the Sieve of Eratosthenes. The celebrated polymath could claim expertise as a mathematician, poet, astronomer, geographer, and (of course) music theorist. Eratosthenes also had potentially the nerdiest day job in the world: chief librarian at the Library of Alexandria.

Oedipus: Live at the Greek Theatre

The Ancient Greeks weren't the first people to mount theatrical productions, but their plays built on earlier traditions, and their big ideas still influence modern theatre. The superstar playwrights of the day, men like Aeschylus, Aristophanes, Euripides, and Sophocles, were what passed for celebrities in Ancient Greece.

One aspect of Greek drama that hasn't found a place in modern drama is 'the chorus.' The chorus was a group of actors who spoke in eerie unison, describing the main action of a play, commenting on the characters, or warning the protagonist of potential danger. With their uniform appearance and creepy masks, they look unsettling, too.

There were two main genres in Greek drama: Tragedy and Comedy. Tragedy dealt with the big themes of love, loss, pride, and the relationships between men and gods. Aeschylus,

Sophocles, and Euripides are the three biggest names of Greek tragedy. Usually, the protagonist of a tragedy unwittingly commits a crime against the gods. Then, as realization dawns, his world crumbles. Aeschylus' *Oedipus Rex* is one such tragedy. It tells the unhappy tale of King Oedipus, whose fate is to unknowingly murder his father and marry his mother, Jocasta. Warned of this by the Sphinx, he attempts to subvert the will of the gods. Nevertheless, he manages to kill Dad and marry Mum anyway. When the horrible truth comes to light, Jocasta commits suicide, and Oedipus blinds himself before going into exile.

Don't expect a Disney cartoon of this one.

Fig. 9: Sometimes the Chorus' rhyming couplets went a little too far (Public Domain and S.E.W.)

The 'Comedy' genre is pretty much as you'd expect, other than that the humor doesn't really translate to the twenty-first century. The master of this form, Aristophanes, used his sharp pen to eviscerate the powerful, vain, and foolish in Athenian society. Not even Socrates was safe from his mocking. Aristophanes' work is the only existing example of Greek satirical dramaturgy of the fifth century BC. In these early comedies, chorus, mime, and dirty jokes still played a considerable part. So did the freedom to critique the political world of Athens.

A third genre, known as Satyr Plays, were performed as light relief in the breaks between acts in a tragedy. The actors gallivanted around dressed as goat-like satyrs, replete with comically oversized strap-on penises. It was all very classy.

Homer: Saw more clearly than any man?

Homer (dates unknown. Probably ninth or eighth century BC) is the most famous of the Greek poets, and one of the most influential writers in history. He is credited as the author of the epic poems *The Iliad* and *The Odyssey*. Little is known of the poet's life, although he was reputedly blind. Of course, legend had it that his blindness occurred in a characteristically Homeric fashion.

Homer was paying homage at the tomb of Achilles and prayed that he might be given a vision of the hero in his battle gear. Miraculously, the specter of Achilles appeared before him. But unfortunately for Homer, he was blinded by the supernatural luminescence of the hero's weapons and armor. Seeing this, Achilles' mother, the goddess Thetis, took pity on Homer, and she and the Muses gifted him with the poetic art as some recompense.

Modern scholars have cast some doubt on Homer's authorship of *The Iliad* and *The Odyssey*. However, it's generally agreed that he composed *The Iliad* as an oral text, which was written down long after his death. *The Odyssey* is unlikely to have been written by Homer, but rather by others inspired by *The Iliad*. Which is just as well, because some scholars believe *The Odyssey* was heavily influenced by *The Epic of Gilgamesh*. I'd hate to think poor old Homer was a plagiarist.

Whatever the real story about *The Iliad* and *The Odyssey*, these two epic poems were the mainstays of education and Greek pop culture in the Classical age. Particularly because of the aretê of the protagonists. Their popularity has endured right up until the present day. *The Iliad* is the tale of the siege of Troy by the Greeks. It focuses on a quarrel between Achilles and King Agamemnon during the last year of the war. *The Odyssey* tells the story of Odysseus' travels home from the Trojan War. He must have been pretty bad at navigation, because the trip home took him ten years. Of course, he and his crew had adventures along the way.

In Book XII of *The Odyssey*, Odysseus encounters two Sirens, half-woman and half-bird monsters whose modus operandi was to lure sailors to their deaths via the medium of song. The story goes that these Sirens were on an island in the sea between Aeaea and the rocks of Scylla. On the advice of a helpful sorceress, the ship's crew escaped the danger of the Siren's song by using wax as primitive noise-canceling headphones. However, Odysseus' desire to hear the Siren's call was so great, he tied himself to the mast so as not to steer the ship to certain doom.

Fig. 10: Odysseus accidentally stumbles upon the Greek island where Mamma Mia was shot (ZU_09 and S.E.W.)

Sappho: Lyric Poet and Gay Icon

The other most famous poet of Ancient Greece was Sappho (c. 630-c. 570 BC). She is renowned for her lyric poetry, which was written to be sung to musical accompaniment. An early reviewer from the Christian church claimed she was also a "sex-crazed whore who sings of her own wantonness," so she was basically an ancient version of Cardi B. In a dissenting view, Plato, who was not always a fan of literature, regarded Sappho as the 'Tenth Muse.'

Like Homer, not much is known about Sappho's life. We know she was from the island of Lesbos. We know she was from a wealthy family and had brothers. Also, like the blind poet, scholars are unsure whether Sappho actually committed much of her poetry to papyrus. The Greek word for the poetry she wrote was *melê*, or 'songs.' They may have been sung for many years before finally being written down.

It would have been something to experience Sappho's songs as they were meant to be heard. In his 2015 article in the New Yorker, Daniel Mendelsohn quotes the following anecdote about the Athenian lawmaker Solon's reaction to Sappho's work:

> *Solon of Athens, son of Execestides, after hearing his nephew singing a song of Sappho's over the wine, liked the song so much that he told the boy to teach it to him. When someone asked him why he was so eager, he replied, "so that I may learn it and then die."*

While her significance as a poet is unquestioned, appreciation of her work has sometimes been overshadowed by discussions of her sexuality. Victorians in particular were both shocked and titillated. Nevertheless, in recent years, Sappho has become a gay icon, with her poetry often interpreted as symbolic of sensual love between women. So much so, that the English word sapphic is derived from her name. For the same reason, the island of her birth gives us the word lesbian.

Urban legends that women from Lesbos were all small 'L'

lesbians couldn't be further from the truth. In ancient times, the people of Lesbos were so renowned for their skill in fellatio, that Mendelsohn points out the Greek verb lesbiazein, meaning 'to act like someone from Lesbos' was Ancient Greek for 'head job.'

Although, I guess that could also have meant the men.

Whether Sappho is famous as a gay icon, lyric poet, or both, she continues to be influential over 2,500 years after her death. And that's a pretty amazing legacy.

Fig. 11: Sappho may forever be misunderstood (clu and S.E.W.)

The Visual Arts
Sculpture

The Archaic period of Greek sculpture (c. 800–c 300 BC) was heavily influenced by the static sculpture of the Egyptians. The most common example of Archaic sculpture is the kouros. Given the Greek predilection for adolescent boys, it is unsurprising that these kouroi (the plural of kouros) were representations of young naked men. The well-muscled youths are depicted blank-faced, standing with their arms to their sides and one foot stepping slightly forward. Kouroi were common throughout the Greek world. They were usually sculpted in marble and are mostly life-sized. However, there are specimens that are as much as 3 meters in height.

The Greeks just couldn't get enough of young, naked dudes.

Fig. 12: A kouros compared to a Roman copy of Praxiteles' Apollo (Public domain)

Comparing the Archaic kouros and Praxiteles' Apollo, it is amazing to see how far Greek sculpture advanced during this period. Their sculptors shrugged off the stifling conventions of the kouroi and began to sculpt realistic, although idealized, depictions of the human body. Gone were the rigid postures of the Archaic period, replaced by fluid, naturalistic poses, full of life and motion. Sculptors such as Praxiteles, Myron, and Pheidias, among others, took cold, hard marble and transformed it into some of the greatest masterpieces of all time. Pheidias created what was considered one of the Seven Wonders of the Ancient World: the statue of the King of the Gods in the Temple of Zeus, Olympia. This ivory and gold statue stood nearly 13 meters high and depicted Zeus seated upon his throne. Unfortunately for posterity, the temple and statue were destroyed by fire and earthquakes, which makes it seem like Zeus was displeased with the work.

It is difficult to overstate the influence of the Classical Greek sculptors. They inspired the Romans and, much later, consummate sculptors such as Michelangelo. Given how the female form has been fetishized for hundreds of years, it's amazing that all this skill and beauty was inspired by the Greeks' need for classy gay soft-core porn.

Pottery

Despite the skill of the Greek sculptors, Roman historian Pliny the Elder makes it clear that painting was the most popular and valued form of Greek art. Regrettably, none of the most well-known examples of panel painting have survived the test of time. The main examples of Greek painting still visible to us are on pottery.

While we see this pottery as precious and beautiful, the Greeks didn't regard it as high art. These pots and vases were utilitarian homewares. The comparison would be a future civilization unable to view our great masterpieces and judging us by 'World's Greatest Mom' mugs and Tupperware. This pottery was usually created on the potter's wheel, and typically the potter and painter were different artisans.

Fig. 13: Black-figure vase paintings often depicted scenes from mythology (SpicyTruffel and S.E.W.)

There were three main types of pottery painting in Ancient Greece: geometric, black on red, and red on black. The first, geometric pottery, came into vogue around 1000 BC. It was decorated using simple geometric patterns. This eventually gave way to black-figure pottery, and this is where we can see a little of what we're missing out on in Greek painting.

The black-figure style was, as the name suggests, known for the way that most figures were painted in black on a red background. This pottery usually shows scenes from mythology and is focused on fine details in the depiction of humans (and gods). Like Classical sculpture, the best examples of black-figure vase painting display figures in graceful action.

The red-figure technique, created by painting outlines with a black background, superseded the black-figure style around 530 BC. This further improved on the depictions of anatomical detail and included attempts showing perspective. These pots often depict mundane scenes of domestic life.

Philosophy: The Theatre of the Mind

We commend the Ancient Greeks because of their invention of democracy, their epic poetry and plays, their extraordinary myths and legends, and because of their heroic deeds in war. However, there is one other reason that the legacy of the Ancient Greeks rings down through the ages: the big ideas of their philosophers. Greek philosophy came to the fore in the 6th century BC, in an era when the Greeks were struggling for their very survival against threats from the East. Philosophy was able to describe the workings of the world and dealt with subjects as diverse as astronomy, mathematics, political theory, ethics, metaphysics, logic, and rhetoric.

Greek philosophy has influenced the Western world for over 2,500 years. Pre-Socratic philosophers such as Pythagoras, Xenophanes, and Heraclitus are still venerated today. These guys rejected mythological explanations in favor of reason and laid the foundation of what came next. But it is the next wave of thinkers who became the first real rockstars of philosophy: Socrates, Plato, and Aristotle.

The School of Athens

For a man who left no written words of his own, Socrates (born c. 470 BC-died 399 BC) had a far-reaching influence on the philosophy of both the ancient and modern world. Although he was treated as something of a joke by some contemporaries such as the comedic playwright Aristophanes, Socrates' enduring legacy was secured by the writings of his students, Plato and Xenophon chief among them. According to their accounts, Socrates was a man of great sagacity, ethics, and argumentative skill. One of his most enduring legacies is the Socratic method, an educational strategy in which students are cross-examined by their teacher to lead them to interrogate their underlying points of view and reach the truth.

The historian Diogenes Laertius wrote that Socrates' views were frequently unpopular, not least because they were expressed with condescension towards his audience. This pissed people off to the point that Laertius observed that "men set upon him with their fists or tore his hair out," but noted that Socrates took all this in his stride. However, it increased his list of enemies.

After a lifetime of teaching, Socrates was tried in 399 BC for two offenses: impiety against the gods, and corruption of the youth of Athens. More on the trial of Socrates later, but spoiler alert: He was convicted and sentenced to death by a jury of his fellow Athenians. Socrates' death was depicted 2,000 years after the event in Jacques Louis David's *The Death of Socrates* (1787); in this painting, an unrepentant Socrates points an accusatory finger to the heavens with one hand and reaches for the fatal chalice of hemlock with the other. I'm not sure how accurate this representation is, as the topless Socrates looks pretty damn ripped for a 70-year-old.

Fig. 14: The Death of Socrates by Jacques Louis David (jorisvo and S.E.W.)

Whether Socrates had abs of steel or not, he would doubtless appear near the top of any hypothetical shortlist for 'Most Influential Teacher of All Time.' His impact on the world of philosophy is incalculable, and one of his pupils was another great, Plato.

Plato (424 BC-347 BC) was the author of philosophical works of unequalled influence. One of his big ideas was Plato's Academy, nominally the forerunner of modern universities. Apart from his significant personal achievements, he is well-known for his association with Socrates, and for the work of his most famous student, Aristotle. Plato believed that happiness was the highest aim of moral thought and conduct and that *aretê* provided the required skill and character to attain it. It is unfortunate that Plato neglected to provide his definition of the conception of 'happiness', an oversight that just wouldn't fly in academia these days.

Plato's Academy was not a physical school or university in a modern sense. It was an informal community of Athenian intellectuals who shared an academic curiosity in philosophic, mathematical, and astronomical matters. It was founded on Plato's belief that knowledge was not the result of introspection but could be obtained through observation and experimentation. As a result, it could be taught to others. These academics would meet in a public grove of olive trees dedicated to the goddess Athena, an idyllic location surrounded by artistic, architectural, and natural beauty. Kind of like intellectual hippies.

Plato's understanding of what constitutes a benefit to humanity varies in the different dialogues, which leads to varying interpretations of his ideas. Was Plato's work a unified whole, or did he undergo a significant transformation in his later years? As Plato never 'speaks' in his own voice, it is unclear which opinions are his and what opinions are those of Socrates or other speakers. Or just the voices in his head.

As if Plato didn't have enough of his own fame to go on with, the artist Raphael used no lesser personage than Leonardo da Vinci as the model for Plato in *The School of Athens* (1511 AD). Aristotle (384-322 BC) is painted beside Plato, and it is unknown who modeled for him, although it looks like it might have been Philosopher Jesus.

Fig. 15: Detail from a reproduction of Raphael's The School of Athens (Johan10 and S.E.W.)

Aristotle is the third of the 'holy trinity' of Greek philosophers. His works have been influential on the study of philosophy all the way until the present. Thirty-one of Aristotle's treatises survive, but he wrote two hundred in his lifetime, on topics spanning a range of disciplines: philosophy, ethics, rhetoric, political theory, and aesthetics. He even delved into fields such as biology. Aristotle also had a famous student, no less a luminary than Alexander the Great, and I can only imagine what it was like keeping the greatest conqueror of all time in line in class. The pressure of such an illustrious student may have driven him to drink. However, history does not record whether Aristotle was indeed "a bugger for the bottle" as Monty Python's *Philosophers' Song* contends.

Stoicism

For many, the deaths of Aristotle and Alexander the Great signaled an end to the greatness of Greece. The Greek city-states were eclipsed as world powers and appeared to be slipping into social and administrative disorder. It was an age of uncertainty, which required a new paradigm of thinking to replace the old ways. Stoicism had its beginnings in this new world, but it was also influenced by precepts of the older philosophies.

Stoicism is a school of philosophy that advocates a way of living that focuses on how to live a virtuous life, maximize happiness, and minimize negative emotions. Over much of human history, many famous people have extolled the virtues of being stoic, and it is enjoying a modern resurgence as it's a bit new-agey. In the third century BC, Zeno of Citium taught his brand of philosophy in the Stoa Poikile, and it is from this 'stōïkos' that Stoicism takes its name. Zeno was a student of Platonic thought in the Academy and incorporated some tenets of this school in his doctrines. He set the Stoic agenda so emphatically that subsequent Stoic philosophers elaborated on his ideas rather than redefined them.

Big Ideas in Greek Mythology

The god Apollo was one of the most important deities in Classical Greek mythology. He was the son of Zeus, so he's right up there in the hierarchy. Apollo also had a literal day job: He had to get up before dawn, harness his four horses to his golden chariot, and then use it to drag the Sun across the sky. But he had a wide variety of portfolios: He was the god of music and dance, healing, truth, and prophecy, among other responsibilities. Ancient Greeks believed Apollo had a responsibility for education, and allied to this, another of his duties was to care for and protect children, boys in particular. Apollo oversaw their education and guided their progression to adulthood.

I think you can see where we're heading here.

That's right, Apollo, the god for whom NASA would later

name their most outstanding technological achievement, was a pederast. As we've already established, this was acceptable in Ancient Greek society, and the myths show Apollo taking serious interest in his part in the *erastes/eromenos* relationship. There's also a Spartan angle to this, as one of Apollo's *eromenos* relationships was with a handsome Spartan prince named Hyacinth. Legend tells us that young Hyacinth wasn't without *erastes* options, as the North Wind Boreas, the West Wind Zephyrus, and the mortal Thamyris, all vied for his attention. However, the hunky and talented Apollo won out, and tutored his pupil in the lyre, hunting, archery, working out, and with less success, the art of prophecy. But circumstance had destined Apollo and Hyacinth to be an all-male version of Romeo and Juliet.

One fine day, Apollo and Hyacinth were having a friendly discus-throwing competition (not a euphemism) when tragedy struck. First up, Apollo launched a god-like throw, which rent the clouds. Hyacinth ill-advisedly tried to catch the projectile as it re-entered Earth's atmosphere and got cracked on the head instead. One wonders, after all that prophecy training, why Hyacinth hadn't seen that coming. While Apollo brought all his medical skills to bear, it was no use. Hyacinth died, likely with a discus embedded in his skull. Never one to waste an opportunity, Apollo struck on a novel use for the blood from Hyacinth's head wound: He created a flower he named the hyacinth after his fallen lover. However, in a happy ending to the tale, Apollo resurrected Hyacinth, who was elevated to god-head.

Which is, ironically, what got him into trouble in the first place.

Fig. 16: Apollo and Hyacinth learn the dangers of Extreme Frisbee (Public domain and S.E.W.)

Hyacinth was far from the only protege Apollo 'tutored.' He taught his sons Asclepius, Anius, Iamus, Melaneus, and his adopted son (and half-brother) Carnus. He gave instruction in medicine, archery, prophecy, and in the case of Iamus, the language of birds, which I'm sure came in useful. However, Apollo's most famous pupil was Chiron.

Chiron was a centaur, but not your common or garden-type centaur: Yes, he had the torso, arms, and head of a man, and the body of a horse. However, tradition dictated his front legs were represented as human, which set him apart from the others of his kind, which had four horse legs. His father was the Titan Cronus, who had taken the form of a horse (because, *of course* he did) to impregnate his mother, the nymph Philyra. Philyra abandoned Chiron after he was born, out of shame from having mated with a horse-shaped god, and maybe because Chiron's congenital anomaly was a bit too much to process.

The young Chiron was then taken in as the foster child of Apollo, who saw something special in him. The god taught Chiron everything he knew, and in time, Chiron became a famous healer. Although he's best known as a teacher. Chiron's students were a veritable who's who of Greek mythology: Theseus, Achilles, Ajax, Jason, even the big guy himself: Heracles. Folklore has it that Chiron died a noble death, sacrificing his immortality to save the life of Prometheus.

Fig. 17: Chiron (without human front legs) gives Achilles (without pants) lyre lessons (Public Domain)

The virgin goddess Athena was also associated with learning and wisdom, with one of her symbols being the owl. The centuries-old debate as to whether Athens was named after Athena or Athena was named after Athens, appears to be resolved, as scholars now agree that the latter is the case. She is a rich vein of material, but as she is partially synonymous with the Roman goddess Minerva, I will cover her legend in the next chapter on Rome. Stay tuned.

A System of Divine Justice

The rule of law has been around since humans began living in small bands, and we already know there were codified laws in Mesopotamia. The Greeks didn't invent the big idea of judicial proceedings, *per se*. However, it's fair to say they tried to put the 'just' in justice.

The Greeks believed that nature was the source of law, and it was the right and duty of Athenian citizens to administer the law. Philosophers such as Plato and Aristotle believed justice was a moral good, and so furthered the ideals of unity, happiness, harmony, and virtue in the state.

Themis was the goddess of divine justice. You may not have heard of Themis, but I guarantee that you've seen her: She is also known as Lady Justice and is still the personification of moral force in Western judicial systems. Themis was pretty well-connected on Mount Olympus; she was the consort of Zeus. One of her powers was the gift of prophecy, which eventually led her to build the Oracle at Delphi.

Fig. 18: Blindfold and sword combo? Don't try this at home, kids (kparis and S.E.W.)

Five Hundred Angry Men

Trial by a jury of one's peers was a big idea pioneered in Ancient Greece. However, it looked a lot different from the trials to which we're accustomed. A hearing required a jury of between 500 and 1,500 people to sit in judgment. As one might expect with juries of that size, coming to a unanimous verdict was nigh on impossible, so a judgment was reached by a simple majority. In a bid to stop frivolous cases, an accuser was required to pay all costs if less than 100 jurors voted to convict.

The aforementioned Trial of Socrates was such a case. It took place in the People's Court over a ten-hour period, with a jury of 500 citizens drawn by lot and sitting on wooden benches. There was a large crowd of spectators. In question was Socrates' continued anti-democratic teachings in a time after democracy had been briefly overthrown. Because of the violence and suffering during that period, Socrates, never the most popular guy around, had his reputation further tarnished. However, there was an added agenda. One of Socrates' accusers, Anytus, had a problem with the philosopher's association with his son. While there's no proof that Socrates had a sexual relationship with Anytus' son, there's no doubt that he liked it both ways and often seduced his students. It's easy to see the double entendre in his evidence in the trial: "I had a brief association with the son of Anytus," Plato quotes him as saying, "and I found him *not lacking in spirit*" (my italics).

Socrates' three-hour-long address to the jury, which we know through Plato and Xenophon's accounts, was defiant and unapologetic: "Men of Athens, I honor and love you; but I shall obey God rather than you, and while I have life and strength I shall never cease from the practice and teaching of philosophy." Socrates left the jury no choice. If they wanted to stop him 'corrupting' the young men of Athens with his dangerous ideas, he had to die. The great philosopher was duly sentenced to death, but Socrates refused to plead for clemency. He believed it an 'unmanly and pathetic practice' and a disgrace to the justice system of Athens.

The outstanding thinkers of Ancient Greece added a significant amount to the discoveries of earlier civilizations, particularly the Egyptians and Mesopotamians, and built a sophisticated culture founded on scientific and philosophical thought. Their contribution to the collective learning of the human race is close to incalculable.

Despite the decline in liberal arts funding, the Greeks still have an immense influence on subsequent cultures up to today. This is true of their love of teaching and learning in particular. However, their love of education via pederastic mentoring relationships never really caught on*.

All-in-all, I think that's for the best.

**Except in the Catholic Church.*

Chapter Ten

Rome (if you want to)
Ancient Rome

> *All right, but apart from the sanitation, the medicine, education, wine, public order, irrigation, roads, the fresh-water system, and public health, what have the Romans ever done for us?*
> Reg, Monty Python's Life of Brian

Despite Reg's grudging admission, Rome brought of all these big ideas and more. They were the pre-eminent world power for hundreds of years, and by the standards of the ancient world, enlightened in their acceptance of the religion and local customs of the peoples they conquered. They didn't always conceive new ideas. Rather, they adapted the big ideas of others, imbued them with true Roman spirit, and launched them back into the world.

Ancient Rome was one of the most successful and long-lived civilizations in history. From its beginnings as a small town on the River Tiber in Italy, it grew into an expansive empire that ultimately incorporated much of continental Europe, most of Asia west of Mesopotamia, North Africa, England, and the Mediterranean. Romans achieved greatness through a combination of military might, strong political and social institutions, as well as through both 'Romanizing' conquered territories and assimilating the benefits of their culture.

The Birth of Rome

Rome itself was a big idea. Legend says it was founded in 753 BC by the twins Romulus and Remus. These two likely lads were the sons of the niece of the King of Alba Longa. She had, in some miraculous way, had been impregnated by Mars, the Roman god of war. This gave Romulus and Remus a formidable heritage, and the king, fearing these boys might become dangerous, set them adrift in a basket, Moses-like, on the Tiber.

In retrospect, this was not the most effective way to rid oneself of a potential threat. The boys survived, thanks to the combined actions of the River God and an obliging she-wolf, who suckled the boys until a shepherd rescued them and raised them as his own. And yep, you guessed it; they went on to defeat their evil uncle and found the city of Rome. But despite a story that seems like a Lion King/Prince of Egypt mash-up, this was no children's movie.

Remus was fated not to survive Rome's foundation day. Depending on who you believe:

A. He argued with, and then by was murdered by, Romulus; or
B. He was killed by one of Romulus' supporters with a spade; or
C. Most ignominiously, he accidentally died after jumping over a wall.

I'm not pointing fingers, but Romulus somehow managed to recover from his grief at the 'untimely' death of his twin and became the first King of Rome. This Rome 1.0 was unrecognizable from the superpower it would become: It was a small, pastoral community with a collective bad temper and delusions of grandeur. The newly-minted Eternal City continued as a monarchy for a couple of hundred years until one of Romulus' successors, the tyrannical King Lucius Tarquinius Superbus, AKA Tarquin the Proud, was overthrown.

One Republic

When Tarquin the Proud was deposed, the Roman people were fed up with kings and proclaimed their city *res publica* (property of the people), or a republic. As we've seen, the Greeks had already experimented with a kind of democracy, and the Romans wanted a chunk of that action. They altered the Greek model, passing the king's powers to two consuls, who were elected each year. Although these consuls were elected by 'the people,' these electors comprised only male descendants of the original senators at the time of Rome's founding. This ruling class was known as the patricians. As a result, there was a lot of argy-bargy in early Republican politics because of the struggles between patricians and lower-class plebeians. The plebs were granted a small amount of political power, in the form of the tribunate, a college of ten tribunes who were a check on the power of the Senate.

Around this time, Romans benefited from assimilating Greek art, religion, and philosophical thought. The first known Roman literature appeared around 240 BC, with translations of Greek classics into Latin. However, this trend for all things Greek had its limits. Romans absolutely drew the line at pederastic mentoring relationships. Marcus Tullius Cicero summed up the attitude of Romans to Greek love: "We must borrow our virtue from Rome and our culture from the Greeks." One can only imagine what the world would be like today if Rome had borrowed their virtue from the Greeks and their culture from Rome.

The last years of the Republic were violent and tumultuous, becoming a time when political assassinations were a way of life.

Political Assassinations: The Only Viable Answer?

Exterminating your rivals wasn't a new idea. It wasn't even a particularly Roman idea. But when the Roman people got their heads around this concept, they found it hard to give up. Don't like your leaders? Just kill them.

However, it wasn't always this way.

When Tarquin the Proud was deposed by Lucius Junius Brutus (the distant ancestor of another Brutus, of whom more later), he was not murdered, but instead, sent into exile. Unfortunately for Tarquin, he threw himself upon the mercy of the Roman garrison at Gabii, where he was assassinated anyway for being such a jerk. It just goes to prove you shouldn't make too many enemies.

Yet, after this, the internal politics of Republican Rome was relatively benign by ancient standards. The rot really set in with the murders of the brothers Tiberius and Gaius Gracchus in 133 BC and 121 BC respectively. It seemed an ultra-conservative senatorial faction, the Optimates, didn't take too kindly to Populares rabble-rousers like the Gracchi trying to give land to veterans and implement social reform. Saturninus and Clodius Pulcher were two other high-profile Populares who felt the cold steel of the assassin's knife. Throughout the days of Gaius Marius' dodgy record of six consulships and Lucius Cornelius Sulla's dictatorship, political violence was the norm in Rome, as right-wing and left-wing bovver-boys clashed in the streets.

Fig. 1: Gaius Julius Caesar: a born shit-stirrer
(Erica Guliane-Nachez and S.E.W.)

However, when it came to pissing off the Optimates, no one did it better than Gaius Julius Caesar. Mind you, Caesar's planet-sized ego had ensured he had loads of enemies. He'd managed to defy the Senate, bribe voters, cross the Rubicon to march an army on Rome, fight a civil war against the likes of Pompey, flaunt his mistress Cleopatra and their love-child Caesarion around Rome, *and* make himself Dictator for life. It was becoming clear to all that Rome was dealing with a man who would be king. By the time Marcus Junius Brutus, Cassius, and their fellow conspirators fell upon him in the Senate, Caesar was probably the only one surprised.

Fig. 2: Forget Shakespeare, these were Caesar's ***real*** *last words (benoitb and S.E.W.)*

After a short-lived period of trying to share power, Octavian and Mark Antony had another little civil war which saw the end of Antony, Cicero, Cato, Cassius, and Brutus. By this time, Romans were so sick of internal strife they were prepared to stomach an autocrat as long as he didn't take up the mantle of king. The triumphant Octavian was proclaimed emperor, reigning as Caesar Augustus. Augustus restored peace and dignity in

Rome after many years of conflict and corruption. Over his 40-year reign, he instituted significant social reforms, and his armies won numerous military victories, heralding the *Pax Romana,* or Roman Peace. This era of relative peace in domestic Roman affairs allowed Roman art, literature, architecture, and education to thrive. Unfortunately, after Augustus' death, things never quite got back on an even keel politically.

Fig. 3: The Senators had no choice but to go with it (Erica Guliane-Nachez and S.E.W.)

Over the next five centuries, a cavalcade of eighty-odd emperors succeeded Augustus. Some were good (Nerva, Trajan, Hadrian Antoninus Pius, and Marcus Aurelius), most mediocre (a list too long to include), and some batshit crazy (Caligula, Nero, Commodus, and Elagabalus).

However, Rome always held tight to its political traditions: A whopping twenty percent of Rome's emperors were assassinated. Clearly, political murder was a big idea the Romans found difficult to give up.

Education: A mind stuffed full

Ancient Rome was a complex and ever-changing civilization that had existed for almost a thousand years, and education was a big idea that kept it ahead of the pack over that time. However, historians are still debating the details of finer points of education in the Republic through to Augustan times.

Roman education in the pre/early Republic was most often practical, comprising instruction in such farm management issues such as how to oversee slaves. However, for warlike people such as the Romans, martial training was of vital importance. Learning also had a moral aspect, establishing a respect for good management and frugality. For these young Romans, education was often just observing and replicating an action. This process served them well in military training, as young men became conditioned to obeying commands without question. Such training was also considered appropriate for politics, where young candidates for the Senate observed their fathers in the Senate chamber, in a kind of "Bring your child to work" day.

Like in much of the ancient world, education began at home for the young Roman. Plutarch's *Life of Marcus Cato* outlines the traditional paterfamilias' (male head of the family) role in the education of children. Cato was the most old-fashioned of men, and was desperate for a return to time-honored Roman values. Cato was suspicious of the new-fangled Greek education that was being introduced to the Republic, and therefore his ideas about education were anachronistic. He took a personal interest in his son's education, teaching him to read, tutoring him in law, and instructing him how to fight, ride a horse, swim, and throw a javelin. Cato even wrote an entire history of Rome for his son's benefit. This was because he felt that it was unseemly for a pedagogue who was invariably a slave, to scold a Roman citizen.

By this time, however, Cato's reactionary brand of 'Make Rome Great Again' education was in decline. This rustic education might have been fine for the forging of a powerful city-state, but it would not do for an expanding empire. To meet that challenge, Rome's leaders needed sophisticated political, administrative, and military training.

The Romans had been well acquainted with the Greeks for hundreds of years, and Greek influence was already apparent in religious matters and the alphabet. However, it was when the Romans subdued mainland Greece in the Achaean War in 146 BC that Greek influence became more pronounced. Greek city-states proved that daily life could be more cultured and comfortable than the Romans experienced at home. Grecian learning influenced Rome in other areas as well: trade, art, literature, philosophy, and science. By the late Republic, Romans weren't considered well educated until they could speak Greek fluently and had honed their knowledge of rhetoric and philosophy by studying in Athens or Rhodes in the original Greek. So it was that the broad-minded and inquiring nature of Greek education eclipsed the more utilitarian nature of traditional Roman education.

> *Captive Greece captivated her rude conqueror and introduced the arts to rustic Latium.*
> Horace

Hellenistic education was considered the ideal for the sons of Roman Patricians, making *paideia* a necessary precondition for assuming a role of power and status in Rome. As a result, many well-to-do Roman fathers turned to Greek slaves to impart education to their sons.

Before we get on to what education was like in Ancient Rome, let's make sure we understand what it wasn't. It wasn't universal. It was only for the wealthy and well-to-do. And it was only for men. This meant that the literacy rate was somewhere between 10 to 15 percent of the population. There were likely large regional differences, as in many Roman provinces the people wouldn't have spoken either Latin or Greek as a first language, or at all. So, while a high rate of literacy is a given for the upper-class Romans, precious few commoners would have possessed that skill. For those without formal education, such as tradesmen, farmers, and artisans, they would have learned their trade from their fathers or as apprentices to craftsmen in the way men had for thousands of years.

Aristocratic boys learned the basics of Greek and Latin from the slave nursemaid in charge of their care. Then, at seven or eight, most boys were given a pedagogue. The role of the pedagogue in Rome differed somewhat from that of the *paidagogos* in Greece. As we have seen in Greece, the *paidagogos* was a slave, often illiterate, whose job was to keep his young charge in line during his education and to make sure unsuitable men did not molest him. The Roman pedagogue was literate, less involved with keeping pedophiles at bay, and more concerned with teaching.

At a certain point, the young master would go to elementary school, and then the pedagogue's role changed to accompanying him to and from school, making sure he was paying attention in class, and tutoring him at home. The *ludi magister* or teacher ran the elementary school or *ludus*, often in a covered outdoor area with open sides.

The *ludi magister* himself was not the social equal of his students. Far from it. He was a man of lower socio-economic status who made his living in a school system in which there was no public sector. The *ludi magister* was the lowest paid of the Roman educators, with the obvious exception of the pedagogues who, as slaves, were not paid at all. This lowly position ensured that their 'betters' often looked down on them. That the phrase: "Your father was a schoolteacher" was the Roman equivalent of "Yo momma's so fat…" speaks volumes of the teacher's inferior social status.

Some things never change.

Around the age of twelve, the boy would progress to secondary school under the tutelage of the *grammaticus*. The syllabus here was the study of language and literature in Greek and Latin. As there was very little Latin literature in the early Republic, there was a focus on classic Greek literature. Only later did the work of Virgil and Horace take their place alongside *The Iliad* and *The Odyssey* as Latin texts studied in secondary school. Students learned by reading and repetition, with the *grammaticus* adding a critique on the style, philosophy, and history inherent in the text.

The big idea of education was not over yet. At sixteen, a boy could burn his boyhood tunic, don the *toga virilis,* and assume the privileges and burdens of manhood. Many of these newly minted men looked forward to an active public life in the Senate or the law courts, and that meant they needed to take the next step in the Roman education process: They needed to study under a *rhetor*, or teacher of rhetoric. The art of rhetoric was to comprehend the theory and practice of public speaking. But speaking well wasn't enough to make a persuasive orator, one needed a quick mind and a background in an array of topics, such as history, law, and philosophy.

As a final level of education, the wealthiest Romans would send their sons to be tutored in Greece. This shows a few things: that 'authentic' Athenian education was considered better than the pale copy of Greek education available at home, there were unique benefits to be gained by the experience, and it enhanced a man's reputation. Given Roman morals, it probably didn't mean that Dad thought Junior could do with a good, old-fashioned buggering. Whatever the case, once a young man returned from Greece with, at the very least, his mind stuffed full, he was ready to take his place in Roman public life.

Teaching at all levels was an inherently violent profession. The poet Horace's nickname for Orbilius, his *ludi magister,* was 'Thrasher.' Quintilian, an educator and rhetorician from the first century AD, warns that the penchant for excessive physical punishment might make a young student unable to resist any 'unspeakable abuse.' Another well-known poet, Marcus Valerius Martialis, regarded schooling and beating as being synonymous.

No wonder political violence and assassination became such a Roman staple.

The College of the Vestal Virgins

The one sure way for a woman to get a formal education in Rome was to be chosen for the College of Vestal Virgins. This group of women enjoyed a special social status because of their fundamental importance to Rome. However, the vestals were a very select group. There was only ever a maximum of eighteen in the college, although only six of these were active vestals at any single moment in time.

The vestals were the custodians of the wills and testaments of the well-born and powerful. They had a special role in Roman religious practice, particularly Vestalia, the annual festival of the goddess Vesta. The Temple of Vesta housed a number of sacred objects and the vestals had responsibility for them. Lastly, it was crucial that the Vestals ensured that the eternal flame in the temple remained alight, as this was a sign that Rome was safe and indestructible.

Because of these important functions, being a member of the College of Vestal Virgins had serious perks. Vestals enjoyed a social status unlike any other women in this most patriarchal of societies: They could own property, write a will, and were allowed to vote. Vestals got V.I.P. transportation in covered carriages that always had right of way. They also got awesome seats for gladiatorial games and were safe wherever they went because their person was sacrosanct. Sounds great, right?

But being a vestal had serious downsides.

The punishments for vestals failing to fulfill their duties were severe. Letting the flame go out was a big no-no. The priestess responsible for such a transgression would be stripped and beaten by the Pontifex Maximus. Also, vestals could not marry until they had completed thirty years' service to the goddess. Before that, they were sworn to a life of celibacy. Failing to live up to this vow had horrific consequences: The transgressing vestal would be permanently locked in a subterranean 'room' under the *Campus Sceleratus* with enough food and water to last a couple of days. As you can imagine, breaches of the chastity rule were exceedingly rare. Not even the most earth-shattering shag was worth being buried alive.

During their thirty years in the College of Vestals, the priestesses went through three distinct stages. For the first ten years, they were novice Vestals and were taught everything they needed to fulfill their role. Their next ten years were as active vestals, tending the flame and undertaking all their other duties. Their last decade as a Vestal was spent teaching the new intake of novices.

Fig. 4: It was always Girls' Night Out at the college of the Vestal Virgins (Benoitb and S.E.W.)

Are You Not Entertained? The Rise of Professional Sports

Already long ago, from when we sold our vote to no man, the People

have abdicated our duties; for the People who once upon a time handed out military command, high civil office, legions — everything, now restrains itself and anxiously hopes for just two things: bread and circuses
Juvenal

In this passage, the poet Juvenal berates the Roman people for allowing themselves to be seduced by slimy politicians who bought their votes with free wheat and expensive circus games. The heavyweight champion of vote-buying was Julius Caesar, who borrowed a fortune to ensure he was elected to the consulship. In later years, elaborate public games were organized to distract citizens from their shrinking rights after the fall of the Republic. Whatever the reason, these public games were where the big idea of professional sport came to the fore.

Professional sport needs a crowd. And crowds need to be accommodated. Enter the Roman circuses. These circuses were not big-top tents full of clowns and carnies. They were large open-air stadia used for what passed for sporting events in Ancient Rome. The best known of these venues were the Colosseum and the Circus Maximus, which were the main venues for large public events, especially chariot racing and gladiatorial games.

The Colosseum

We all know the Colosseum. Despite its antiquity, it is still the largest amphitheater in the world. Unlike most amphitheaters, the Colosseum is a freestanding structure of concrete and stone. Built around 70 AD, it still stands, a time-honored testament to the Roman fascination with spectacle. In its heyday, it's estimated it could hold between 50,000 and 80,000 spectators, a capacity comparable to most large modern stadiums. The Colosseum's main function was to house events such as gladiatorial games, executions, and dramatic re-creations of mythological stories. It was even filled with water and used for reenactments of famous naval engagements.

Fig. 5: The crowds in the Colosseum liked a bit of fight in their entertainment (Luis Louro and S.E.W.)

Today we often view the martyrdom of large numbers of Christians (usually as lion fodder) as the highlight of a fun day in the Colosseum. While Christians were certainly martyred, and big cats were almost inevitably involved, the supporting evidence that these martyrdoms were the main event in the Colosseum is slight. The simple fact is that watching helpless people being torn apart by wild animals was only a curtain-raiser in Roman games.

The Circus Maximus

The Circus Maximus or 'biggest circus' was the largest sporting arena of the ancient world and could reputedly hold up to 200,000 people. Unlike the ovoid Colosseum, the Circus Maximus was cigar-shaped. It was purpose-built for staging chariot races, with two long straightaways that were half a Roman mile long.

It reached its full glory during the time of the Caesars, but the development of the Circus Maximus dates to the time of the Roman kings. The venue remained in use as a circus through the Republican and Imperial eras, up until the mid-fifth century AD. Although it is famed for hosting Ben Hur-style chariot races, the Circus Maximus was also the preferred venue for religious processions. It was even used to stage games where wild beasts were stalked by Bestiarii, or wild beast hunters.

There were professional bestiarii, who made a conscious choice to put their lives on the line for prize money. There were also enthusiastic amateurs, such as the Emperors Nero and Commodus, who fought lions and other dangerous animals just for the hell of it. They probably went into battle armed to the teeth (and, if I know anything, against beasts that had been handicapped in some way).

However, this was also a mode of capital punishment. In contrast to Roman noblemen, the condemned were sent into the circus without clothes or weapons. And if by some miracle some poor naked guy managed to choke a lion with his bare hands, he had not earned his freedom. Oh no. This was just the signal for another wild beast to be loosed upon him.

As you can imagine, things never ended well for these bestiarii.

Fig. 6: Not a big top or clown in sight (antique images and S.E.W.)

Gladiatorial Games: The Perfect Funeral Entertainment

The Roman tradition of public gladiatorial combat began when gladiators were engaged to fight to the death during the funeral of Junius Brutus (another early relation of the Brutus who murdered Caesar) in 264 BC. While it may sound insane to us, it made perfect sense to the militant Romans. What better way to express profound grief at the loss of a loved one than watching two men hack each other to death?

If nothing else, it must have been a distraction.

For the most part, the ranks of the gladiators were made up of slaves, condemned criminals, and prisoners of war. They were men with nothing to lose and very little reason to live. However, like the bestiarii, there were some volunteers who were in it for cold hard cash, thrills, and celebrity. Like today's professional sportspeople, gladiators were not considered respectable citizens.

Nevertheless, there were a small number of well-to-do Romans who did compete in the arena. These rich thrill-seekers were unusual in the world of Roman entertainment, and catered to a niche market. It was a similar story for the rare gladiatrices (female gladiators). Before competing, all gladiators swore a sacred oath: "I will endure to be burned, to be bound, to be beaten, and to be killed by the sword." I can only presume they did this under duress, because no sane person would utter such words.

Fig. 7: All in a day's work (Archivist and S.E.W.)

There were many types of gladiators. They could be distinguished by their equipment and their style of combat. Their fights commonly pitted two different categories of gladiator. For instance, it was common for a Retiarius or 'netman' to fight a Secutor or 'pursuer.' The Retiarius wore only arm and shoulder protectors, and was armed with a net, a trident, and a dagger. The Secutor wore a helmet, a shin protector, and arm protector (only one of each) and carried a rectangular shield and sword. If this seems like a weird pairing for a fight, it was. But the audiences in the Colosseum lapped it up.

There were a number of other types of gladiators, and it was typical for a gladiator to fight in one category for his career. Given the highly specialized nature of the equipment, it's easy to understand why this was the case. Not everyone is handy with a net and a trident.

A Lovely Day out at the Arena

A typical day in the Colosseum went something like this: First, the sponsor of the games, in Imperial times, most often the Emperor, would lead a parade of gladiators around the arena. There would then be a display of trained animals doing tricks, and then wild beasts would be set loose against each other. If they couldn't avoid it, sometimes bestiarii would also be involved. All this would wrap up at, what nowadays we'd term, 'half-time.'

Like today, the crowd was treated to some half-time entertainment. However, instead of Coldplay or Lady Gaga, the halftime show was something a little more to Roman taste: wanton slaughter. In particular, the execution of criminals for transgressions such as arson, murder, and sacrilege. The nature of these punishments often involved people being fed to hungry animals. The painful, degrading, and public nature of these executions made them a stark deterrent for all in attendance.

Half-time blessedly over, the games continued.

Now came the main event, the individual gladiatorial combats. Unfortunately for fans of gladiator movies, there is little evidence that the gladiators uttered the words "Those who are about to die salute you," before their contests began. However, a wounded gladiator could concede defeat by holding up an index finger. From here on, he was at the mercy of the mob. The beaten gladiator's fate was determined by hand gestures from the crowd. Scholars debate whether the hand gestures were the classic 'thumbs down' for death and 'thumbs up' for life, but whatever the signals were, it was the ultimate in crowd participation.

It kind of puts beer snakes and 'the wave' to shame.

Chariot Racing: Bigger than Ben Hur

The Romans certainly didn't invent chariot racing, but they were the ones who made it big business. This popularity should come as no surprise, because chariot races provided the kind of thrills and spills that Formula One racing provides today. With the exception that horrific crashes and death were far more likely in the Circus Maximus. As you may already have worked out by now, Roman audiences *loved* them some blood and guts.

Such was the popularity of the chariot races, the streets of Rome would be eerily deserted when they took place. It was *the* Roman event and had more in common with roller derby or stock car racing than today's equine 'sport of kings.' Twelve chariots would race in teams, or factions. These factions didn't have fancy names; they were just known as Green, Blue, Red, and White. While this seems like a missed merchandising opportunity, it didn't worry Roman sports fans. They chose their team color and followed them with the same quasi-religious fervor of modern sports fanatics.

There were superstar charioteers, daredevils whose prowess

captured the imagination of the crowds. One such hotshot was Gaius Appuleius Diocles. He was a stalwart of the Red faction who not only survived, but thrived. He placed first or second in nearly 70% of his races over the course of a twenty-four-year career. Earnings-wise, he was the LeBron James of the Roman world. When he retired at 42, having somehow not died in a horrific chariot crash, he was richer than all but the wealthiest Roman senators.

While Gaius Appuleius Diocles led a charmed life, the same cannot be said for a rookie charioteer named Scorpius. A rising star of the Green team, young Scorpius had the world at his feet: great talent, burgeoning fame, and an awesome moniker. That was, until a horrific accident in the Circus Maximus. In a tight race to the line, Scorpius managed to drive his chariot directly into the finishing post at top speed. Unsurprisingly, he didn't survive.

*Fig. 8: Unfortunately, Scorpius couldn't quite make **every** post a winner (Archivist and S.E.W.)*

Philosophy: What Every Young Man Needs to Know

Given the Roman worship of the Hellenistic world, it's no

surprise that Greek philosophy was high on the list of 'things every educated Roman should know'. The Roman pilgrimage to what amounted to Greek Finishing School meant that Greek thought dominated Roman philosophy. However, there was one realm of philosophy where Rome surpassed its teacher: Stoicism.

Roman Stoicism had several high-profile proponents, not least of which was Marcus Cato the Younger, the same guy who wouldn't let slaves teach his son. Cato felt so strongly about Julius Caesar's victory over Republican forces that he committed suicide, although that was less to do with him being a Stoic and more to do with being inflexible and bloody-minded. Another famous Roman Stoic was Lucius Annaeus Seneca, who was a major philosophical figure of Imperial times. He was a statesman and writer who could explain Stoicism in an easy-to-understand way. Seneca's practical advice about topics such as friendship, morality, and altruism still resonates with readers in the modern era.

However, the most famous Roman Stoic philosopher was Emperor Marcus Aurelius. Unless you're a student of Stoic philosophy or Roman history, your exposure to the Philosopher King was likely his portrayal by Richard Harris in the Academy Award-winning film, *Gladiator*. We can't be sure if he spoke in Harris' husky-velvet whisper, but he was a writer whose voice still speaks to us through the ages. His book, *the Meditations,* has been very influential over two millennia, but is seen by some as a rehashing of earlier Stoic philosophy. However, Marcus Aurelius would have done well in the era of the internet, as his pithy Stoic quotes like "Do every act of your life as though it were the very last act of your life" are the stuff of self-actualization memes. But beware—not all Marcus Aurelius quotes are authentic:

Fig. 9: Isn't the internet great? (mmac72 and S.E.W.)

Warfare: Travel the World, Meet Interesting People, and Subjugate them

As we've seen a number of times, the Romans adopted and refined big ideas rather than invented them. The clearest example of this is warfare. Humans had been waging war since the year dot. It took the Romans to polish this idea until it shone, ensuring that their armies ruled most of the known world.

Roman politics and warfare had a symbiotic relationship. Rare was the man of senatorial class whose step up to the consulship hadn't been boosted by a successful military campaign. Equally rare was the successful general who didn't have his eyes on power, and in the Imperial age, becoming emperor. Gaius Julius Caesar was the pinnacle of the former and the trendsetter of the latter.

Fig. 10: Brutus didn't appreciate Caesar's trendsetting (Patrick Guenette and S.E.W.)

While Roman armies were known for their intelligent use of military tactics, organized strategic warfare was not a Roman innovation. The ancient Sumerians, Assyrians, Babylonians, Persians, Spartans, and Macedonians all used versions of the phalanx formation. This was a rectangular formation of heavy infantry, usually armed with spears.

The early Roman generals adapted the unwieldy phalanx, dividing it into two 'centuries,' which provided more flexibility. They called these two centuries a maniple. Each century was commanded by a centurion. If you imagine this centurion like the screaming, spittle-expectorating drill sergeant from *Full Metal Jacket*, you'll get the idea.

The Roman's level of martial organization didn't stop there, though. Usually, ten maniples were arranged into battle lines, and there were three battle lines. Later, when the Roman army became professionalized under Gaius Marius, this formation was further refined. Eight centuries were arranged into a cohort, and ten cohorts became the famous Roman legion. Legions were drilled in the many tactical formations they could assume in certain battle conditions.

One of the most famous formations Roman legions could form into one command was the testudo or 'tortoise' formation. The tortoise got its name from the way the ranks would use their large shields to form a protective shell around the formation, just like the eponymous reptile. The front rank of the formation would interlock their shields and kneel. Then each subsequent row of soldiers would hold their shields above the heads of the men immediately in front of them. In certain circumstances, the men on both flanks and at the rear could also interlock their shields. The curved face of the upturned shields provided an excellent defense against incoming arrows.

Another well-known formation was 'the wedge.' On command, legionaries would form into a triangle formation and charge the opposition. The leading edge of the wedge would pierce the front line of enemy soldiers, and the widening of the V spears into the opponent's line, dividing their forces and allowing other legionaries to move into the gap. It was a neat trick.

All Roman foot soldiers used the same equipment and were trained in the same tactics, making them interchangeable cogs in a machine. These soldiers had an unerring belief in the superiority of Roman military might. They had intense loyalty to their legion and would, without question, respond to commands that every soldier implicitly understood.

Fig. 11: Not all legionaries were as tough as nails
(Vladimirs Poplavskis and S.E.W.)

Legionaries were highly disciplined troops. Sometimes because of a love of Rome, but usually because of the army's strict rules and the penalties they could incur for breaking them. Lying was a big no-no. 'Unmanly acts' (the mind boggles) were also punishable. For these relatively minor infringements, the legionary might only have to pay a fine, although they could be whipped or even executed, depending on the severity of the offense.

For entire army units that deserted, or were considered cowardly or mutinous in battle, the punishment was decimation. This was decimation in its literal, Roman sense, meaning that every tenth offender was terminated. It usually happened in this manner: Cohorts would be divided into groups of ten legionaries. The soldiers would then draw lots (or play a *very* intense game of Scissors, Paper, Rock) and the loser was killed by the other nine, usually by clubbing or by the sword. Roman generals found this kind of discipline tended to focus the mind.

However, warfare for Romans was more than just discipline, martial ability, and tactics. Roman military logistics were also second to none. Before commencing a campaign, they would create an operational base that was strategically positioned for easy resupply. This operational base would then be connected via a supply line to a tactical base near the front line. Superior logistics allowed the Romans to campaign in remote areas over extended periods. A definite advantage, and a big idea that would resonate with would-be conquerors from Napoleon to Hitler. And beyond.

The Roman army left a lasting impression wherever it went. The legionaries were famous for road building, with many Roman roads still existing today. These roads are often considered a key to Roman military superiority, as they allowed even the most isolated Roman province to be quickly reinforced if necessary. These roads enabled the Romanisation of conquered lands. But, like all roads, they ran in both directions, allowing the flow of cultural influences from the provinces back to Rome.

These guys could really build.

Roman Architecture: Imitation and Innovation

As with seemingly every other innovation for which the Romans were responsible, their architecture was heavily influenced by other cultures. And yet again, after the initial copying stage, the Romans introduced new technology such as true arches, vaults, and concrete, to take architecture to new creative heights. This originality didn't take place until the Imperial era. Before that, in the Republican era, they created buildings that harked back to their Etruscan roots, or paid homage to Greek architecture.

Augustus' funeral inscription, the *Res Gestae,* boasted: "I found Rome a city of bricks and left it a city of marble." While true, he could also rightly have claimed to have left Rome a city of concrete, but that doesn't sound nearly so sexy. However you term it, the Augustan age saw a construction boom, with ground-breaking designs, and yes, lavish use of marble.

Fig. 12: And a fair bit of marble, too (antiqueimages and S.E.W.)

Yet, it was humble concrete that allowed the Romans to create some of their most amazing pieces of architectural engineering. The dome of Pantheon is one such wonder. The building, initially commissioned during Augustus' reign by Marcus Agrippa, burned down and was reconstructed by Hadrian. Even after nearly two millennia, it remains the largest unsupported concrete dome ever constructed. Its 43-meter-wide dome weighs 4535 tonnes.

Egyptians, Babylonians, and Greeks had used arches and vaults for many hundreds of years. However, these were only used on a small scale to support roofs or other smaller structures. The Romans' engineering expertise allowed them to perfect these features, and they were used in the construction of bridges and aqueducts.

I'm getting a little sick of writing this, but aqueducts were not a Roman innovation. They had been used by the Assyrians, Babylonians, Minoans, and Greeks to bring fresh water to urban centers. It was the immense scale of Roman aqueducts that made them memorable, as they carried water over vast distances on a slight gradient. Aqueducts were first built in Rome in 312 BC, and eventually, arched aqueducts became commonplace throughout the empire. The Romans used similar technology to build great bridges that spanned rivers and gorges.

As Reg from the People's Front of Judea acknowledged at the beginning of this chapter, Roman colonization brought sanitation. Vaulted sewers carried away water from individual homes, which connected to the main sewage system of *Cloaca Maxima*, which drained into the Tiber. It goes without saying that while the Romans weren't the first to do this, they did it best.

Big Ideas in Roman Mythology

It was routine for Romans to adopt their gods from existing Greek and Etruscan counterparts, although they made an effort to Romanise them. This means there are direct swaps for gods, such as Jupiter for Zeus, Venus for Aphrodite, Neptune for Poseidon. The legends associated with these gods were usually the same, but with the Roman names substituted for the Greek. The one exception to this rule is our old friend Apollo. We've already covered Apollo and his decidedly unRoman sexual preferences, but somewhat surprisingly, they didn't seek to censor him. While there were only a couple of temples dedicated to Apollo during the Republic, Emperor Augustus' admiration of him made his stocks rise in the early years of empire.

However, when it comes to Roman deities of big ideas, we need to look no further than the goddess Minerva. In stark contrast to Apollo's carbon-copy import into Rome, Minerva evolved from the home-grown Etruscan goddess Menvra. As Rome became Hellenised, they equated Menvra with the Greek goddess Athena, and over time, she became Minerva. Because of her hybrid nature, Minerva continued to display some quintessentially Roman attributes. She was the virgin goddess of wisdom, medicine, weaving, and school children. Artists of the time often depicted Minerva with her sacred pet, an owl known as the "owl of Minerva," symbolizing her association with wisdom and knowledge. She is portrayed as a tall woman with an athletic build, clad in armor, and carrying a spear.

Despite her Etruscan beginnings, Minerva's origin story is lifted straight from the Greek story of the birth of Athena. And, as we now expect with the birth of ancient gods, there is a lot of shape-shifting and weird sex. For a start, Jupiter, king of the gods and presumably a being with unlimited sexual options, nevertheless chose to rape the titaness Metis, who had the power to shape-shift. At this point, Jupiter recalled the prophecy that his son would overthrow him. Fearing he had impregnated Metis with his hyper-virility, he decided he must do something to forestall this. So, he tricked Metis into changing into a fly, and then promptly swallowed her. Disaster averted. Or so he thought.

Of course, Jupiter had indeed got Metis up-the-duff, and she continued to live and have her pregnancy progress while residing inside the king of the gods. While still within Jupiter's body, Metis gave birth to Minerva, then as you do, she forged weapons and armor for her newborn daughter. As anyone who has heard metalworking can attest, it is a cacophonous process. All the constant hammering, clanging, and ringing left Jupiter with a horrible migraine. Jupiter's ham-fisted and not-too-bright buddy Vulcan helped relieve Jupiter's agony by using a hammer to split his head open. From the resulting crater, Minerva popped out, an already grown woman and kitted out in the armor crafted by her mom. You may be surprised that Jupiter recovered completely after this forced cranial caesarian. Doctors don't recommend this treatment for headache or childbirth, so don't try this at home, kids.

Like many of the Greek and Roman gods, Minerva's immortality and power amplified her very human faults. For instance, she could be inordinately jealous. How jealous? Just ask Medusa. Despite our image of Medusa as a hideous monster with hissing snakes for hair, she was once a beautiful, mortal human who boasted that her good looks rivaled those of Minerva. Big mistake. Minerva, already rubbed up the wrong way by Medusa's vain boasts, got a teensy bit steamed up after catching Neptune and Medusa bonking in her own temple, and decided to teach Medusa a lesson. Minerva turned Medusa into a hideous creature, replacing her glorious flowing locks with the hair extensions from hell. Not only did Minerva wipe away Medusa's beauty and charm, she also made it so any living creature who looked directly into Medusa's eyes would be turned into stone. That's why when the hero Perseus went after Medusa, he avoided eye contact by looking into the reflection in a mirrored shield (given to him by Minerva). He then promptly beheaded Medusa and FedExed the severed head to Minerva, making her insane revenge fantasy complete.

Medusa is not the only mortal to suffer because of Minerva's psychotic brand of moral education. Witness the story of Arachne, a mortal girl with a spectacular talent for weaving. It was a talent of which Arachne was very proud. A little too proud, perhaps, as without heed to her personal safety, she announced she was a superior weaver to Minerva. This was a red rag to a bull, and Minerva approached Arachne in disguise as an old crone, offering her a chance to recant her boastfulness. Arachne refused and it was then that Minerva revealed her true self. A titanic handicraft-based version of a rap-battle ensued, with the mortal woman and goddess trading insults via the novel medium of weaving and embroidery. When Minerva finally had enough, she just touched Arachne's forehead and made her feel shame for her actions. So much shame, in fact, that Arachne committed suicide by hanging herself. A somewhat remorseful Minerva, realizing that she had perhaps gone too far, brought Arachne back from the dead. But lest we think that Minerva had learned a lesson of her own, she transformed Arachne into a spider as a constant reminder that her actions offended the gods. Or at least the goddess of school children.

Fig. 13: Arachne: about to discover the fragility of a god's ego (Public Domain and S.E.W.)

Christianity in Rome: From Pogroms to Power

The Apostle Paul began teaching in Rome about 60 AD, but it is an understatement to say that for the longest time, he and his fellow Christians weren't that well-received. They were seen as superstitious followers of a dangerous sect which refused to acknowledge the primacy of the Roman gods. Their unpopularity made it easy for Emperor Nero to frame them for the Great Fire of Rome in 64 AD. According to the historian Tacitus, after a show trial, Nero had some of the Christians crucified, others burned alive, and still others dressed in animal skins then sent into the arena and torn apart by ravenous dogs. Saint Paul, traditionally acknowledged as the first Pope, was martyred when he was beheaded after being sentenced to death by Nero. If nothing else, the emperor liked a little variety in his executions.

Fig. 14: Lions 15 - Christians 0 (Erica Guilane-Nachez and S.E.W.)

The Romans' distaste of Christians wasn't helped by adverse publicity, particularly as they viewed some Christian rituals (such as transubstantiation) as cannibalistic. The Christians' deep unpopularity was illustrated by the high frequency with which they were denounced by their fellow Romans. The punishment for being Christian varied: They could get a slap on the wrist or be fed to the lions, or somewhere in between. However, they could sometimes save themselves from the worst by making an offering to appease the Roman gods. As the years went by, Christianity's PR problems continued, and they were often the focus of violent mobs and increasing institutional persecution.

All-in-all, while Jesus loved them, it really wasn't the greatest time in history to love Jesus.

That is until Emperor Constantine changed the game with his conversion to Christianity. The Christians' lot had already improved sometime earlier: The Edict of Milan in AD 313, agreed to by co-emperors Constantine and Licinius, gave Christianity legal status and a reprieve from persecution within the Roman

Empire. No more anti-Christian pogroms; two thumbs-up.

Constantine's changes of policy towards Christianity altered Roman society in all aspects, both public and private. Education was not immune to these changes, raising the question of what teaching was to be given regarding the rights and responsibilities of the individual. St Basil and other Christian teachers devised a hybrid Christian/Hellenic curriculum, and Eusebius of Caesarea, a scholar and adviser to the emperor, presented this curriculum in terms of a mash-up of Christian education and the traditional Roman curriculum. While Constantine's successors, Constantine II, Constantius II, and Constans I, also ruled as Christians, the problem of reconciling Christian and Roman education was short-lived. This is because the next emperor, Julian the Apostate, brought back the 'good old days' of traditional Roman religion. But only for a time. His ill-fated clashes with the clergy underlined the diminishment of his power and the rising power of the church.

In 354, Aurelius Augustinus, or as history would know him, St Augustine, was born in North Africa. He was the child of a Christian mother and a pagan father (who, in the style of the time, converted to Christianity on his deathbed). Augustine's education was typical of the era: It was expensive and dispiriting, focusing on rote learning with an emphasis upon individual words to the neglect of the bigger picture. He was despondent about learning to read and write in Greek, something with which he never felt comfortable. He recalled his school days as a tedious time, punctuated with numerous beatings.

Augustine is a prominent figure in the history of education. His book, *De Magistro* (On the Teacher), details his thoughts about teaching and learning. He was a prolific writer, and over one hundred of his works survive, most of which are devoted to discussion of the ecclesiastical controversies of his time. He had some far-sighted ideas, such as championing the use of critical thinking skills and advocating the adaptation of educational practices to suit the students' background. Augustine's posthumous impact on the post-Roman world is incalculable. He continues to be influential in Christian theological thought. Several orders of friars were founded on his teachings, and any self-respecting medieval library stocked a number of his books. He was the Dan Brown of the Middle Ages.

In 380 AD, the Edict of Thessalonica declared Christianity to be the state religion of the Roman Empire. Unfortunately, not long after that breakthrough, the wheels fell off. The Roman Empire imploded under pressure from a wide range of causes, including invading barbarian tribes, a weakened military, internal social divisions, religious and political disunity, and corruption, to name but a few. The next couple of hundred years were the darkest Rome had ever seen, and that's *really* saying something. Barbarian hordes sacked Rome several times and reduced it to a fraction of its former glory. For a time, it was even depopulated. As one might expect, having one's civilization dismantled by barbarian hordes had a deleterious effect on the Roman Empire. The last Roman emperor was Julius Nepos and, after his assassination in 480 AD, the position of Emperor was abolished.

It's impossible to tell at what point the 'Dark Ages' began, because things had been dark in Rome for many years. Let's just say it happened somewhere in the last paragraph.

Innovative Imitation

No ancient culture has influenced the modern world as directly as the Romans. They were innovators in science, the military, law, politics, art, architecture, and so many other fields. However, as must be very obvious by now, nearly every big idea for which the Romans were responsible was influenced by those of other, earlier cultures.

Nevertheless, they were still innovators.

You see, what the Romans did better than anyone else was

to take good ideas and improve upon them. Often to the point where they're almost indistinguishable from the original. Roman armies wiped the floor with virtually every other fighting force, thanks to their creative tweaks to the traditional phalanx. Roman architecture was initially a slavish copy of Greek architecture, until it morphed into something totally different and original. They took the pantheon of Greek gods and gave them a very Roman flavor (with the notable exception of Apollo). Then when they got sick of that, they took a fringe monotheistic religion and turned it into the biggest religion in the world.

If, by my Star Trek analogy, the Athenians were the Federation and the Spartans were the Klingons, then Rome's ability to assimilate ideas makes them the Borg. This works for their military as well, because most of the time, resistance was futile.

In short, the Romans nailed collective learning, and that was what made them the only superpower of their day. The problem was, when they fell, there was no similarly civilized superpower to take up their mantle.

This was the dawn of the Middle Ages.

Conclusion

Getting Better
The End of the Beginning

Sometimes, things just don't turn out like you imagine.

In the introduction, I told the story of how the most ambitious idea of all, the Moon landing, sparked my interest in humanity's lightbulb moments. Six-year-old me fully expected that more than 50 years in the future there'd be Moon and Mars bases aplenty. Maybe even some massive space stations like in *2001: A Space Odyssey*. I wasn't the only one. The head of the Apollo program, Wernher von Braun, turned his attention to planning a mission to Mars the moment Apollo 11 touched down.

Unfortunately, it wasn't to be. The problems posed by a Mars mission were far more complex than the already immensely complicated Moon shot. The bottom line was that an Austin Powers level of technology just wasn't going to get the job done. Not for the first time, our ideas and initiative had outstripped our abilities. This gap between what humans *can do* and what they *want to do* is what Russian educational theorist Lev Vygotsky called the Zone of Proximal Development (ZPG). The ZPG is where all the creative thought and problem-solving happens. In education, this gap is filled by a teacher who guides the student from what they *want to do* towards what they *can do*. In the wider world of human development, it's bridged by lightbulb moments.

Since the end of the Apollo program, humans have been working to fill this gulf. Finally, Mars beckons, but that's a story for another book. Although, on the subject of astronauts, I would be remiss in not mentioning this book's nemesis, Erich von Däniken. I've mercilessly mocked him throughout *Lightbulb Moments in Human History*, and with good reason: He's a charlatan and conspiracy theorist who's done irreparable damage to the way many view the ancient world. Nevertheless, he sparked my interest in human civilization in the strangest possible way. So thank you, Erich von Däniken.

I hope no one takes your work seriously again. No offense.

Are Things Really Getting Better?

> *Over the last several decades, extreme poverty, victims of war, child mortality, crime, famine, child labour, deaths in natural disasters and the number of plane crashes have all plummeted. We're living in the richest, safest, healthiest era ever.*
>
> Rutger Bregman: Humankind: A Hopeful History

As a species, *Homo sapiens* has conceived many big ideas in the past 300,000 years. Our challenge has been to use those ideas to build a better civilization. Sometimes we don't get a choice. A form of ideas-based natural selection takes place and the juggernaut of big ideas rolls on. Civilization takes on a life of its own.

A theory put forward by primatologist Frans de Waal proposed that civilization is a thin veneer papering over humanity's animalistic instincts. If this veneer is damaged, our baser tendencies bubble to the surface. However, Rutger Bregman in his book *Humankind,* disputes de Waal's claim, making a strong case that humans are hard-wired to be cooperative, decent, and kind.

I wholeheartedly agree with Bregman's take. Co-operation, decency, and kindness are the keys. Together, they continue to inspire humans to find ever more effective ways to communicate and record collective learning. However, I'm a pragmatist. If de Waal is right, I believe that collective learning over millennia has hardened the veneer to an impenetrable shell. So, whether Bregman or de Wall is correct is immaterial to my argument.

In the introduction, I wrote that over Big History periods

of time, lightbulb moments serve to make the world a better place. I don't back away from that one iota. The question is: Have I proven it? Do we even have the data to make a useful comparison?

Nowadays, there are a number of ways to compare the success of countries. There's the Human Development Index, a statistical measure that incorporates "education, life expectancy, and per capita income." The World Happiness Report derives a score by examining "income, freedom, trust in government, healthy life expectancy, social support from family and friends, and generosity." We could use the Global Liveability Survey, which gives scores calculated on "stability, healthcare, culture and environment, education and infrastructure." Or there's the OECD's Better Life Index, which scores for "housing, income, jobs, community, education, environment, civic engagement, health, life satisfaction, safety, and work-life balance."

There are many more ways to evaluate success, but you get the picture.

Of course, if we can't decide on how to assess present-day countries when we are awash in statistics, how can we possibly judge ancient civilizations? *And*, even if we agreed on methodology, something important is missing: There's no ancient data to plug into these models. So how *can* we tell?

That's a great question for which I don't have a definitive answer. Yet. The good news is, even though I can't empirically prove life is getting better, there is something significant that's easy to prove.

It's *Almost* Too Easy

Throughout *Lightbulb Moments in Human History,* we've seen the staggering scope of human achievement during civilization's infancy. Humans had inherited valuable traits from our animal forebears, but could not initially communicate complex ideas. We had no means of long-term information preservation. Then we invented complex language, which enabled us to teach and made collective learning possible.

The invention of writing was crucial to passing on and increasing knowledge. Following that development, the sheer volume of big ideas was overwhelming. Big ideas generated more big ideas. They were combined and synthesized. There was an exponential growth of interconnected ideas. The critical mass of intellectual property that humanity continues to accumulate is staggering.

Paleo-hippies argue that our hunter-gatherer past was perfect until it was wrecked by human progress. This view of our distant past is based on wish fulfillment, guesswork, and ignorance. I can easily imagine one of these anti-progress truthers paraphrasing Reg from *the Life of Brian*: "Well, apart from language, writing, the wheel, domesticated animals, literature, philosophy, equality, medicine, science, teaching, art, architecture, mathematics, and law, what have humanity's lightbulb moments ever given us?"

Fig. 1: Bloody Paleo-hippies have no appreciation for lightbulb moments (alfa27 and S.E.W.)

It's almost too easy to refute such arguments, as we are judging from such a low base. Most people in the past had desperately shitty, subsistence lifestyles. Judging comparative levels of shittiness in the short-term is difficult, but big ideas have a long-term cumulative effect. Life gets consistently less shitty: Infant mortality drops; levels of education rise; fewer people have their hearts sliced out. When viewed over Big History time frames it's almost impossible to argue that the journey from cave to colosseum was anything other than a procession of human achievement (albeit with a few stumbles along the way).

But almost impossible isn't enough to prove my point. The problem is, it's a controversial idea that runs contrary to current historical thought.

In 1979, Carl Sagan wrote that 'extraordinary claims require extraordinary evidence.' Given that my claim is somewhat extraordinary, I haven't yet met the requirement for 'extraordinary evidence.' Strong though I believe it is, my thesis relies on anecdotal evidence and a great, steaming dollop of interpretation. Luckily for me, the story of humanity's lightbulb moments doesn't end with the fall of Rome.

Something tells me I've got more research into the past in my future.

Acknowledgments

Something as all-consuming as a book doesn't happen without a lot of help, encouragement, and a certain amount of collateral damage. As a result, there are some people who must be thanked for enabling, supporting, cajoling, and inspiring me through the creation of *Lightbulb Moments in Human History*. And there are a few who must be commended for persevering with me through the process.

Let's deal with the 'collateral damage' first. My kids Sarah Williams, Sebastian Harvey, and Cate Williams Harvey have occasionally had a somewhat preoccupied Dad. Sarah in the 1990s during my abortive attempt to write a novel. Seb and Cate more recently with the writing of *Lightbulb Moments in Human History*. Thanks for your love, support, and understanding. I love you guys!

This book wouldn't have happened without the inspiration, encouragement, and feedback of my good friend Elizabeth Gascoigne Rosa. Thank you, Elizabeth.

What can I say about the Holy Trinity of Colin Howe, Elwood Scott, and Adam Parker? These guys gave me invaluable feedback on the appropriateness of my humor. If you're offended by any content in *Lightbulb Moments in Human History*, it's likely you would've been *more* offended without Colin, Elwood, and Adam's interventions. Well done, lads.

To my mentors and teachers, some of whom get a mention in the text, I give my thanks.

I had a lot of help in the editing of this book. Back when the working title was *Brainchild*, I had assistance from Hannah Wolfram, who gave great feedback from a Gen Z perspective. Then, Virginia Lloyd challenged me to lift my game and helped me craft, what I flatter myself is, a coherent thesis. She also talked me out of the name *Brainchild* (the loss still stings, Virginia)!

Finally, I acknowledge the invaluable assistance of Jim Bessey of So Write Editing. Jim usually edits novels, but he took an interest in my book as a beta reader and one thing led to another. He picked up my egregious errors, gaps in logic, made excellent suggested changes, and added seemingly millions of curly quotes, helping me create a book of which I'm proud. Thank you, Jim.

I kept the writing of this book close to my chest, and the big reveal came as a surprise to many of my friends, particularly my colleagues at A.P.S. Three people who *weren't* surprised were my sisters Leigh, Vicki, and Merilyn. It's deeply unfortunate that *Lightbulb Moments in Human History* isn't a genre any of them would ever choose to read, but I thank them for their encouragement and apologize about my constant von Däniken bashing.

Finally, to the team at JHP and Chronos Books: *Lightbulb Moments in Human History* would not be seeing the light of day without your belief, advice, and backing. It is appreciated.

Scott Edwin Williams

Sydney

February 2022

References

All About Bottlenose Dolphins - Communication & Echolocation | SeaWorld Parks & Entertainment 2019, Seaworld.org.

Amemiya, T. 2008, 'Economy and Economics of Ancient Greece. London and New York: Routledge, 2007. Pp. xxiv, 184. $125.', *The Journal of Economic History*, vol. 68, no. 1, pp. 300–301.

Apel, T n.d., *Apollo*, Mythopedia, viewed 30 September 2020, <https://mythopedia.com/roman-mythology/gods/apollo/>.

— n.d., *Minerva*, Mythopedia, viewed 30 September 2020, <https://mythopedia.com/roman-mythology/gods/minerva/>.

Armitage, D. 2012, 'What's the Big Idea? Intellectual History and the Longue Durée', *History of European Ideas*, vol. 38, no. 4, pp. 493–507.

AusSMC. 2017, *Dr Diane Colombelli Negrel says different penguin calls are 'key' to conservation, YouTube*, viewed 22 September 2020, <https://www.youtube.com/watch?v=8vJjFiz6iqE>.

Baird Rattini, K. 2019, *Cyrus the Great: History's most merciful conqueror?*, Culture.

Baker, D. 2010, *Collective Learning as a Key Concept in Big History*, Sociostudies.org.

Baraniuk, C. 2019, *Crows could be the smartest animal other than primates*, Bbc.com, BBC Future.

Bauer, SW. 2007, *The history of the ancient world: from the earliest accounts to the fall of Rome*, W.W. Norton, New York.

— 2010, *The history of the medieval world: from the conversion of Constantine to the First Crusade*, W.W. Norton, New York.

Bender, CE, Herzing, DL & Bjorklund, DF. 2008, 'Evidence of teaching in atlantic spotted dolphins (Stenella frontalis) by mother dolphins foraging in the presence of their calves', *Animal Cognition*, vol. 12, no. 1, pp. 43–53.

Berndt, RM & Tonkinson, R. 2019, *Australian Aboriginal peoples | History, Facts, & Culture, Encyclopædia Britannica*.

Birch-Chapman, S, Jenkins, E, Coward, F & Maltby, M 2017, 'Estimating population size, density and dynamics of Pre-Pottery Neolithic villages in the central and southern Levant: an analysis of Beidha, southern Jordan', *Levant,* vol. 49, no. 1, pp. 1–23.

Bishop, M. 2015, *Do animals have language?, TED Ed*.

Black, R. 2012, *The Idiocy, Fabrications and Lies of Ancient Aliens,* Smithsonian, Smithsonian.com.

Bowen, S, Nocerino, FR & Shapiro, J. 1988, *Mysteries of the crystal skulls revealed,* J & S Aquarian Networking, Pacifica, Calif.

Bowman, AK & Dorman, PF. 2019, *ancient Egypt | Civilization, Geography, & History, Encyclopædia Britannica.*

Bregman, R. 2018, *Utopia for Realists,* Bloomsbury Publishing, London.

— 2020, *Humankind: a hopeful history,* Bloomsbury Publishing, London.

Budin, SL, Cifarelli, M, Garcia-Ventura A, Millet Albà A & Pròxim D. 2019, *Gender and methodology in the ancient Near East : approaches from Assyriology and beyond,* Universitat De Barcelona Edicions, Barcelona.

Building Stonehenge 2019, English Heritage. https://www.english-heritage.org.uk/visit/places/stonehenge/history-and-stories/building-stonehenge/

Carmody, RN, Dannemann, M, Briggs, AW, Nickel, B, Groopman, EE, Wrangham, RW & Kelso, J. 2016, 'Genetic Evidence of Human Adaptation to a Cooked Diet', *Genome Biology and Evolution*, vol. 8, no. 4, pp. 1091–1103.

Caro, T & Hauser, MD. 1992, 'Is There Teaching in Nonhuman Animals?', *The Quarterly Review of Biology*.

Cartwright, M. 2014, *Minerva,* Ancient History Encyclopedia, Ancient History Encyclopedia.

— 2015, *Saraswati,* Ancient History Encyclopedia, Ancient History Encyclopedia.

Cassidy, C. 2021, *Who ate the First Oyster?: the extraordinary people behind the greatest firsts in history.*, Headline Book Publishing, S.L.

Chan, H & Franke, H. 2019, *China | Culture, History, & People, Encyclopædia Britannica.*

Chariots of the Gods (documentary/movie 1970)

Choi, D. 2020, *History's First Astronaut*, Medium, viewed 9 June 2021, <https://historyofyesterday.com/historys-first-astronaut-c27f32b3e8b5>.

Christian, D. 2019, *Origin story: a big history of everything*, Penguin Books, Uk.

Collado-Vázquez, S & Carrillo, JM. 2014, 'Cranial trepanation in The Egyptian', *Neurología (English Edition)*, vol. 29, no. 7, pp. 433–440, viewed 28 April 2020, <https://www.elsevier.es/en-revista-neurologia-english-edition--495-articulo-cranial-trepanation-in-the-egyptian-S2173580814000959>.

Crisostomo, CJ. 2016, 'Writing Sumerian, Creating Texts: Reflections on Text-building Practices in Old Babylonian Schools', *Journal of Ancient Near Eastern Religions*, vol. 15, no. 2, pp. 121–142.

Crook, JA n.d., *Marcus Aurelius - The Meditations*, Encyclopedia Britannica, viewed 5 October 2020, <https://www.britannica.com/biography/Marcus-Aurelius-Roman-emperor/The-Meditations>.

Crow that bent wire to retrieve food was acting naturally, scientists discover 2016, the Guardian, viewed 5 September 2021, <https://www.theguardian.com/science/2016/aug/10/crow-that-bent-wire-to-retrieve-food-was-acting-naturally-scientists-discover#:~:text=A%20crow%20that%20astonished%20the>.

Curry, A. 2008, *Gobekli Tepe: The World's First Temple?*, Smithsonian, Smithsonian.com.

Daily Stoic. 2019, *Have Better Days With Marcus Aurelius' Daily Routine | Ryan Holiday on Practicing Stoicism, YouTube*, viewed 5 October 2020, <https://www.youtube.com/watch?v=OiMbKCXAV8k>.

Daly, LW. 1950, 'Roman Study Abroad', *The American Journal of Philology*, vol. 71, no. 1, p. 40.

Davenport, C & Malik, S. 2018, *Mythbusting Ancient Rome – throwing Christians to the lions*, The Conversation.

Deadly Story n.d., *Food and Agriculture*, www.deadlystory.com.

Diamond, J. 1987, *The Worst Mistake in the History of the Human Race*, viewed 2 August 2021, <https://web.cs.ucdavis.edu/~rogaway/classes/188/materials/diamond#:~:text=While%20farmers%20concentrate%20on%20high>.

— 2007, *The rise and fall of the third chimpanzee*, Vintage, London.

— 2019, *Guns, germs and steel: a short history of everybody for the last 13,000 years*, Vintage, London.

Downey, G. 1957, 'Education in the Christian Roman Empire: Christian and Pagan Theories under Constantine and His Successors', *Speculum*, vol. 32, no. 1, pp. 48–61.

Durant, W. 2003, *The greatest minds and ideas of all time*, Simon & Schuster International, London.

EIU digital solutions 2019, *Liveability Report | The Economist Intelligence Unit*, Eiu.com.

Ervin, FR, Palmour, RM, Young, SN, Guzman-Flores, C & Juarez, J. 1990, 'Voluntary consumption of beverage alcohol by vervet monkeys: Population screening, descriptive behavior and biochemical measures', *Pharmacology Biochemistry and Behavior*, vol. 36, no. 2, pp. 367–373.

Evans, R. 2016, *A (brief) history of vice: how bad behavior built civilization*, A Plume Book, New York, New York.

Fagan, G. 2019, *Chariot Racing in Ancient Rome - The History, Fans and Facts*, The Great Courses Daily.

Fanous, AA & Couldwell, WT. 2012, 'Transnasal excerebration surgery in ancient Egypt: Historical vignette', *Journal of Neurosurgery*, vol. 116, no. 4, pp. 743–748, viewed 19 May 2020, <https://thejns.org/view/journals/j-neurosurg/116/4/article-p743.xml>.

Finch, D et al. 2021, *Australia's oldest known Aboriginal rock paintings*,

Pursuit, viewed 7 April 2021, <https://pursuit.unimelb.edu.au/articles/australia-s-oldest-known-aboriginal-rock-paintings#:~:text=The%20painting%20itself%20we%20have>.

Finn, JK, Tregenza, T & Norman, MD. 2009, 'Defensive tool use in a coconut-carrying octopus', *Current Biology*, vol. 19, no. 23, pp. R1069–R1070.

Fitch, W Tecumseh. 2011, 'Speech Perception: A Language-Trained Chimpanzee Weighs In', *Current Biology*, vol. 21, no. 14, pp. R543–R546.

Flemming, R. 2007, 'Women, Writing and Medicine in the Classical World', *The Classical Quarterly*, vol. 57, no. 1, pp. 257–279.

Frede, D. 2017, *Plato's Ethics: An Overview*, in EN Zalta (ed.), Stanford Encyclopedia of Philosophy, Winter 2017, Metaphysics Research Lab, Stanford University.

Gadotti, A & Kleinerman, A. 2017, '"The Rules of the School"', *Journal of the American Oriental Society*, vol. 137.1.

Garcia, B. 2018, *Romulus and Remus*, Ancient History Encyclopedia.

Gärdenfors, P & Högberg, A. 2017, 'The Archaeology of Teaching and the Evolution ofHomo docens', *Current Anthropology*, vol. 58, no. 2, pp. 188–208.

Geggel, L. 2019, *Did the Maya Really Sacrifice Their Ballgame Players?*, livescience.com, Live Science.

George, AR. 2001, 'In search of the é.dub.ba.a: the ancient Mesopotamian school in literature and reality*'.

Gerritsen, R. 2008, *Australia and the origins of agriculture*, Archaeopress, Oxford, England.

Gill, NS. 2019, *The 9 Most Important Ancient Chinese Inventions*, ThoughtCo.

Gladiatorial Games n.d., vroma.org.

González JL. 2010, *The story of Christianity*, Harperone, New York.

Gottlieb, A. 2016, *The dream of reason: a history of western philosophy from the Greeks to the Renaissance*, W.W. Norton & Company, New York.

Griffin, W. 2019, *The Gestural Precursor to Protolanguage and Teaching in Early Hominid Evolution*.

Guardian Staff. 2015, *Hitler really did have only one testicle, German researcher claims*, the Guardian, viewed 28 April 2021, <https://www.theguardian.com/world/2015/dec/19/hitler-really-did-have-only-one-testicle-german-researcher-claims>.

Hand Stencils, Prehistoric Rock Art: Oldest Painted Handprints n.d., www.visual-arts-cork.com.

Harari, YN. 2018, *Homo deus: a brief history of tomorrow*, Harper Perennial, New York, Ny.

Harari, YN. 2019, *Sapiens.*, Random House Uk.

Harris, R. 2021, *Anthropologist and archaeologist say Dark Emu was littered with weak evidence and unsourced claims*, The Age, viewed 16 June 2021, <https://www.theage.com.au/politics/federal/anthropologist-and-archaeologist-say-dark-emu-was-littered-with-weak-evidence-and-unsourced-claims-20210611-p58089.html>.

Harris, WV. 2009, *Ancient literacy*, Harvard University Press, Cambridge; London.

Hayden, B, Canuel, N & Shanse, J. 2012, 'What Was Brewing in the Natufian? An Archaeological Assessment of Brewing Technology in the Epipaleolithic', *Journal of Archaeological Method and Theory*, vol. 20, no. 1, pp. 102–150.

Heinzelin, JD. 1999, 'Environment and Behavior of 2.5-Million-Year-Old Bouri Hominids', *Science*, vol. 284, no. 5414, pp. 625–629.

Hewlett, BS & Roulette, CJ. 2016, 'Teaching in hunter–gatherer infancy', *Royal Society Open Science*, vol. 3, no. 1, p. 150403.

Highlights | Global Slavery Index 2018, Global Slavery Index.

History of Information n.d., www.historyofinformation.com, viewed 21 April 2021, <https://www.historyofinformation.com/>.

History.com Editors. 2018, *Printing Press*, HISTORY, A&E Television Networks.

Holmen, N. 2010, 'Examining Greek Pederastic Relationships', *Inquiries Journal*, vol. 2, Inquiries Journal, no. 02.

Hornblower, S. 2018, *ancient Greek civilization | History, Map, & Facts, Encyclopædia Britannica.*

https://www.facebook.com/Lachlanbrownhs 2018, *15 Aboriginal Australian Quotes That Will Change Your Perspective On Life*, Ideapod.

Idiocracy 2006, Twentieth Century Fox.

Invicta n.d., *Why Didn't Anyone Copy the Roman Army? - The Imitation Legions DOCUMENTARY*, www.youtube.com, viewed 15 August 2021, <https://www.youtube.com/watch?v=dfKNbuxekEo>.

Ishaan Tharoor. 2015, 'The dark side of Winston Churchill's legacy no one should forget', *The Washington Post*, 3 February.

It's official: Admiral Zheng beat Cook to Australia 2002, The Age, viewed 19 March 2021, <https://www.theage.com.au/world/its-official-admiral-zheng-beat-cook-to-australia-20021125-gdutvo.html>.

Jay, M. 2017, '"Hey! What's the Big Idea?": Ruminations on the Question of Scale in Intellectual History', *New Literary History*, vol. 48, no. 4, pp. 617–631.

Jesper Majbom Madsen & Rees, R. 2014, *Roman rule in Greek and Latin writing: double vision*, Brill, Leiden.

King, BJ. 1991, 'Social information transfer in monkeys, apes, and hominids', *American Journal of Physical Anthropology*, vol. 34, no. S13, pp. 97–115.

Kraut, R 2019, *Socrates | Biography, Philosophy, Beliefs, & Facts, Encyclopædia Britannica.*

Langley, L. 2016, *Schooled: Animals That Teach Their Young*, National Geographic News, viewed 22 September 2020, <https://www.nationalgeographic.com/news/2016/05/160507-animals-teaching-parents-science-meerkats/>.

Le Gallou, S. 2018, *Alcohol brewed from trees and other fermented drinks in Indigenous history | Faculty of Sciences | University of Adelaide,* sciences.adelaide.edu.au, viewed 15 June 2021, <https://sciences.adelaide.edu.au/news/list/2018/10/29/alcohol-brewed-from-trees-and-other-fermented-drinks-in-indigenous-history>.

León V. 2011, *4,000 Years Of Uppity Women: Rebellious Belles, Daring Dames, And Headstrong Heroines Through The Ages,* Mjf Books, New York.

Lewis, N. 1985, *Papyrology,* Cambridge [U.A.] Cambridge Univ. Press.

Linder, DO. 2019, *The Trial of Socrates,* Famous-trials.com.

Lopez, R. 2019, *Did sons and daughters get the same education in ancient Greece?,* Nationalgeographic.com.

Lovett, RA & Hoffman, S. 2017, *Crystal Skulls Are Shrouded in Mystery and Fascination,* History, viewed 25 August 2021, <https://www.nationalgeographic.com/history/article/crystal-skulls?loggedin=true>.

MacDonald, S & Kretzmann, N n.d., *Medieval philosophy - Routledge Encyclopedia of Philosophy,* www.rep.routledge.com, viewed 17 October 2020, <https://www.rep.routledge.com/articles/overview/medieval-philosophy/v-1>.

Mark, J n.d., *Beer,* World History Encyclopedia, viewed 29 May 2021, <https://www.worldhistory.org/Beer/#:~:text=Mesopotamian%20beer%20was%20a%20thick>.

— n.d., *Beer in Ancient Egypt,* World History Encyclopedia.

— n.d., *Pets in Ancient Egypt,* World History Encyclopedia.

Mark, JJ. 2012, *Ancient China,* Ancient History Encyclopedia, Ancient History Encyclopedia.

Marr, A & British Broadcasting Corporation. 2012, *A history of the world,* Macmillan, London.

Marshall, M. 2021, *Humans may have domesticated dogs by accident by sharing excess meat,* New Scientist.

McGroarty, AB. 2020, *New World Happiness Report,* Global

Wellness Institute.

Mendelsohn, D. 2015, *How Gay Was Sappho?*, The New Yorker, The New Yorker.

Menzies, G. 2002, *1421: the year China discovered the world*, Bantam, London.

Merton, RK. 1965, *On the shoulders of giants: a Shandean postscript*, Univ. Of Chicago Press, Chicago U.A.

Millman, M. 2008, *Ancient Egyptian Inventions*, Discovering Ancient Egypt.

Mintz, A n.d., *Sparta, Athens, and the Surprising Roots of Common Schooling*.

Mithen, S. 2007, 'Did farming arise from a misapplication of social intelligence?', *Philosophical Transactions of the Royal Society B: Biological Sciences*, vol. 362, no. 1480, pp. 705–718.

Monty Python and the Holy Grail. 1975, Cinema 5 Distributing.

Monty Python's The Life of Brian 1979, London:Eyre Methuen.

Moore, I n.d., *Bloodletting and Piercing in Mayan Culture*, HistoricalMX.

Morell, V. 2011, *Why Dolphins Wear Sponges*, Science | AAAS.

Mukti Jain Campion. 2014, 'How the world loved the swastika - until Hitler stole it', *BBC News*, 23 October.

Mythbusters n.d., *Wan-Hu Ming Dynasty Astronaut?*, www.youtube.com, viewed 11 June 2021, <https://www.youtube.com/watch?v=2hdoLh2DODQ>.

Niek Veldhuis. 1997, *Elementary education at Nippur : the lists of trees and wooden objects*, Groningen.

Nogendra Nath Mazumder. 2010, *History of education in ancient india.*, Nabu Press.

Nuwer, R. 2014, *This Guy Simultaneously Raised a Chimp and a Baby in Exactly the Same Way To See What Would Happen*, Smithsonian, Smithsonian.com.

Ofek, H. 2011, *Why the Arabic World Turned Away from Science*, The New Atlantis.

Osamede Okundaye, J. 2020, *No joke: ironic racism in comedy is just not funny*, the Guardian.

Palmer, JA, Bresler, L & Cooper, DE. 2001, *Fifty modern thinkers on education: from Confucius to Dewey*, Routledge, London; New York.

Palmour, RM, Mulligan, J, Howbert, JJ & Ervin, F. 1997, 'Of Monkeys and Men: Vervets and the Genetics of Human-Like Behaviors', *The American Journal of Human Genetics*, vol. 61, no. 3, pp. 481–488.

Patterson, G & Commission, R n.d., *The Children's Employment Commission, 1842*, Durham County Local History Society

Peers, C. 2006, 'What does a pedagogue look like? Masculinity and the repression of sexual difference in ancient education', *Discourse: Studies in the Cultural Politics of Education*, vol. 27, no. 2, pp. 189–208.

Peters, Joris & Schmidt, Klaus. 2004, Animals in the Symbolic World of Pre-Pottery Neolithic Göbekli Tepe, South-eastern Turkey: A Preliminary Assessment. *Anthropozoologica*. 39.

Petit, P & Thomson, N. 2018, *ancient Rome | Facts, Maps, & History, Encyclopædia Britannica*.

Pinker, S. 2012, *The better angels of our nature: why violence has declined*, Penguin Books, New York, New York.

— 2018, *Is the world getting better or worse? A look at the numbers*, www.ted.com, viewed 4 May 2021, <https://www.ted.com/talks/steven_pinker_is_the_world_getting_better_or_worse_a_look_at_the_numbers?language=en#t-90606>.

Plato. 2012, *Plato's phaedo.*, Hardpress Publishing.

Pollock, S. 2008, *Ancient Mesopotamia: the eden that never was*, Cambridge University Press, Cambridge.

Powell, K. 2002, 'Stone Age man kept a dog', *Nature*.

Price, M. 2021, *Tool Talk, Apa.org, viewed 8 November 2021, <https://www.apa.org/monitor/2010/03/tools>.*

Rabe, M n.d., *Sexual Imagery on the 'Phantasmagorical Castles' at Khajuraho» International Journal of Tantric Studies Vol. 2 No. 2» Asiatica Association*, asiatica.org, viewed 19 June 2021, <http://

asiatica.org/ijts/vol2_no2/sexual-imagery-phantasmagorical-castles-khajuraho/>.

ReligionForBreakfast. 2020, *The Reason Why They Gave Jesus a Beard*, YouTube, viewed 2 December 2020, <http://youtube.com/watch?v=7DUekrCnye8&feature=emb_logo>.

Rendell, L & Whitehead, H. 2001, 'Culture in whales and dolphins', *Behavioral and Brain Sciences*, vol. 24, no. 2, pp. 309–324.

Roger S. Bagnall, Kai Brodersen, Craige B. Champion, Andrew Erskine, and Sabine R. Huebner. 2013, *The Encyclopedia of Ancient History, First Edition. Roger S. Bagnall, Kai Brodersen, Craige B. Champion, Andrew Erskine, and Sabine R. Huebner, print pages 2318–2323. © DOI: 10.1002/9781444338386.wbeah15122*, Blackwell Publishing Ltd. Published 2013 by Blackwell Publishing Ltd.

Rosati, A. 2018, *Food for Thought: Was Cooking a Pivotal Step in Human Evolution?*, Scientific American.

Roser, M & Ortiz-ospina, E. 2018, *Literacy*, Our World in Data.

Russell, M & Wheeler, S. 2016, *Apocrypha now*, Top Shelf Productions, Éditeur: Marietta, Ga, Usa.

Ryan, C & Cacilda Jethá. 2011, *Sex at dawn: how we mate, why we stray, and what it means for modern relationships*, Harper, New York, NY.

Sat Bir Singh Khalsa, Cohen, L, Mccall, TB & Telles, S 2017, *The principles and practice of yoga in health care*, Sage Publications, Inc, New Delhi, India ; Thousand Oaks, California.

Sax, M, Walsh, JM, Freestone, IC, Rankin, AH & Meeks, ND. 2008, 'The origins of two purportedly pre-Columbian Mexican crystal skulls', *Journal of Archaeological Science*, vol. 35, no. 10, pp. 2751–2760.

Schlossberg, T. 2018, *The State of Publishing: Literacy Rates*, McSweeney's Internet Tendency.

Smith, JN, Goldizen, AW, Dunlop, RA & Noad, MJ. 2008, 'Songs of male humpback whales, Megaptera novaeangliae, are involved in intersexual interactions', *Animal Behaviour*, vol. 76, no. 2, pp. 467–477.

Smolker, R, Richards, A, Connor, R, Mann, J & Berggren, P. 2010, 'Sponge Carrying by Dolphins (Delphinidae, Tursiops sp.): A Foraging Specialization Involving Tool Use?', *Ethology*, vol. 103, no. 6, pp. 454–465.

Snowden, J. 2014, *How did they make papyrus? | All About History*, Historyanswers.co.uk.

Sorkin, A. 2012, 'The Newsroom', 1, HBO.

Southon, E & Matthewson, J n.d., Episode 60: How Smelly Was the Past?, History Is Sexy, viewed 30 September 2021, <https://historyissexy.com/show-notes/episode-60-how-smelly-was-the-past>.

STD Facts - Syphilis (Detailed) 2019, www.cdc.gov.

Tharoor, I. 2014, 'Did Chinese mariners reach Australia before the Europeans?', *Washington Post*.

The Devil's Hellish History: Satan in the Middle Ages 2018, History.

The Editors of Encyclopaedia Britannica 2019a, *Chariot | vehicle, Encyclopedia Britannica.*

— n.d., *Graphic design - Early printing and graphic design, Encyclopedia Britannica.*

— *n.d., Hand tool - Neolithic tools, Encyclopedia Britannica.*

— 2019b, *Minerva | Roman goddess | Britannica, Encyclopedia Britannica.*

— *Education - Roman adoption of Hellenistic education, Encyclopedia Britannica.*

— 2017, *Egyptian calendar | dating system, Encyclopedia Britannica.*

— 2018a, *Indus civilization | History, Location, Map, Art, & Facts, Encyclopedia Britannica.*

— 2018b, *Sparta | History & Facts, Encyclopedia Britannica.*

The Editors of the Merriam-Webster Dictionary 2019, *Merriam-Webster Dictionary*, Merriam-webster.com.

The Enigma of the Menhirs - Standing Stones of the Land's End Peninsula n.d., www.ancientpenwith.org, viewed 15 October

2021, <https://www.ancientpenwith.org/menhirs/enigma-of-menhirs.html>.

The First Lunar Landing 2018, Nasa.gov.

The Sacred Animals of Hinduism 2019, Hinduwebsite.com.

Thornton, A & Raihani, N. 2008, 'The Evolution of Teaching', *ANIMAL BEHAVIOUR*, vol. 75, pp. 1823–1836.

Tiwary, S & Saurabh, S. 2018, 'Archaeological Evidences of Toilet System in Ancient India', *Heritage: Journal of Multidisciplinary Studies in Archaeology*, vol. 6,.

Toivanen, O & Väänänen, L. 2016, 'Education and Invention', *Review of Economics and Statistics*, vol. 98, no. 2, pp. 382–396, viewed 22 May 2021, <http://aalto-econ.fi/toivanen/Toivanen_Vaananen_REStat16.pdf>.

Turney, A n.d., *Privilege and punishment: the Vestal Virgins in Ancient Rome*, Through Eternity Tours.

Tuttle, C n.d., *Child Labor during the British Industrial Revolution*, eh.net.

Tyldesley, J. 2011, *BBC - History - Ancient History in depth: The Private Lives of the Pyramid-builders*, BBC.co.uk.

Underwood, EA. 2020, *History of medicine - Traditional medicine and surgery in Asia | Britannica, Encyclopædia Britannica.*

University Of Wollongong. Woolyungah Indigenous Centre 2019, *You can't say that! : hints and tips*, University Of Wollongong, March, Wollongong, New South Wales.

Van De Mieroop, M. 1999, *The ancient Mesopotamian city*, Oxford University Press, Oxford.

Vestal Virgins | UNRV.com Roman History n.d., www.unrv.com.

von Daniken, E n.d., *Chariots of the Gods?, Internet Archive.*

Walton, DP. 2020, 'Experimental Archaeology: Making, Understanding, Story-telling', *Ethnoarchaeology*, vol. 12, no. 2, pp. 154–156.

Wentz, Evans. 1911 *402 note: also quoting from Jubainville Le culte des menhirs dans le monde celtique printed in Rev.Celt.*, xxvii: 313

What is Yoga? – Yoga Australia n.d., www.yogaaustralia.org.au.

Wickham, C. 2010, *The inheritance of Rom : a history of Europe from 400 to 1000*, Allen Lane, London; Penguin.

Wikipedia Contributors n.d., *Ludi magister* - Wikipedia, Wikimedia Foundation.

— 2018, *Women in ancient Sparta*, Wikipedia, Wikimedia Foundation.

— 2019b, *Archimedes*, Wikipedia, Wikimedia Foundation.

— 2019c, *Great Fire of Rome*, Wikipedia, Wikimedia Foundation.

— 2019d, *History of education in China*, Wikipedia, Wikimedia Foundation.

— 2019e, *Marcus Aurelius*, Wikipedia, Wikimedia Foundation.

— 2019f, *Pederasty in ancient Greece*, Wikipedia, Wikimedia Foundation.

— 2019i, *Sacred fire of Vesta*, Wikipedia.

— 2019j, *Sanskrit*, Wikipedia, Wikimedia Foundation.

— 2019k, *Sparta*, Wikipedia, Wikimedia Foundation.

— 2019l, *Venus of Willendorf*, Wikipedia, Wikimedia Foundation.

— 2019m, *Washoe (chimpanzee)*, Wikipedia, Wikimedia Foundation.

— 2020a, *Agoge*, Wikipedia, Wikimedia Foundation.

— 2020b, *Ancient Greek philosophy*, Wikipedia, Wikimedia Foundation.

— 2020c, *Chiron*, Wikipedia, Wikimedia Foundation.

— 2020d, *Fire-stick farming*, Wikipedia, Wikimedia Foundation.

— 2020e, *Isocrates*, Wikipedia, Wikipedia, Wikimedia Foundation.

— 2020f, *Khajuraho Group of Monuments*, Wikipedia, Wikimedia Foundation.

— 2020g, *Minerva*, Wikipedia, Wikimedia Foundation.

— 2020h, *Owl of Athena*, Wikipedia, Wikimedia Foundation.

— 2020i, *Social learning in animals*, Wikipedia, Wikimedia Foundation.

— 2020j, *Vestal Virgin*, Wikipedia, Wikimedia Foundation.

— 2021a, *Bi Sheng*, Wikipedia, Wikimedia Foundation.

— 2021b, *Crystal skull*, Wikipedia, Wikimedia Foundation.

Winston, RML. 2011, *Bad ideas? : an arresting history of our inventions*, Bantam Books, London.

writer873. 2012a, *Vestal Virgins of Rome: Privileged Keepers of Rome's Home Fires*, Ancient History Encyclopedia, viewed 18 January 2021, <https://www.ancient.eu/article/146/vestal-virgins-of-rome-privileged-keepers-of-romes/>.

— 2012b, *Vestal Virgins of Rome: The Price of Civic Duty and Privilege*, Ancient History Encyclopedia.

Yong, E. 2010, *Bee-ware – bees use warning buzz to refute the waggle dance*, Science, viewed 15 May 2021, <https://www.nationalgeographic.com/science/article/bee-ware-bees-use-warning-buzz-to-refute-the-waggle-dance>.

— 2016, The Origin of Dogs: When, Where, and How Many Times Were They Domesticated?, *The Atlantic*, The Atlantic. <https://www.theatlantic.com/science/archive/2016/06/the-origin-of-dogs/484976/>

Zuk. M. 2014, *Paleofantasy: what evolution really tells us about sex, diet, and how we live*, W. W. Norton & Company, New York.

CHRONOS
BOOKS

HISTORY

Chronos Books is an historical non-fiction imprint. Chronos publishes real history for real people; bringing to life people, places and events in an imaginative, easy-to-digest and accessible way - histories that pass on their stories to a generation of new readers.

If you have enjoyed this book, why not tell other readers by posting a review on your preferred book site.

Recent bestsellers from Chronos Books are:

Lady Katherine Knollys

The Unacknowledged Daughter of King Henry VIII

Sarah-Beth Watkins

A comprehensive account of Katherine Knollys' questionable paternity, her previously unexplored life in the Tudor court and her intriguing relationship with Elizabeth I.

Paperback: 978-1-78279-585-8 ebook: 978-1-78279-584-1

Cromwell was Framed

Ireland 1649

Tom Reilly

Revealed: The definitive research that proves the Irish nation owes Oliver Cromwell a huge posthumous apology for wrongly convicting him of civilian atrocities in 1649.

Paperback: 978-1-78279-516-2 ebook: 978-1-78279-515-5

Why The CIA Killed JFK and Malcolm X

The Secret Drug Trade in Laos

John Koerner

A new groundbreaking work presenting evidence that the CIA silenced JFK to protect its secret drug trade in Laos.

Paperback: 978-1-78279-701-2 ebook: 978-1-78279-700-5

The Disappearing Ninth Legion

A Popular History

Mark Olly

The Disappearing Ninth Legion examines hard evidence for the foundation, development, mysterious disappearance, or possible continuation of Rome's lost Legion.

Paperback: 978-1-84694-559-5 ebook: 978-1-84694-931-9

Beaten But Not Defeated

Siegfried Moos - A German anti-Nazi who settled in Britain

Merilyn Moos

Siegi Moos, an anti-Nazi and active member of the German Communist Party, escaped Germany in 1933 and, exiled in Britain, sought another route to the transformation of capitalism.

Paperback: 978-1-78279-677-0 ebook: 978-1-78279-676-3

A Schoolboy's Wartime Letters

An evacuee's life in WWII — A Personal Memoir

Geoffrey Iley

A boy writes home during WWII, revealing his own fascinating story, full of zest for life, information and humour.

Paperback: 978-1-78279-504-9 ebook: 978-1-78279-503-2

The Life & Times of the Real Robyn Hoode

Mark Olly

A journey of discovery. The chronicles of the genuine historical character, Robyn Hoode, and how he became one of England's greatest legends.

Paperback: 978-1-78535-059-7 ebook: 978-1-78535-060-3